KT-568-253

N E FIFE

NF022663

THE CREATIVE
COOK

THE CREATIVE
Cook

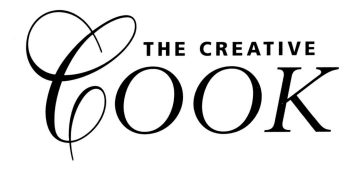

CONRAN OCTOPUS

Please note the following:

Quantities given in all the recipes serve 4 people unless otherwise stated.

Spoon measurements are level unless otherwise stated.

Metric and imperial measures are both given, use one or the other as the two are not interchangeable.

Flour used is plain white flour, unless otherwise stated.

Preparation of ingredients, such as cleaning, trimming and peeling of vegetables and fruit, is presumed and the text only refers to any aspect of this if unusual, such as onions used unpeeled etc.

Citrus fruit is generally coated in a layer of preservative wax. For this reason, whenever a recipe uses the rind of oranges, lemons or limes the text specifies unwaxed fruit. If organic uncoated fruit is not available, scrub the fruit vigorously in hot soapy water, rinse well and pat dry.

Eggs used are size 3(65g/2¼ oz) unless otherwise specified. The Government recommends that eggs should not be consumed raw, and people most at risk, such as children, old people, invalids and pregnant women should not eat them lightly cooked. This book includes recipes with raw and lightly cooked eggs, which should not be eaten by the above categories. Once prepared, these dishes should be kept refrigerated and used promptly.

This edition published in 1995 by
Conran Octopus Limited

First appeared as *The Creative Cook* series:
Appetizing Outdoor Eating (1994), Aromatic Herbs (1992), Compulsive Cakes and Gâteaux (1993), Easy Oriental (1992), Mouthwatering Mediterranean (1992), Tempting Tarts (1992), Traditional Country (1992), Versatile Vegetables and Salads (1992).

Text copyright ©: Richard Cawley, Lewis Esson, Janice Murfitt, Lyn Rutherford, Sally-Anne Scott, Jane Suthering (see details on p. 256)
Photography copyright ©: Julie Fisher, Michelle Garrett, Deborah Patterson, Pia Tryde (see details on p. 256)
Illustration copyright ©: Alison Barratt
Design and layout copyright ©: Conran Octopus 1995

All rights reserved. No part of this book may be reproduced, stored in a retrieval system or transmitted in any form or by any means, electronic, electrostatic, magnetic tape, mechanical, photocopying, recording or otherwise, without the prior permission in writing of the publisher.

British Library Cataloguing in Publication Data
A catalogue record for this book is available from the British Library

ISBN 1-85029-790-8

Printed and bound in Hong Kong

NORTH EAST FIFE DISTRICT LIBRARY

CLASS	641.5
COPY	022663
VENDOR	H5
PURCHASE DATE	8/96
PRICE	£14.99

CONTENTS

INTRODUCTION

Over the last few years there has been a revolution in the way that we cook. Inspired by the wonderful array of new produce available in our supermarkets and multi-ethnic markets and stimulated by more foreign travel and eating out, we have become a nation of increasingly adventurous cooks. Even the housewife and mother who has to produce daily meals for a demanding and picky family now tends to lean on dishes like pasta and curries in a way that her parents' generation would have found unthinkable.

Health concerns have also played a big part in reshaping our eating habits. Gone are the fry-ups and stodgy puddings that were once such mainstays of our national diet. Instead we are now making much more use of vegetables and fruits, rice, grains and pulses; replacing butter, suet and lard with olive, nut and vegetable oils; and favouring white meat and fish over red meat. To make the most of such ingredients we have broadened our horizons to embrace ideas from nations whose diets have long been based on such healthier tenets – like those of the Orient and the Mediterranean region.

The Creative Cook provides an amazing wealth of recipes to help you make the most of both tried-and-tested ingredients and today's new exotica. There are recipes for traditional favourites – often given new life with an unusual and refreshing twist – alongside lots of innovative ideas, many of which are inspired by the best that the fascinating cuisines of the world have to offer.

The book begins with some basic stocks and sauces and a range of delicious soups. There are also chapters on Starters and Snacks, Rice, Grains and Pasta, Vegetables and Salads and Puddings and Desserts. Main courses are presented by ingredients, with separate sections on each different type of meat, as well as poultry and game, fish and shellfish. To make the book even more useful for today's cook, there are substantial sections on Oriental Cooking and one on Vegetarian Main Courses. The book finishes with a section on Baking, giving an assortment of simple treats you can make at home for morning coffee and afternoon tea. Throughout, the book is also dotted with invaluable marginal notes, which provide useful hints and tips, information on more unusual ingredients, interesting serving suggestions and clever ideas for variations.

There is something for everyone and every occasion in this bible for the cooking of today. Whether you simply want some fresh ideas for family meals or are planning a special meal for a celebration or to impress your friends, you will find no end of exciting ideas every time you dip into it. With this book on your shelf, you need never again allow your cooking to get into a rut – even your family favourites can be given a new lease of life.

STOCKS, SAUCES AND SOUPS

A well-flavoured stock is at the heart of most good cooking, and although there are many high-quality bottled and chilled stocks readily available, you will find that making your own stock is relatively easy, very economical and gives an unbeatable freshness and depth of flavour to any dish in which it is used.

From good stocks it is one short step to making a wide range of nourishing soups, from those suitable for a dinner party, like Artichoke Soup with Lemon Grass, to others, like Lentil and Ham Soup with Mushroom Toasts, which are whole meals in themselves.

Many sauces are also based on stocks, like the classic rich reductions of *haute cuisine* as well as good giblet gravy for roast poultry. This chapter, however, also features milk-based Béchamel or basic white sauce, the emulsion sauces like Mayonnaise and Hollandaise and salad dressings like vinaigrette and French dressing, as well as some tasty relishes.

Left to right: a jar of French Dressing (page 14); a plate and bowl of Low-calorie Yogurt Dressing (page 14); a spoonful of Rouille (page 100); Strawberry Vinaigrette (page 15); Mango Vinaigrette (page 15); and Mayonnaise (page 13)

NF022663

*Make CHICKEN
STOCK as per the
BASIC BOUILLON
recipe, but using no
beef. Use 2 or 3
chicken carcasses and
some giblets or
trimmings such as
feet for even more
flavour. Leftover
carcasses from roast
chickens can make
good stock.*

*Make FISH STOCK
with 675 g/1½ lb of
fish heads and
trimmings, 3 onions,
3 bay leaves and a
bunch of parsley.
Cover with water,
bring to the boil and
simmer for 20
minutes only.*

VEGETABLE STOCK

MAKES ABOUT 1.1 LITRE/2 PT

*225 g/8 oz haricot beans, soaked in cold water overnight
45 g/1½ oz butter
1 tbsp sunflower oil
1 garlic clove
1 stalk of celery
6 carrots, coarsely chopped
3 leeks, coarsely chopped
3 turnips, diced large
2 onions
12 cloves
1 parsnip
small sprig of thyme
3 bay leaves
small bunch of parsley
salt and freshly ground black pepper*

Drain the haricot beans, rinse and put them in a saucepan. Cover them with fresh cold water and bring to the boil. Drain, rinse and cover with more fresh cold water. Bring to the boil again and then drain.

Melt the butter with the oil in a large heavy-based saucepan over a moderate heat. Sauté the garlic in it for 2 minutes.

Add the celery, carrots, leeks, turnips, onions stuck with the cloves and the parsnip. Cook for 5-7 minutes, stirring constantly.

Remove from the heat and add the drained beans, followed by 3 litre/5 pt of water, the thyme, bay leaves and the parsley, complete with stalks. Bring to the boil, cover and simmer gently for 1½ hours.

Remove from the heat and leave to cool for about 2 hours.

Return the pan to a low heat and cook for 15 minutes. Strain the stock through a sieve, return it to the pan and boil rapidly to reduce it by about half.

Allow any stock not being used immediately to cool and then store it in the refrigerator.

BASIC BOUILLON OR ENRICHED MEAT STOCK

MAKES ABOUT 850 ML/1½ PT

*675-900 g/1½-2 lb shin of beef
carcass of 1 fresh chicken
1 onion, coarsely chopped
3 carrots, coarsely chopped
bouquet garni
2 stalks of celery, coarsely chopped
8 black peppercorns*

Chop the meat and chicken into manageable pieces and place them in a large flameproof casserole. Cover with 2.25 litre/4 pt of cold water and bring to the boil.

Reduce the heat and add the other ingredients. Cover and cook gently for about 1½ hours, skimming as necessary.

Remove all the larger solids from the pan, then strain the stock through a muslin-lined sieve.

Return the liquid to the heat and boil it rapidly to reduce it by about half. Strain it through muslin again before use.

Allow any stock not being used immediately to cool and then store in the refrigerator.

PEANUT AND PEPPER RELISH

115 g/4 oz salted peanuts, chopped
½ red or yellow sweet pepper, deseeded and finely chopped
½ tsp curry powder
1 small garlic clove, crushed
3 tbsp Greek yogurt
2 tbsp chopped flat-leaf parsley

Mix all the ingredients and chill for at least 1 hour, or up to 24, to allow the flavours to develop fully.

MANGO SAMBAL

½ large ripe mango, peeled and coarsely chopped
2 spring onions, thinly sliced
⅛ cucumber, coarsely chopped
1 chilli pepper, deseeded and finely chopped
juice of 1 lime or lemon
1 heaped tbsp chopped coriander

Combine all the ingredients except the coriander and chill for at least 1 hour, or up to 24, to allow the flavours to develop fully.

Just before serving, mix in the coriander.

COCONUT SAMBAL

85 g/3 oz freshly grated coconut
55 g/2 oz mild onions, thinly sliced
1 chilli pepper, deseeded and finely chopped
juice of 1 lime or lemon
¼ tsp salt

Mix all the ingredients together well and chill for at least 1 hour, or up to 24, to allow the flavours to develop fully.

CUCUMBER AND CARROT RELISH

2 tbsp sugar
juice of ½ lime
¼ cucumber, finely chopped
2 shallots, thinly sliced
1 small carrot, grated
1 large red or green chilli pepper or more to taste, deseeded and finely chopped

In a small bowl, dissolve the sugar in 2 tablespoons of hot water. Mix in all the other ingredients.

Leave for at least an hour to allow the flavours to develop fully, but use within 24 hours. Keep refrigerated.

PLUM SAUCE

55 g/2 oz Oriental 'Preserved Bottled Plums'
450 g/1 lb granulated sugar
2-3 large red chilli peppers, deseeded and very finely chopped
1 red sweet pepper, deseeded and very finely chopped
4 tbsp malt or white wine vinegar

Rub the plums through the fingers to break up the flesh, but do not discard the stones.

Put the sugar and 300 ml/10 fl oz of water in a medium saucepan and bring to the boil over a moderate heat. When the syrup is boiling well add the chopped chilli peppers, the sweet pepper and the plums with their stones. Bring back to the boil and allow to boil for 2-3 minutes, then add the vinegar. The resulting sauce will be sweet-and-sour.

Allow to cool, remove the stones and discard. Pour into warmed sterile bottles or jars and seal or tightly stopper. This sauce will stay fresh for several weeks in the refrigerator.

Thick sweet spicy PLUM SAUCE *is traditionally served by the Chinese as a dip with dumplings or seafood and with poultry dishes, especially duck.*

ORIENTAL *'*PRESERVED BOTTLED PLUMS'*, pickled in a spiced vinegar, are available from Oriental supermarkets. A blender or food processor easily gets the peppers chopped to the correct degree of fineness.*

SAMBALS *are Indonesian relishes, usually spiced with chilli peppers.*

Variations on
BÉCHAMEL *include*
AURORE SAUCE
*which contains
added tomato pulp
or purée and*
MORNAY *which
is flavoured with
grated cheese.*

QUICK TOMATO SAUCE

MAKES ABOUT 250 ML/8 FL OZ

*125 ml/4 fl oz olive oil
1 large onion, sliced
2 garlic cloves, crushed
4 tbsp tomato paste
salt and freshly ground black pepper*

Heat the oil over a moderate heat and cook the onion and garlic in it for 3-5 minutes, stirring constantly, until soft.

Add the tomato paste and 1 tablespoon of water. Season to taste and mix well.

BÉCHAMEL SAUCE

MAKES ABOUT 300 ML/½ PT

*300 ml/½ pt milk
1 small onion
¼ tsp freshly grated nutmeg
1 bay leaf
sprig of thyme
30 g/1 oz butter
30 g/1 oz flour
salt and freshly ground black pepper*

Place the milk in a saucepan together with the onion, nutmeg, bay leaf and thyme. Very slowly bring to the boil. Immediately remove from the heat and leave to infuse for 20 minutes.

Melt the butter in a heavy-based saucepan. Stir in the flour and cook thoroughly, stirring constantly, for about 4 minutes. Remove from the heat.

Strain the infused milk through a sieve and then gradually add it to the flour in the pan. Mix thoroughly and then return to the heat and bring to the boil, stirring constantly.

Reduce the heat and simmer for 3-4 minutes, still stirring. Season with salt and pepper and a little more nutmeg, if wished.

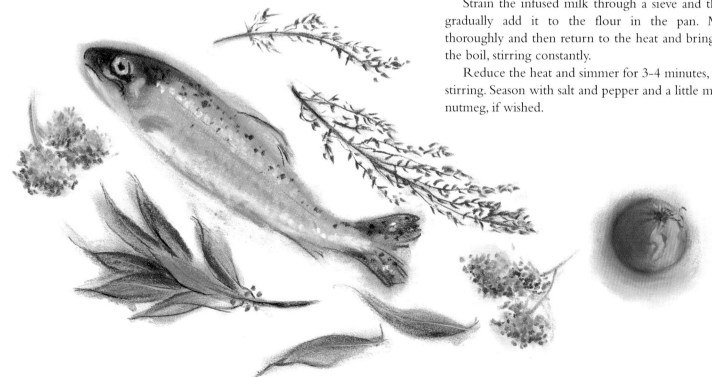

HOLLANDAISE SAUCE

MAKES ABOUT 300 ML/½ PT

200 g/7 oz unsalted butter
3 egg yolks
1 tbsp lemon juice
1 tbsp dry white wine
salt and freshly ground black pepper

Melt 170 g/6 oz of the butter in a heavy-bottomed pan over a gentle heat. Transfer to a warmed jug.

Place the egg yolks in the same pan and beat them quickly with a whisk. Add half the lemon juice, the wine and a pinch of salt. Beat again. Add half the remaining unmelted butter and place the pan in a bain-marie or double boiler.

Whisking steadily, cook gently until the egg yolks are creamy in texture and beginning to thicken. Immediately remove the pan from heat and stir in the remaining unmelted butter until it dissolves.

Dribble the melted butter into the yolk mixture, whisking fast. Add the butter more rapidly as the sauce thickens. When the sauce is the consistency of double cream, add the remaining lemon juice and adjust the seasoning.

NOTES: if the sauce is too thick it can be thinned down with 1 tablespoon of water.

Hollandaise not being used immediately should be stored in the refrigerator for a day or two only.

Try adding 3 tablespoons of freshly grated Parmesan cheese to the sauce for extra flavour.

MAYONNAISE

MAKES ABOUT 200 ML/7 FL OZ

1 egg yolk
½ level tsp salt
½ level tsp dry mustard
150 ml/¼ pt olive oil
1 tbsp white wine vinegar or lemon juice
pinch of caster sugar (optional)
freshly ground black pepper

In a bowl beat the egg yolk until thick. Then beat in the salt, mustard and black pepper to taste.

Add the oil very slowly, drop by drop, whisking continuously to absorb the oil evenly. As the mayonnaise thickens and becomes shiny, add the oil in a thin steady stream. Finally blend in the vinegar or lemon juice and sugar, if using.

NOTES: any mayonnaise not being used immediately should be stored in the refrigerator for a day or two only.

Try flavouring the mayonnaise with 2 or 3 crushed garlic cloves, 2 tablespoons chopped fresh herbs or 1 tablespoon grated orange or lemon zest.

Make BÉARNAISE SAUCE in the same way as HOLLANDAISE, but first flavour the vinegar by boiling it with some chopped shallots, tarragon and black peppercorns.

For really exciting salad dressings, use the wide variety of flavoured oils and vinegars now readily available. As appropriate, more exotic items, such as nut oils - like sesame, walnut and hazelnut - soy sauce, tahini (sesame seed paste) and Japanese rice vinegar are also very useful. It is also quite easy to make flavoured oils and vinegars at home by adding flavouring ingredients such as fresh herbs like tarragon or rosemary, 3 or 4 garlic cloves, 1 or 2 small whole chilli peppers or some berry fruit to good-quality oil or white wine vinegar, and leaving it in a cool place for several weeks.

LOW-CALORIE YOGURT DRESSING

MAKES 450 ML/¾ PT

3 egg yolks
250 ml/8 fl oz plain Greek yogurt
2 tsp lime or lemon juice
2 tsp Dijon mustard
1 tbsp finely chopped parsley
salt and freshly ground black pepper

In a bowl, beat the egg yolks, yogurt and lemon juice together until creamy.

Stand the bowl in a pan of very gently simmering water and cook for about 15 minutes, stirring continuously, until the dressing has thickened to a coating consistency.

Add the mustard, season with salt and pepper and leave to cool. Stir in the parsley just before use.

Store any not being used immediately in a screw-top jar in the refrigerator for a day or two only.

FRENCH DRESSING

MAKES ABOUT 150 ML/¼ PT

2-3 garlic cloves, crushed
6 tbsp olive oil
2 tbsp wine vinegar
2 level tsp French mustard
salt and freshly ground black pepper
pinch of caster sugar (optional)

Put all the ingredients in a bowl. Season to taste and add the sugar, if using. Whisk together well.

If not using immediately, transfer to a screw-top jar and store in the refrigerator.

NOTE: use more or less garlic to taste. Try flavouring the dressing with the additions as listed for basic vinaigrette.

BASIC VINAIGRETTE

MAKES ABOUT 150 ML/¼ PT

6 tbsp olive oil
2 tbsp wine vinegar
salt and freshly ground black pepper

Pour the oil and vinegar into a screw-top jar. Seal and shake vigorously. Season and shake again.

NOTES: add 2 tablespoons of finely chopped fresh herbs, such as parsley, chervil or chives, for a herb vinaigrette.

Instead of these herbs, the vinaigrette may be flavoured with 2 tablespoons of chopped tarragon, 1 tablespoon of tomato paste with a pinch of paprika, 2 tablespoons each of finely chopped onions and parsley, or 1 tablespoon of finely chopped anchovy.

STRAWBERRY VINAIGRETTE

MAKES ABOUT 175 ML/6 FL OZ

55 g/2 oz strawberries
1½ tbsp strawberry vinegar or lemon juice
6 tbsp grapeseed oil
salt and freshly ground black pepper

Put the strawberries in a blender or food processor with the vinegar or lemon juice. Pulse briefly until the mixture is smooth.

With the machine running, gradually add the oil until it is all incorporated and the mixture is thick and smooth. Sieve out the pips if wished. Season.

NOTE: serve this unusual dressing over cucumber salad or with cold poached chicken or salmon.

MANGO VINAIGRETTE

MAKES ABOUT 175 ML/6 FL OZ

1 very ripe mango, peeled
1½ tbsp red wine vinegar or lemon juice
5 tbsp sunflower oil
1 tbsp finely chopped parsley
salt and freshly ground black pepper

Slice away the mango flesh coarsely from the stone.

Put the mango flesh in a blender or food processor with the vinegar or lemon juice. Pulse briefly until the mixture is smooth.

With the machine running, gradually add the oil until it is all incorporated and the mixture is thick and smooth. Stir in the parsley and season.

NOTE: serve with smoked chicken salads or flavour with chopped dill or mint and serve with smoked fish. Try flavouring it with some mustard.

Left: Strawberry Vinaigrette; right: Mango Vinaigrette

Other blue cheeses, such as Dolcelatte, Stilton or Danish Blue, may be substituted for Roquefort in this soup, but the flavour will not be quite the same.

LEEK AND POTATO SOUP

SERVES 6-8

55 g/2 oz butter
900 g/2 lb leeks, sliced into 6 mm/¼ in pieces
450 g/1 lb thin-skinned potatoes (preferably reds), unpeeled and coarsely diced
2 large stalks of celery, chopped
575 ml/1 pt chicken stock
575 ml/1 pint semi-skimmed milk
½ tsp freshly grated nutmeg
300 ml/½ pt double cream
salt and freshly ground black pepper
finely chopped parsley, to garnish

Melt the butter in a large heavy-based pan over a moderate heat. Add the leeks and potatoes and cook gently for 7-10 minutes, stirring constantly.

Add the celery. Stir in the stock and milk and bring to the boil. Add the nutmeg and season with salt and pepper. Reduce the heat and simmer for 30 minutes.

If serving cold, allow to cool completely then liquidize in a blender or food processor. Stir in the cream and chill for at least 2 hours. Adjust the seasoning, if necessary, and serve garnished with parsley.

If serving hot, stir in the cream and allow to warm through gently, without allowing to boil. Adjust the seasoning, if necessary, pour into warmed bowls and garnish with the parsley.

NOTE: for a hot smooth soup, allow the mixture to cool before blending and then reheat.

ROQUEFORT AND SAVOY CABBAGE SOUP

SERVES 6-8

225 g/8 oz rindless streaky bacon, cut into strips
10 cloves
2 onions, quartered
3 leeks, chopped
4 carrots, chopped
1 large savoy cabbage
4 potatoes, diced
6-8 slices of brown granary bread, lightly toasted
225 g/8 oz Roquefort cheese
salt and freshly ground black pepper

Put 2 litre/3½ pt of cold water in a pan and place over a moderate heat. Add the bacon and bring to the boil. Skim, then simmer for 15 minutes. Skim again.

Stick the cloves into the onion quarters, and add these to the stock together with the leeks and carrots. Simmer for a further 30 minutes.

Quarter the cabbage, cutting out the core and any thick ribs on outer leaves. Blanch for 3 minutes in a large pan of boiling water. Drain and refresh under cold running water, then cut into strips.

Add the cabbage strips to the stock and cook for a further 20 minutes over a moderate heat. Add the potatoes and simmer for another 30 minutes or so, until they are tender. Remove the cloves, if preferred.

Place a slice of toast in the bottom of each of the warmed bowls and crumble the cheese over it.

Season the soup with pepper (little added salt should be necessary due to the high salt content of the cheese), pour it into the bowls and serve.

BEEF TOMATO AND OKRA SOUP

55 g/2 oz butter
6 spring onions (including the green tops), sliced
225 g/8 oz okra, sliced
1 garlic clove, crushed
3 large beef tomatoes, peeled, deseeded and sliced
1 tbsp demerara sugar
1 tsp soy sauce
850 ml/1½ pt vegetable stock
1 tbsp juice and 1 level tsp zest from an unwaxed lemon
1 heaped tbsp chopped coriander leaves, to garnish
salt and freshly ground black pepper

Melt the butter in a heavy-based pan over a moderate heat. Add the spring onions, okra, garlic and tomatoes and sauté gently for 7 minutes.

Add the remaining ingredients, cover and simmer for a further 10 minutes.

Season and add the coriander just before serving.

PETIT POIS AND LEMON GRASS SOUP

2 stalks of lemon grass
850 ml/1½ pt vegetable stock
55 g/2 oz butter
1 large onion, diced
2 large potatoes, peeled and diced
350 g/12 oz frozen petits pois, defrosted
salt and freshly ground black pepper

Using a rolling pin, crush the bulbous part of the lemon grass stalks and place them in a pan. Add one-third of the stock. Cover, bring just to a simmer and cook over a very low heat for 30 minutes.

Meanwhile, melt the butter in a large pan over a moderate heat and toss the onion and potatoes in it for 5 minutes. Add the remaining stock and bring to the boil. Cover and simmer for 30 minutes.

Remove the pan with the lemon grass from the heat. Discard the lemon grass, then add the petits pois. Allow to sit for 15 minutes off the heat.

Add the contents of this pan to the other. Season and allow to cool, then liquidize in a blender or food processor. Warm the soup through for serving, being careful not to allow it to boil.

LE PUY LENTIL SOUP WITH FRESH GINGER

225 g/8 oz le Puy lentils, soaked overnight (see p.24)
1 large onion, diced
1 large purple garlic clove, crushed
2 tbsp corn oil
300 ml/½ pt vegetable stock
300 ml/½ pt semi-skimmed milk
30 g/1 oz peeled fresh root ginger, grated
55 g/2 oz sesame seeds, roasted
1 tbsp chopped parsley, to garnish

Wash the lentils thoroughly, then boil them rapidly in 450 ml/¾ pt of water for 10 minutes. Then simmer for 15–20 minutes, until tender.

In a large heavy-based pan, sauté the onion and garlic in the corn oil until translucent. Add the vegetable stock and milk. Bring to the boil and simmer for 10 minutes. Add the lentils with their stock and the ginger. Season, then simmer for a further 15 minutes. Allow to cool, then liquidize in a blender or food processor.

Reheat to serve, being careful not to allow it to boil. Put some of the sesame seeds in the base of each of the warmed serving bowls, reserving some for garnish. Fill the bowls with soup and garnish with the remaining sesame seeds and the parsley.

The BUTTERNUT SQUASH is the distinctively peanut-shaped, pale yellowy-orange variety of winter squash. If unavailable, any hard-skinned squash or pumpkin will work in this recipe.

SPICED GOLDEN SQUASH SOUP

SERVES 6

900 g/2 lb butternut squash
55 g/2 oz butter
white parts only of 4 leeks, thinly sliced
1 tbsp coriander seeds, crushed
large pinch of ground allspice
large pinch of freshly grated nutmeg
700 ml/1¼ pt chicken stock
300 ml/½ pt milk
salt and freshly ground black pepper
6 tbsp single cream, to garnish

Peel the squash, cut the flesh into 2.5 cm/1 in cubes and discard the seeds.

Melt the butter in a large saucepan over a moderate heat. Add the leeks and cook, stirring, for 5-6 minutes until they are soft and beginning to colour. Stir in the squash, coriander seeds, allspice and nutmeg and cook for 1 minute.

Stir in the stock, season with salt and pepper and bring to the boil. Cover and simmer for about 35 minutes, until the squash is very soft.

Purée the soup, in batches, using a blender or food processor. Return the puréed soup to the pan and stir in the milk. Reheat gently and adjust the seasoning to taste.

Serve garnished with swirls of cream.

TOMATO AND RICE SOUP WITH BASIL

SERVES 4-6

1 tbsp olive oil
1 large onion, finely chopped
1 garlic clove, crushed
1 small red sweet pepper, deseeded and chopped
45 g/1½ oz Milano or other Italian salami, chopped
900 g/2 lb ripe tomatoes, peeled, deseeded and chopped
1 tbsp tomato paste
sprig of oregano
200 ml/7 fl oz dry white wine
575 ml/1 pt chicken or vegetable stock
45 g/1½ oz risotto rice, preferably arborio
3 tbsp chopped basil
salt and freshly ground black pepper
bread sticks or crusty Italian bread, to serve

Heat the oil in a large heavy-based saucepan over a moderate heat, add the onion and garlic and cook for 5 minutes, without browning. Stir in the red pepper and salami and cook for 2 minutes.

Add the tomatoes, tomato paste and oregano and stir in the wine and stock. Season, bring to the boil then lower the heat, cover and simmer for 20 minutes.

Add the rice and basil to the pan, cover and continue cooking for 15 minutes, until the rice is tender.

Serve accompanied by bread sticks or crusty Italian bread.

CREAM OF MUSHROOM SOUP WITH MARSALA

45 g/1½ oz butter
675 g/1½ lb mushrooms, roughly chopped
1 shallot, finely chopped
½ garlic clove, chopped
2 tbsp flour
100 ml/3½ fl oz Marsala
700 ml/1¼ pt well-flavoured chicken or vegetable stock
175 ml/6 fl oz double cream
salt and freshly ground black pepper
chopped flat-leaf parsley or chervil, to garnish

Melt the butter in a large heavy-based saucepan. Add the mushrooms, shallot and garlic and cook, stirring, for 4 minutes.

Stir in the flour and continue cooking for 1 minute. Gradually stir in the Marsala and stock. Season and bring to the boil. Then lower the heat, cover and simmer for 20 minutes.

Purée the soup in a blender or food processor, in batches if necessary, until smooth and then return it to the pan.

Just before serving, stir in all but 4 tablespoons of the cream and heat the soup through gently. Adjust the seasoning and serve garnished with swirls of the reserved cream and the parsley or chervil.

NOTE: if available, field mushrooms will give a much better flavour than cultivated ones. A mixture of mushroom varieties is best, particularly if it includes a few ceps.

BORSCHT

SERVES 6

350 g/12 oz cooked beetroot, peeled and grated
2 carrots, grated
1 onion, finely chopped
1 celery stalk, finely chopped
850 ml/1½ pt beef stock
strip of zest and 1 tbsp juice from an unwaxed lemon
bouquet garni
175 ml/6 fl oz sour cream
salt and freshly ground black pepper

Put the beetroot in a large pan with the carrots, onion and celery. Stir in the stock, lemon zest and bouquet garni. Season with salt and pepper. Bring to the boil then lower the heat, cover and simmer for 40 minutes.

Remove the lemon zest and bouquet garni. Purée the soup, in batches, using a blender or food processor. Strain into a bowl or serving tureen and leave to cool.

When the soup is completely cold, stir in the lemon juice and all but 6 tablespoons of the sour cream. Adjust the seasoning to taste. Cover and chill for at least 2 hours.

Swirl the reserved sour cream into the soup to serve.

Versions of BORSCHT, or beetroot soup, are traditional throughout Eastern Europe. The soup may be served either hot or cold, with sour cream swirled into it.

HERBED CREAM OF CARROT SOUP

SERVES 4-6

450 g / 1 lb carrots, chopped
450 ml / ¾ pt vegetable stock
30 g / 1 oz butter
1 large onion, diced
1 tsp celery salt
300 ml / ½ pt single cream
½ tbsp each finely chopped watercress, parsley and chives
freshly ground black pepper

Put the carrots and the vegetable stock in a large pan and gently bring to the boil. Reduce the heat, cover and simmer for about 15 minutes, until the carrots are tender. Leave to cool in the pan.

Melt the butter in a frying pan over a moderate heat and sauté the onion until translucent. Add the celery, salt and stir thoroughly. Remove from the heat and allow to cool.

Transfer the carrots and their stock to a blender or food processor. Add the onion and blend until smooth.

Return this to the saucepan and bring almost to the boil. Remove from the heat and add the cream. Season with pepper only and stir thoroughly over a gentle heat just to warm through. Do not allow to boil or the cream will curdle.

Pour the soup into warmed bowls and sprinkle a little of each of the 3 herbs over each bowl.

HERBED VEGETABLE SOUP WITH VERMICELLI

SERVES 6

1 tbsp butter or vegetable margarine
1 large onion, diced
2 crisp stalks of white celery, chopped
2 large carrots, chopped
2 heads of broccoli, chopped
1 large potato, diced
1 tbsp chopped oregano
1.5 litre / 2½ pt vegetable stock
85 g / 3 oz vermicelli
1 tbsp chopped flat-leaf parsley
1 tbsp chopped chives
salt and freshly ground black pepper

Melt the butter or margarine in a large heavy-based pan over a moderate heat and sauté the onion until translucent.

Add the other vegetables and sauté for 5 minutes, stirring constantly. Add the oregano and sauté for a further 2 minutes.

Add the stock and bring it gently to the boil. Cover and simmer gently for 10 minutes.

Add the vermicelli, increase the heat to moderate again and cook until the vermicelli is tender.

Adjust the seasoning, then add the parsley and chives just before serving.

CHILLED CELERIAC AND APPLE SOUP WITH CHIVES

55 g/2 oz butter
1½ large onions, sliced
½ tsp freshly grated nutmeg
3 hard green cooking apples, unpeeled and coarsely chopped
1 celeriac root, peeled and cut into small cubes
3 chicken stock cubes
2 tsp lime juice
bunch of chives
salt and freshly ground black pepper

Melt the butter in a large heavy-based pan over a moderate heat and sauté the onions in it for about 2-4 minutes, until translucent.

Sprinkle in the nutmeg and cook for another 1 minute. Add the apples and celeriac and cook for 5 minutes more, stirring constantly.

Dissolve the chicken stock cubes in 1.1 litre/2 pt of hot water and add this to the pan. Reduce the heat, cover and simmer for 30 minutes.

Remove the pan from the heat and allow to cool a little before adding the lime juice.

When cold, purée the soup in a blender or food processor. Then chill overnight.

Adjust the seasoning of the chilled soup and pour it into serving bowls. Finely snip the chives over the bowls to garnish.

CHILLED AVOCADO SOUP WITH CORIANDER

2 ripe avocados
juice of ½ lemon
1 tsp chilli oil
3 tbsp finely chopped coriander
225 g/8 oz plain yogurt, preferably Greek
300 ml/½ pt crème fraîche
300 ml/½ pt fresh tomato juice
450 ml/¾ pt vegetable stock
½ onion, finely shredded
salt and freshly ground black pepper

Halve and stone the avocados. Peel them and place the flesh in a large bowl with the lemon juice. Mash with a fork or hand blender until smooth.

Stir in the chilli oil and two-thirds of the coriander. Cover and chill for 30 minutes.

Gently blend in the yogurt and crème fraîche, followed by the tomato juice and finally the stock. Stir in the shredded onion, season and chill for 2 hours.

Adjust the seasoning, if necessary, and garnish with the remaining coriander to serve.

CELERIAC *is a variety of celery grown for its large spherical fleshy white root. Long a favourite in France, it has recently become more widely available in this country. Usually boiled and puréed with potatoes, it is also popular shredded raw in salads.*

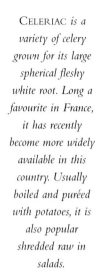

As in GARLICKY FIVE-BEAN SOUP WITH GOOSEBERRY, *an alternative to spooning swirls of cream decoratively into soups before serving is to add fruit and vegetable purées with complementary colours and flavours. Try avocado purée in tomato soup, tomato purée in spinach or sorrel soup and apple sauce in pea and ham soup.*

CHILLED BEETROOT AND HORSERADISH SOUP

SERVES 6-8

6 raw beetroots (see below)
1.5 litre/2½ pt chicken stock
8 spring onions (including green tops), chopped
½ cucumber, peeled, halved lengthwise and deseeded
juice of ½ lime
1 tsp dark brown sugar
2 tsp freshly grated horseradish root
150 ml/¼ pt single cream
6-8 tbsp sour cream
salt and freshly ground black pepper
2 large gherkins, thinly sliced, to garnish
½ tbsp finely chopped dill leaves, to garnish

Try to buy beetroots which still have their stems and leaves and an intact skin. It is also a good idea to buy ones of a uniform size so that they will cook in the same time.

Put the stock in a large pan and bring to the boil. Place the beetroots gently in the stock, cover and simmer for 15-20 minutes, until they are completely tender.

Trying to avoid breaking the skins, remove the beetroots from the stock. Leave to cool completely and reserve the stock.

Once cool, peel and coarsely dice the beetroots and chop their leaves. Liquidize them in a blender or food processor, together with the spring onions and cucumber.

Mix with the reserved stock, lime juice, sugar, horseradish and cream. Chill for at least 3 hours.

Adjust the seasoning and pour the chilled soup into bowls. Place a spoonful of the sour cream in the middle of each bowl, then garnish with the slices of gherkin and some finely chopped dill leaves.

GARLICKY FIVE-BEAN SOUP WITH GOOSEBERRY

SERVES 6

45 g/1½ oz butter
1 tbsp olive oil
3 garlic cloves, sliced
1 large onion, sliced
2 leeks, cut into 1 cm/½ in slices
850 ml/1½ pt vegetable stock
225 g/8 oz potatoes, cut into small chunks
225 g/8 oz fresh gooseberries, halved
350 g/12 oz mixed cooked beans: kidney, flageolet, butter, haricot and black-eyed
salt and freshly ground pepper

Melt the butter with the oil in a large heavy-based pan over a low heat. Add the garlic and cook gently for 3 minutes, stirring constantly. Add the onion and leeks and sauté for 5 minutes.

Add the stock and bring to the boil. Reduce the heat, add the potatoes and simmer for 15-20 minutes, until they are tender.

Place the gooseberries in a small pan with a few spoonfuls of water and bring to the boil. Simmer until they are reduced to a pulp. Remove from the heat, allow to cool a little and then push them through a sieve to make a coulis.

Add the cooked beans to the potato and vegetable stock. Heat through, but do not bring to the boil.

Season and pour into warmed soup bowls. Dribble some of the gooseberry coulis into each and serve immediately.

Left: Garlicky Five-Bean Soup with Gooseberry; right: Chilled Beetroot and Horseradish Soup

The very fine green LENTILS FROM LE PUY *in France are actually almost purple in colour. They have an incomparable flavour and cook very quickly. If none are available use any green lentils, but they will need longer cooking.*

GREEN LENTIL SOUP WITH HERBES DE PROVENCE

225 g/8 oz green lentils, preferably Le Puy (soaked overnight)
30 g/1 oz butter
1 large onion, coarsely chopped
225 g/8 oz tomatoes, coarsely chopped
1 tbsp herbes de Provence
salt and freshly ground black pepper
1 tbsp chopped flat-leaf parsley, to garnish

Wash the lentils thoroughly, then put them in a large heavy-based pan with 850 ml/1½ pt of water. Bring to the boil, boil rapidly for 10 minutes then simmer gently for 15-20 minutes until the lentils are tender. Set them aside in their stock.

Melt the butter in a frying pan over a moderate heat and add the onion. Sauté until translucent, then add the tomatoes and herbs and stir constantly for 5 minutes. Transfer the contents of the frying pan to the lentil pot. Season, cover and leave to cool.

When cool, purée the soup in a blender or food processor or push it through a sieve. Return to a moderate heat and gently warm it through.

Transfer the soup to warmed bowls and sprinkle with parsley to serve.

CREAM OF BLACK-EYED BEAN SOUP

SERVES 6-8

350 g/12 oz black-eyed beans, soaked overnight in cold water
85 g/3 oz butter
3 onions, chopped
85 g/3 oz carrots, chopped
85 g/3 oz celery, chopped
2 garlic cloves, crushed
1.5 litre/2½ pt vegetable stock
bouquet garni
1 tsp lemon juice
250 ml/8 fl oz single cream
1-2 tbsp cranberry sauce
salt and freshly ground black pepper
1 tbsp finely chopped parsley, to garnish

Drain the beans, put them in a pan and cover with fresh cold water. Bring to the boil, and boil rapidly for 10 minutes. Bring to the boil once more, cover and simmer for 40 minutes, or until tender.

Melt the butter in a frying pan over a low to moderate heat. Add the onion, carrot, celery and garlic and sauté for 10 minutes. Transfer the vegetables to a large pan, add the vegetable stock, cooked beans and the bouquet garni. Bring to the boil, cover and simmer for 20 minutes.

Discard the bouquet garni. Add the lemon juice and season the soup to taste. Leave to cool.

When cool, liquidize the soup in a blender or food processor. Stir in the cream, then heat through, being careful not to allow it to boil.

Ladle the soup into 6-8 warmed bowls and spoon some of the cranberry sauce in the centre of each. Garnish with parsley to serve.

LENTIL AND HAM SOUP WITH MUSHROOM TOASTS

SERVES 6

30 g/1 oz butter
1 large onion, chopped
1 garlic clove, crushed
1 carrot, finely diced
1 celery stalk, finely diced
350 g/12 oz red lentils
1 bay leaf
sprig of thyme
1 tbsp chopped parsley (optional)
salt and freshly ground black pepper
FOR THE HAM STOCK
1 smoked ham joint, weighing about 675 g/1½ lb
1 onion, quartered
1 carrot, quartered
6 black peppercorns
FOR THE MUSHROOM TOASTS
45 g/1½ oz butter
55 g/2 oz mushrooms, finely chopped
2 tsp chopped parsley
½ garlic clove, crushed
6 small slices of French bread

First prepare the ham stock: put the ham joint in a large pan, cover it with water and bring to the boil. Boil for 1 minute, then discard the salty cooking water.

Add 1.5 litre/2½ pt of fresh cold water to the pan with the onion, carrot and peppercorns. Return to the boil, then lower the heat, cover and simmer for about 1½ hours, until the ham is tender.

Transfer the ham to a plate and leave to cool. Then cut it into small dice or flake it with a fork and set aside. Leave the stock to cool, then remove the fat which rises to the surface. Strain the stock and reserve.

Melt the butter in a large saucepan over a moderate heat. Add the onion, garlic, carrot and celery and cook, stirring, for 3-4 minutes. Stir in the lentils, bay leaf and thyme and add the reserved ham stock. Bring to the boil then lower the heat, cover and simmer for 1-1½ hours.

About 10 minutes before serving, make the mushroom toasts: first preheat a hot grill.

Melt the butter in a small heavy-based pan over a moderate to high heat. Add the mushrooms, parsley and garlic and cook, stirring frequently, until all the liquid which exudes from the mushrooms is evaporated. Season with salt and pepper.

Toast the bread slices on one side under the grill. Then turn them over and divide the mushroom mixture between them. Return them to the grill for 1 minute only, until well heated through.

Season the soup with salt and pepper. Remove and discard the bay and thyme and stir in the parsley, if using. Serve piping hot, accompanied by the mushroom toasts.

The MUSHROOM TOASTS *make good starters or snacks on their own. Just double or triple the quantities, depending on appetites.*

MINESTRONE SOUP

SERVES 6-8

170 g/6 oz piece of unsmoked bacon, chopped
1 large onion, finely chopped
1 garlic clove, crushed
3 carrots, diced
3 celery stalks, thinly sliced
225 g/8 oz potatoes, diced
450 g/1 lb tomatoes, peeled and chopped
170 g/6 oz dried cannellini beans, soaked overnight in
cold water
1.1 litre/2 pt stock or water
½ small white cabbage, finely shredded
2 courgettes, thinly sliced
170 g/6 oz fresh or frozen garden peas
140 g/5 oz macaroni or other small pasta
2 tbsp chopped flat-leaf parsley
handful of basil leaves, shredded
salt and freshly ground black pepper
6-8 tbsp freshly grated Parmesan cheese, to serve

Put the bacon in a large heavy-based saucepan over a moderate heat and cook for a few minutes until the fat begins to melt. Add the onion and cook for about 5 minutes more until that is soft.

Stir in the garlic, carrots, celery, potatoes, tomatoes and drained beans. Pour in the stock and bring to the boil. Lower the heat, cover and simmer for about 2 hours, until the beans are tender.

Add the cabbage, courgettes, peas, macaroni and parsley to the pan, cover and cook for a further 20 minutes.

Just before serving, stir in the basil and season with salt and pepper. Serve piping hot, sprinkled with freshly grated Parmesan.

Clockwise from the top centre: Minestrone Soup, Lentil and Ham Soup (page 25) and Cream of Mushroom Soup with Marsala (page 19)

SPRING CHICKEN AND LEEK SOUP

5 tbsp olive oil
1 large onion, chopped
2 bay leaves
sprig of thyme
2 dressed poussins, each weighing about 450 g/1 lb
150 ml/¼ pt dry white wine
450 g/1 lb leeks, diced
115 g/4 oz potatoes, diced
large pinch of freshly grated nutmeg
150 ml/¼ pt double cream
salt and freshly ground black pepper

Heat 2 tablespoons of the oil in a large heavy-based saucepan over a moderate heat, add the onion and cook, stirring, for about 10 minutes until it is pale golden in colour.

Add the bay leaves, thyme and poussins to the pan and pour over the wine. Add just enough water to cover the birds (about 850 ml/1½ pt). Bring to the boil then lower the heat, cover and simmer for 30-40 minutes, until the poussins are cooked.

Remove the birds from the stock and set aside until cool enough to handle. Strain the stock into a large bowl, discarding the herbs and onion.

Heat the remaining oil in the saucepan. Add the leeks and potatoes and sauté for 2-3 minutes. Pour over the reserved stock and bring to the boil. Season with freshly grated nutmeg, salt and pepper. Cover and simmer for 25-30 minutes, stirring occasionally.

Meanwhile, remove the flesh from the poussins, cut it into dice or strips and add these to the soup.

Just before serving, stir the cream into the soup and warm through gently. Adjust the seasoning to taste, if necessary.

The exact recipe for MINESTRONE, *the classic vegetable soup of Italy, varies from region to region. Generally, however, it is garnished with pasta and sprinkled with grated Parmesan cheese.*

LEMON GRASS *is native to South-east Asia and its citrus tang is a basic flavour in much of the cooking of the area, especially Thai cuisine. It remains fibrous even after lengthy cooking so is best removed after it has imparted its flavour. Once available only from specialist food stores, or in its powdered form, known as* SEREH, *the long pale green stalks with bulbous bases are now a common sight in some supermarkets.*

ARTICHOKE SOUP WITH LEMON GRASS

SERVES 6

2 stalks of lemon grass
450 g/1 lb large Jerusalem artichokes, unpeeled and coarsely chopped
85 g/3 oz butter
2 large onions, sliced
1 garlic clove, finely chopped
1.1 litre/2 pt chicken stock
4 tbsp single cream (optional)
1 tbsp finely chopped parsley, to garnish

Bring a large pan of water to the boil.

Crush the bulb ends of the lemon grass stalks, then place them in the pan of water with the artichokes and simmer them for 10 minutes. Strain the artichokes, reserving the lemon grass.

Melt the butter in a large heavy-based pan over a moderate heat. Add the onions and garlic and sauté them for about 3 minutes. Reduce the heat, cover and simmer for a further 5 minutes.

Add the pieces of artichoke and stir them into the onions and garlic. Then add the stock and bring to the boil. Add the reserved lemon grass, cover and simmer for 20 minutes. Remove from heat and allow to cool. Remove and discard the lemon grass.

Liquidize the mixture in a blender or food processor. Return it to the pan and re-heat gently. Stir in the cream, if using, and adjust the seasoning.

Pour the soup into warmed serving bowls and garnish with parsley.

FISH CHOWDER WITH HORSERADISH

SERVES 6

450 g/1 lb skinned cod fillet
450 g/1 lb skinned smoked haddock fillet
1.1 litre/2 pt milk
450 g/1 lb potatoes, peeled and diced
575 ml/1 pt fish stock
55 g/2 oz butter
225 g/8 oz onions, sliced
1 tbsp finely grated fresh horseradish root
juice of ½ lemon
115 g/4 oz canned sweetcorn kernels (optional)
salt and freshly ground black pepper

Put the fish in a large pan and cover with the milk. Bring to just below the boil over a moderate heat and simmer gently for 20 minutes, or until the flesh flakes readily.

In another pan, put the potatoes and the fish stock. Bring to the boil and cook for 15 minutes.

Melt the butter in a frying pan over a moderate heat and sauté the onions for about 5 minutes, until translucent.

Pour the potatoes and their stock into the fish pan, then add the onions in their butter. Sprinkle the horseradish on top and mix gently. Add the lemon juice.

Slowly bring the contents of the pan to a simmer and cook very gently for 15 minutes. Season and add the sweetcorn, if using.

Pour into warmed bowls and serve immediately.

Clockwise from the left: Herbed Cream of Carrot Soup (page 20), Artichoke Soup with Lemon Grass and Fish Chowder with Horseradish

The flavour of THAI PRAWN SOUP *relies on fragrant* LEMON GRASS *and* KAFFIR LIME LEAVES *which add a strong citrus note without acidity. These are available, fresh or dried, from Oriental shops. Lemon or lime rind may be used instead, but will not give the same distinctive taste.* GALANGAL, *a spice related to ginger, is available from Oriental suppliers and some supermarkets. Fresh ginger may be substituted.*

QUICK CHICKEN AND COCONUT SOUP

450 ml/¾ pt chicken stock
grated zest and juice of ½ unwaxed lime,
plus juice of 1 more lime
3 tbsp fish sauce
1 tsp ground ginger
½ tsp chilli powder
300 ml/½ pt thick coconut milk
170 g/6 oz skinned boneless chicken breasts, cut across
into thin slices
chopped fresh coriander, to garnish
sliced deseeded chilli peppers, to garnish (optional)

Put the stock in a saucepan with the lime zest and juice, the fish sauce, ginger and chilli powder and simmer for 5 minutes.

Add the coconut milk and chicken slices and simmer for 2 or 3 more minutes, until the chicken is just cooked through.

Pour into 4 warmed bowls and garnish with coriander and chilli slices, if using.

THAI PRAWN SOUP

350 g/12 oz raw prawns in their shells, heads removed
3 chilli peppers
1 tbsp vegetable oil
2 stalks of lemon grass, thinly sliced
3 Kaffir lime leaves
3 slices of galangal, each about 1 cm/½ in thick
2 garlic cloves, chopped
2 tbsp fish sauce, or more according to taste
juice of ½ lime
1 tbsp chopped coriander, to garnish
3 chopped spring onions, to garnish

Remove the shells from the prawns, put the meat to one side and reserve the shells. Deseed the chilli peppers. Coarsely chop 2 of them and thinly slice the third.

Heat the oil in a saucepan over a moderate heat and fry the prawn shells for 1-2 minutes, or until they turn pink.

Add 1.5 litre/2½ pt of water, the coarsely chopped chilli peppers, the lemon grass, Kaffir lime leaves, galangal, garlic and fresh sauce. Bring to the boil, reduce the heat and simmer for 20 minutes. Strain into a clean pan and discard the solids.

Add the shelled prawns and cook for 3-4 minutes, or until the prawns are just cooked through. Do not overcook or the prawns will become tough and tasteless.

Add the lime juice and, if the soup seems too bland, add a little more fish sauce to taste.

Pour into 4 warmed bowls and garnish with the slices of chilli pepper, the coriander and the chopped spring onion.

SWEETCORN AND CRAB SOUP

850 ml/1½ pt chicken stock
1 cm/½ in cube of peeled fresh root ginger, crushed through
a garlic press or very finely chopped
1 tsp soy sauce
1 tsp sugar
350 g/12 oz canned or frozen sweetcorn kernels, drained
or defrosted
1 tbsp cornflour
3 tbsp dry sherry
170 g/6 oz canned crab meat, drained
white of 1 egg, lightly beaten
1 tsp sesame oil
55 g/2 oz chopped cooked ham, to garnish (optional)
1 thinly sliced spring onion, to garnish

Put the chicken stock in a saucepan with the ginger, soy sauce, sugar and sweetcorn. Bring to the boil and then reduce the heat and simmer the mixture for 2-3 minutes.

In a small bowl, mix the cornflour mixture with the sherry. Remove the pan from the heat and whisk the cornflour mixture into the soup. Simmer for 2 minutes more, until the soup thickens.

Add the crab meat and cook for another minute or so to warm it through.

Remove the soup from the heat once more. Whisk the egg white with the sesame oil and then vigorously whisk this into the soup so that it forms white strands.

Pour into 4 warmed bowls and sprinkle with chopped ham, if using, and the chopped spring onion.

HOT AND SOUR SOUP

4 Chinese dried mushrooms
1.1 litre/2 pt chicken stock
115 g/4 oz chicken breast fillet, cut into thin slivers
85 g/3 oz peeled cooked prawns
115 g/4 oz tofu, cut into 1 cm/½ in cubes
55 g/2 oz canned bamboo shoots, drained and cut into
short pieces
55 g/2 oz frozen peas
2 spring onions, chopped
2 tbsp soy sauce
3 tbsp white wine vinegar
2 tbsp cornflour
salt and freshly ground black pepper
1 tsp Oriental sesame oil, to serve

Soak the dried mushrooms in warm water for 30 minutes. Drain them, remove and discard the stalks and slice the caps thinly.

Bring the stock to the boil in a saucepan, add the mushrooms and chicken and simmer the mixture for 10 minutes.

Add the prawns, tofu, bamboo shoots, peas and spring onions and simmer the mixture for 2 more minutes.

In a bowl, mix together the soy sauce, vinegar, cornflour and 85 ml/3 fl oz of water. Season with salt and plenty of pepper to give the soup its characteristic 'hot' flavour.

Stir this mixture into the soup and simmer for another 2 minutes until the soup thickens.

Pour the soup into warmed bowls and add a few drops of sesame oil to each to serve.

A wide variety of bottled FISH SAUCES *is made from fermented fish by various Oriental nations. This salty condiment, used as a flavour enhancer and not just in fish dishes, is available from Oriental supermarkets.*

TOFU, *or soy bean curd, is available from better supermarkets and health-food shops as well as Oriental supermarkets.*

STARTERS AND SNACKS

The worldwide popularity and influence of Mediterranean-style cuisine have made us all familiar with the *tapas* of Spain and the *mezze* of the Aegean and Middle-east. These assortments of little titbits may be served just to accompany drinks, as first courses prior to a simple main dish of plainly cooked fish or meat, or they can even make meals in themselves.

What characterizes the dishes in this chapter is their flexibility. Some, like Bresaola with Lemon Vinaigrette or the devilishly easy Peppered Smoked Mackerel Pâté with Horseradish, make perfect first courses for formal meals. Others, like Spicy Hummus with Tahini and Assorted Filo Pastry Parcels, are classic *mezze*. Many, like Bruschette with Tomatoes and Crostini with Wild Mushrooms, make elegant and satisfying snacks at any time of the day. All may be used singly or in conjunction with others to make meals for any occasion.

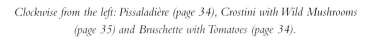

Clockwise from the left: Pissaladière (page 34), Crostini with Wild Mushrooms (page 35) and Bruschette with Tomatoes (page 34).

PISSALADIÈRE

FOR THE DOUGH
½ sachet (5.5 g / 1½ tsp) active dried yeast
250 g / 8½ oz flour, plus more for dusting
1 egg, lightly beaten
½ tsp salt
1 tbsp olive oil
FOR THE TOPPING
5 tbsp olive oil
1 kg / 2¼ lb onions, very thinly sliced
3 garlic cloves, crushed
bay leaf
1 tsp chopped fresh thyme or ½ tsp dried thyme
1 tsp chopped fresh basil or ½ tsp dried basil
1 tsp chopped fresh rosemary or ½ tsp dried rosemary
3 tbsp red wine
1 tbsp capers, drained and mashed
225 g / 8 oz canned chopped plum tomatoes, drained
24 canned anchovy fillets, drained and cut in half lengthwise
24 small black stoned olives
salt and freshly ground black pepper

PISSALADIÈRES, a speciality of the Provence region of France, are flat open tarts not dissimilar to Italian pizzas.

First make the dough: dissolve the yeast in 5 tablespoonfuls of warm water. Sift the flour into a warm bowl and form a well in the centre of it.

When the yeast mixture is spongy, pour it into the middle of the well together with the egg and salt. Gradually mix in the flour from the edges until the mixture forms a smooth dough.

Turn it out on a floured surface and knead for 5 minutes until smooth and elastic.

Generously grease a bowl with the oil, place the ball of dough in it and turn the ball well to coat it thoroughly with the oil. Cover with a damp cloth and leave in a warm place to rise for 1 hour, or until it has risen to about twice its original size.

Meanwhile make the topping: put 4 tablespoons of oil in a large frying pan (preferably with a lid) over a moderate heat and add the onions, garlic, bay leaf and other herbs. Season well and cook gently for about 5 minutes until the onions are translucent. Add the wine, capers and tomatoes. Stir well, cover and cook very gently for about 30 minutes more, until the onions are very soft.

Preheat the oven to 250C/475F/gas 9 and grease a 25.5 cm/10 in pie or pizza pan, or a baking sheet, with a little of the remaining olive oil.

Remove the risen dough from the bowl and knead it briefly on a lightly floured surface to knock it back slightly and incorporate the oil. Then roll it out and use it to line the pie or pizza dish or simply press it into the dish so that it is higher at the edges and there is a hollow in the centre. Alternatively, form the dough into such a round shape on the prepared baking sheet.

Adjust the seasoning of the onion mixture and spoon it into the centre of the pie, leaving a broad rim round the edge. Using the strips of anchovy, make a lattice pattern on top of the filling and press the olives into the spaces between. Brush the uncovered rim with the remaining olive oil and leave the pissaladière in a warm place for about 15 minutes to rise a little more.

Bake for 20-25 minutes, until the dough is crisp and brown, and serve hot or warm.

NOTE: defrosted frozen bread dough, pizza dough or shortcrust pastry works very well in this recipe.

BRUSCHETTE WITH TOMATOES

2 ciabatta loaves
2 large garlic cloves, crushed
4 tbsp extra virgin olive oil
4 large very ripe tomatoes, halved
salt and freshly ground black pepper
tiny basil or tarragon leaves, to garnish (optional)

Prepare a hot grill.

Split each loaf across in half lengthwise (start by cutting the crusts with a knife, but try to prise the halves apart and not to slice all through cleanly, as it is necessary to create a rough surface on which to rub the tomatoes). Then cut each of these pieces in half.

Grill the pieces of bread, rough sides uppermost, until they are just beginning to brown around the top edges.

While the bread is still very warm, spread each piece with some crushed garlic, brush generously with oil and then smear a tomato half all over its surface to spread the tomato pulp on it. Season well.

Return to the grill briefly just to warm through for serving and then garnish with the leaves, if using.

BRESAOLA WITH LEMON MUSTARD VINAIGRETTE

2 unwaxed lemons
5 tbsp extra virgin olive oil
2 tsp English mustard
20 slices of bresaola
2 tbsp finely chopped flat-leaf parsley
salt and freshly ground black pepper
about 12 tiny cherry tomatoes, to garnish
radicchio leaves, to garnish

Finely grate 2 teaspoons of zest from one of the lemons and extract 1 tablespoon of its juice. Cut the other lemon into wedges.

In a small bowl, blend the lemon zest and juice with the oil, mustard and seasoning to taste.

Fan the slices of beef out decoratively on a plate. Just before serving, mix the dressing together well again and dribble it over the slices of beef.

Sprinkle with the parsley, garnish with the cherry tomatoes nestling in radicchio leaves and serve with the lemon wedges.

CROSTINI WITH WILD MUSHROOMS

4 tbsp extra virgin olive oil
4 garlic cloves, finely chopped
255 g/9 oz mixed sliced wild mushrooms, preferably including some ceps
3 tbsp lemon juice
2 tbsp chopped flat-leaf parsley
8 thick slices of crusty white bread
3 tsp anchovy paste
1 buffalo Mozzarella cheese, thinly sliced
salt and freshly ground black pepper
cayenne pepper

Preheat a hot grill or the oven to 180C/350F/gas 4.

In a large frying pan, heat 2 tablespoons of the oil over a moderate heat and sauté the garlic gently until translucent. Add the mushroom slices and sauté over a moderate to high heat until the mushrooms are just beginning to give off their liquid.

Increase the heat and cook briskly for a few minutes until the liquid is driven off and the mushrooms are beginning to brown. Stir in the lemon juice, together with most of the parsley. Season.

Meanwhile lightly grill the slices of bread, or bake them, until they are just beginning to brown.

Spread the toasted slices of bread sparingly with the anchovy paste and then brush them with the remaining oil. Spoon the sautéed mushroom mixture in heaps in the centres of them, reserving some of the better-looking mushroom slices for garnish.

Cover the mushrooms with slices of Mozzarella and sprinkle some pepper over the cheese. Grill or bake in the oven until the cheese is bubbling.

Garnish with the reserved mushrooms and parsley and dust lightly with cayenne before serving piping hot.

BRESAOLA is a speciality of Italy's Lombardy province. Best quality beef is sliced very thinly and air-cured.

BRUSCHETTE may be described as Italian garlic bread while CROSTINI are more like a type of toasted sandwich, although in Italy both are mostly cooked in the oven.

If wild mushrooms are difficult to obtain for the CROSTINI, use equal parts button mushrooms, oyster mushrooms, or brown caps and dried ceps (porcini), soaked in warm water for 20 minutes.

SPICY HUMMUS WITH TAHINI

Now familiar all over the world, the Middle-eastern chickpea purée HUMMUS *traditionally appears on most mezze tables. Such purées may simply be flavoured with garlic and salt, or - as here - with lemon juice, cumin and tahini paste, made from crushed sesame seeds, to give a fine nutty flavour. The earthy taste of tahini is also essential to the classic Turkish aubergine dip* BABA GHANOUJ. *The aubergines must also first be charred to impart the right degree of smokiness. Serve both these dips with strips of pitta bread or crudités, such as celery stalks, sticks of cucumber and courgette, and sweet pepper strips.*

225 g/8 oz dried chickpeas, soaked overnight, or 450 g/1 lb
canned cooked chickpeas, drained
3 or 4 large garlic cloves, crushed
juice of 3 lemons
3 tbsp extra virgin olive oil
2 tsp ground cumin
150 ml/¼ pt tahini paste
2 tbsp finely chopped flat-leaf parsley
salt
cayenne pepper
1 tbsp toasted pine kernels, to garnish (optional)
pitta bread, cut into strips, to serve

Rinse the chickpeas thoroughly (carefully removing any debris and shed skins). Cover the dried chickpeas with water, bring to the boil and boil fast for 10 minutes, then simmer them until quite tender (just over 1 hour). The canned chickpeas need just a 10-15 minute simmer.

Drain thoroughly, reserving a little of the liquid, and put the chickpeas into a food processor or mash them in a bowl. Add the garlic, lemon juice, 2 or 3 tablespoons of the cooking liquid, 1 tablespoon of oil, 1 teaspoon of cumin, a generous pinch of salt and a pinch of cayenne.

Add most of the tahini paste and mix again to a good thick creamy consistency. Adjust the consistency, if necessary, with more tahini paste or cooking liquid or lemon juice. Adjust the seasoning with more salt and cayenne.

Turn the mixture out into a shallow soup bowl. Mix the remaining oil with a pinch of the cayenne and a pinch of the cumin. Dribble this over the top.

Sprinkle with the parsley and decorate with the remaining cumin and some more cayenne (a star pattern is traditional). Dot with the pine kernels, if using. Serve with pitta strips or crudités.

BABA GHANOUJ

2-3 large aubergines
3 large garlic cloves, crushed
1 small onion, grated
pinch of paprika
juice of 2 large lemons
100 ml/3½ fl oz tahini paste
salt
2 tsp finely chopped mint, coriander or flat-leaf
parsley, to garnish
tiny stoned black olives, to garnish
1 tbsp olive oil, to serve
pitta bread or crudités, to serve

Preheat a fairly hot grill or the oven to 230C/450F/gas 8.

Either grill the aubergines, turning them regularly, or bake them in the oven for about 30 minutes, until the skins are black and blistered.

Allow them to cool slightly and then peel off the charred skin. Wash the aubergines and squeeze them firmly to extract their bitter juices.

Chop the aubergine flesh coarsely and put into a blender or mash it in a bowl. Add the garlic, onion, a large pinch of salt, paprika and some of the lemon juice. Blend lightly and then add alternating small amounts of the tahini paste and remaining lemon juice. The final consistency should be thick and smooth. Adjust this and the seasoning with more salt, tahini or lemon juice.

Turn out into a serving bowl and garnish with the herbs and olives. Just before serving with pitta bread or crudités, dribble the oil over the top.

Clockwise from the top left: Assorted Filo Pastry Parcels (page 38), Vine Leaves Stuffed with Seafood Mousse (page 39), Baba Ghanouj, baby aubergines, black olives and Spicy Hummus with Tahini served with crudités

ASSORTED FILO PASTRY PARCELS

MAKES ABOUT 48

450 g/1 lb frozen filo pastry, defrosted
olive oil, for greasing
salt and freshly ground black pepper
FOR THE CHEESE FILLING
250 g/8½ oz Feta cheese
2 tbsp finely chopped walnuts
2 tbsp finely chopped fresh chervil or chives
1 large egg, separated
FOR THE PRAWN FILLING
55 g/2 oz crab meat
2 garlic cloves, crushed
2 spring onions, finely chopped
3 tbsp mayonnaise
2 tbsp finely chopped flat-leaf parsley
juice of 1 lemon
15 large frozen shelled cooked prawns, defrosted
FOR THE SAUSAGE FILLING
4 spicy chorizo sausages, cut across into quarters
2 tbsp finely chopped flat-leaf parsley
cayenne pepper

Preheat the oven to 190C/375F/gas 5 and grease 2 baking sheets with oil.

First make the fillings. For the cheese pastries, crumble the cheese into a bowl and stir in the nuts, herbs and lightly beaten egg yolk. Season and add just enough lightly beaten egg white to give a mixture with a good thick but spoonable consistency.

For the prawn pastries, in a bowl mix all the ingredients but the lemon juice and prawns. Season and add just enough of the lemon juice to give a good sharp flavour and a thick but spoonable consistency.

Remove the sheets of filo pastry from their packet only 2 or 3 at a time, reseal the packet and return to the refrigerator. Use a damp cloth to cover those sheets not being worked with at any given time to prevent them drying out.

For the prawn purses, cut 3 sheets of filo into 10 cm/4 in squares. Oil lightly and then arrange 3 on top of one another so that the corners form a star shape. Put some filling in the centre, press a prawn into it and then pull up the edges and twist around to form the purse. Make sure the pastry is not too tightly wrapped around the filling. Brush the outsides lightly all over with oil.

For the cheese triangles: cut the filo in long strips about 7.5 cm/3 in wide and brush these lightly with oil. Place a generous spoonful of the mixture on one end of the strip about 2.5 cm/1 in away from that end and slightly off centre. Lifting the corner of the end farther away from the filling, fold the pastry in to cover it and form a triangle. Then fold this stuffed triangle on its side parallel to the short edge of the strip of pastry up and over on the strip. Next fold this triangle on its diagonal slide over on to the strip of pastry. Continue until all the strip is used. Press the edges lightly to seal the parcel well, and brush the outsides lightly with oil.

For the sausage 'cigars': cut the pastry into the same long strips as for the cheese triangles and lightly oil them. Place a piece of sausage at one end parallel to the short ends, sprinkle with a little cayenne and some parsley and simply roll the filo strip up, tucking in the edges as you go. Brush the finished 'cigars' lightly with oil.

Arrange on the baking sheets and bake for about 25 minutes, until just golden. Serve hot or warm with drinks or as part of a buffet meal.

VINE LEAVES STUFFED WITH SEAFOOD MOUSSE

MAKES 18

2 unwaxed lemons
4 large garlic cloves
1 tbsp oil
1 onion, finely chopped
2 tsp finely chopped fresh root ginger
2 tbsp finely chopped bulb fennel
225 g/8 oz white fish fillets, skinned
1 celery stalk, chopped into small dice
3 tbsp finely chopped coriander
1 egg, separated
85 g/3 oz cooked rice
85 g/3 oz tiny frozen prawns, defrosted
85 g/3 oz canned shelled baby clams, drained
about 24 good large vine leaves
2 tbsp finely chopped flat-leaf parsley
400 g/14 oz canned chopped plum tomatoes
1 tbsp tomato paste
salt and freshly ground black pepper
more lemon slices, to serve

Finely grate 1 teaspoon of zest from one of the lemons and extract the juice from both. Cut 1 of the garlic cloves into fine slivers and crush the rest.

Put the oil in a sauté pan over a moderate heat. Add the onion, three-quarters of the crushed garlic, the ginger and fennel and sauté gently until the onion is soft but not browned.

In a food processor, blend the fish together with the celery, coriander, egg yolk, the grated lemon zest, half the lemon juice and the sautéed mixture. Be careful not to over-process! Stir in the rice, prawns and clams. Season generously.

Whisk the egg white to stiff peaks and then stir a spoonful into the stuffing to loosen it. Gently fold the remaining egg white into the mixture.

If using vine leaves preserved in brine, cover with boiling water, stir well and leave to soak for about 30 minutes. Drain and rinse with cold water. Repeat the process. If using fresh leaves, blanch for about 15 minutes in boiling water and then drain well.

Arrange 18 of the best leaves (don't use any with holes or tears) with vein sides up. Put a generous tablespoonful of stuffing on each leaf, near its base. Roll up the leaf from the base, tucking in the sides as you go. Take care not to wrap the filling too tightly as it needs a little room to expand. Squeeze the parcel gently in the palm to secure it.

Line a large heavy-based saucepan with the remaining vine leaves and arrange the rolled leaves on them with the tips tucked underneath to keep them rolled during cooking. Add the remaining lemon juice and chopped garlic to the tomatoes and their liquid, together with the parsley, garlic slivers and tomato paste. Season and pour over the parcels. Cover and simmer very gently for 30 minutes.

Serve the stuffed vine leaves hot, with a little of the cooking juices and accompanied by lemon slices.

Sweet peppers grilled as in the MARINATED PEPPERS recipe develop a unique smoky flavour. Do not peel them under running water (as some other recipes suggest) or you will lose all the flavourful juices.

MARINATED PEPPERS WITH PINE KERNELS AND CAPERS

4-6 (depending on size) red or yellow sweet peppers, quartered and deseeded
1 tbsp pine kernels
1 tbsp capers, rinsed and drained
FOR THE GARLIC VINAIGRETTE
1 tbsp vinegar
3 tbsp extra virgin olive oil, plus more for greasing
1 garlic clove, crushed
salt and pepper
crusty bread, such as ciabatta, to serve

Prepare a hot grill. Line the grill pan with foil and lightly grease it with olive oil.

Place the pepper quarters, skin side up, in a single layer in the prepared grill pan and grill until all the skin is blackened.

Put the pepper quarters in a plastic bag. Seal the bag and allow the peppers to cook in their own steam for 5 minutes. Then remove the blackened skin, but do not rinse the peppers as this will wash away the precious tasty juices.

Make the garlic vinaigrette by combining the ingredients in a bowl with some seasoning. Add the pepper pieces and toss gently but thoroughly to coat them well. Cover the bowl with film and leave to marinate at room temperature for 1-2 hours, or in the refrigerator for up to 24.

To serve: arrange the pepper pieces in one layer on an attractive serving plate and drizzle over any dressing remaining in the bowl. Scatter over the pine kernels and capers. Accompany with crusty bread to mop up the juices.

AÏOLI WITH QUAILS' EGGS, PRAWNS AND CRUDITÉS

12 quails' eggs
about 450 g/1 lb mixed raw vegetables (such as carrots, celery, cucumber, radishes, cherry tomatoes, deseeded sweet peppers, broccoli, cauliflower, courgettes, sugar peas, mange-tout peas and button mushrooms), cut into sticks or bite-sized pieces as necessary
12 large shelled cooked prawns
FOR THE AÏOLI
2 garlic cloves, crushed
1 egg
175 ml/6 fl oz sunflower or corn oil
1 tsp white wine vinegar or lemon juice
salt and pepper

First make the aïoli: put the garlic and egg in the bowl of a blender or food processor and season generously with salt and pepper.

With the motor running, add the oil in a slow trickle from a jug. The sauce will thicken. Add the vinegar or lemon juice and whizz for a couple of seconds more.

Transfer the aïoli to a serving bowl and leave it for at least 30 minutes before serving, to allow the rich flavours to develop fully.

Meanwhile, boil the quails' eggs for 3 minutes, then cool them under cold running water.

To serve: place the bowl of aïoli in the middle of a large plate and surround it with the vegetable crudités, quails' eggs and prawns for dipping.

Top: Aïoli with Quails' Eggs, Prawns and Crudités; bottom: Marinated Peppers with Pine Kernels and Capers.

For the AÏOLI WITH QUAILS' EGGS, PRAWNS AND CRUDITÉS *you can make your own selection of vegetables according to what are the freshest and best available.* AÏOLI *is the Provençal garlic-flavoured mayonnaise which is a traditional accompaniment to many fish and seafood dishes.*

TORTILLAS, *or*
Spanish omelettes,
are a mainstay of
the traditional
selections of snacks
served in tapas bars.
They are served
warm or cold, cut
into thick wedges or
squares.

SALSA *is the*
Spanish and Italian
word for sauce, but it
is now commonly
used in English for
dressings spiced with
chilli.

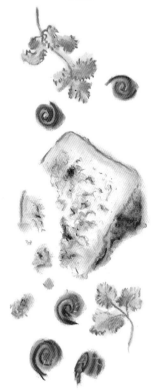

COURGETTE TORTILLA WITH A HERB SALSA

SERVES 4-6

2 large potatoes, diced small
30 g/1 oz butter
2 tbsp olive oil
2 onions, finely chopped
3 garlic cloves, finely chopped
3 large courgettes, thinly sliced
8 eggs, beaten
2 tbsp chopped flat-leaf parsley
salt and freshly ground black pepper
FOR THE HERB SALSA
5 tbsp olive oil
1 tbsp red wine vinegar
1 tsp grainy mustard
5 tbsp canned chopped plum tomatoes, drained
pinch of chilli powder
2 tbsp each chopped chives and flat-leaf parsley

In a large pan of boiling salted water, blanch the potato dice for 2 or 3 minutes. Refresh under cold running water, drain well and pat dry.

In a 25.5 cm/10 in frying or omelette pan, preferably with a lid, melt the butter with the oil over a moderate heat.

Sauté the onion and garlic until the onion is translucent and soft. Add the courgettes and potatoes and sauté for a few minutes more, taking care that the onion and garlic do not get too brown.

Season the eggs and stir in most of the parsley. Stir into the pan, cover and cook over a gentle heat for about 10 minutes, until the eggs are just set.

Meanwhile, preheat a hot grill. Finish the omelette off under it until the top is well browned.

While the tortilla is cooking, make the salsa by mixing all the ingredients and seasoning to taste.

Serve the tortilla warm or cold, sprinkled with the remaining parsley. Serve the salsa separately.

GORGONZOLA AND ANCHOVY SOUFFLÉ

55 g/2 oz unsalted butter
55 g/2 oz canned anchovy fillets, drained
1 level tbsp flour
150 ml/¼ pt milk
3 eggs, separated
85 g/3 oz Gorgonzola cheese, crumbled or cubed
freshly ground black pepper
cayenne pepper

Preheat the oven to 190C/375F/gas 5 and heat a baking sheet in the centre of it. Carefully grease a 15 cm/6 in soufflé dish with 15 g/½ oz of the butter. Make sure that the rim is well greased to prevent the soufflé catching as it rises.

Rinse the anchovies to remove excess saltiness, pat them dry and cut them into small strips.

In a large heavy-based pan, melt two-thirds of the remaining butter over a low heat and stir in the flour. Cook for a minute or two, stirring continuously. Gradually add the milk, still stirring, and cook until smooth and thick.

Off the heat, stir the egg yolks into the sauce, one at a time. Then stir in the cheese and anchovies. Adjust the seasoning with pepper and cayenne pepper (the seasoning should be quite forceful as it will be cut by the unseasoned egg white). Set aside.

Whisk the egg whites to stiff peaks. Spoon a little of the beaten egg white into the cheese mixture and stir well to 'slacken' the mixture. Carefully fold the remaining egg white into the mixture.

Pour the mixture into the prepared soufflé dish. Tap the base fairly hard on a work surface and place in the oven on the hot baking sheet.

Bake for 20-25 minutes, until well risen and golden. Serve immediately, dusted with cayenne.

Courgette Tortilla with a Herb Salsa.

CEVICHE

2 whole fresh mackerel or 4 skinned mackerel fillets
5 tbsp lime juice
5 tbsp lemon juice
3 tbsp extra virgin olive oil
1 tbsp red wine vinegar
1 large onion, finely chopped
1 tsp chopped coriander
2 tbsp chopped flat-leaf parsley
1 fresh chilli pepper, deseeded and finely chopped
2 large tomatoes, peeled and chopped
1 ripe avocado
salt and freshly ground black pepper
tortilla chips, to serve

If using whole fresh fish, press out the backbone of each and remove. Cut the fish or the fillets into chunks about 1 cm/½ in across.

Place the pieces of fish in a shallow dish and pour over the lime and lemon juice. Season, cover and leave to marinate for 6 hours, turning once or twice.

Put the oil, vinegar, onion, coriander, parsley, chilli and tomatoes in another bowl and mix together thoroughly.

Drain the fish, reserving the juice. Mix the fish in with the herb and tomato mixture and transfer to a serving dish.

Halve and stone the avocado. Peel and slice the flesh thinly, then arrange the slices on top of the fish mixture. Using a pastry brush, coat the avocado with the reserved juice to prevent discoloration.

Season with salt and pepper and serve with tortilla chips.

Top: Smoked Trout and Dill in Halibut Cornets; bottom: Ceviche.

PEPPERED SMOKED MACKEREL PÂTÉ WITH HORSERADISH

4 peppered smoked mackerel fillets, skinned
30 g/1 oz butter, softened
150 ml/¼ pt single cream
3 tbsp coarsely chopped hazelnuts
1 tbsp lime juice
1 tbsp horseradish sauce
salt and freshly ground black pepper
slices of warm toast, to serve

Put all the ingredients into a blender or food processor with some seasoning. Process until smooth, then transfer to a serving bowl.

Serve with slices of warm toast.

SMOKED TROUT AND DILL IN HALIBUT CORNETS

170 g/6 oz smoked trout fillets, skinned and flaked
1 tbsp finely chopped dill
1 tbsp horseradish cream
350 g/12 oz very thin slices of smoked or fresh halibut
2 slices of brown toast
small bunch of chervil
juice of ½ lemon
juice of 1 lime
salt and freshly ground black pepper

Place the smoked trout, dill and horseradish in a small bowl. Season and mix together thoroughly.

Lay the halibut slices on a flat surface and cut them into 8 strips. Spread each piece with the smoked trout mixture, then roll up into a cornet.

Cut each slice of toast into 4 rectangles. Place on a serving dish, then sit the cornets on top of them.

Garnish with chervil. Dribble the fruit juice over and sprinkle with pepper just before serving.

CEVICHE *is a dish native to South America in which raw fish virtually 'cooks' in a lime juice marinade.*

Fresh and smoked HALIBUT *are available sliced like smoked salmon from better fishmongers and some supermarkets. Smoked eel or smoked salmon may be substituted.*

When buying
Camembert cheese
for the
CAMEMBERT AND
CRANBERRY
BARQUETTES, *try
to buy a slightly
under-ripe cheese as
this will slice more
easily.*

For the GOATS'
CHEESE AND
HERB TARTLETS,
*buy a goats' cheese
which has no
flavoured coating
and is quite soft in
texture.*

PROSCIUTTO *(also
known as Parma
ham) is a traditional
Italian ham. The
pigs are fed on a
diet of whey left over
from making the
local Parmesan
cheese and the ham
is dry-cured under
weights and left to
mature for one year.
It is very thinly
sliced and served raw
as an appetizer or
used as a flavouring
in cooking.*

CAMEMBERT AND CRANBERRY BARQUETTES

MAKES 16

FOR THE PASTRY
115 g/4 oz flour
½ tsp salt
½ tsp English mustard powder
85 g/3 oz butter, cut into small pieces
1 egg yolk
FOR THE FILLING
2 tbsp orange juice
1 tbsp caster sugar
55 g/2 oz cranberries
115 g/4 oz Camembert cheese, thinly sliced

To make the pastry: sift the flour, salt and mustard powder into a bowl, add the butter and rub it in finely with the fingertips. Stir in the egg yolk and mix together with a fork to form a firm dough.

Knead the dough on a lightly floured surface until smooth. Roll it out thinly and use to line sixteen 10 cm/4 in fluted barquette moulds. Chill for 30 minutes.

Preheat the oven to 200C/400F/gas 6.

Bake the pastry cases blind for 10 minutes, or until lightly browned at the edges and cooked at their bases.

While they are baking make the filling: place the orange juice, sugar and cranberries in a small saucepan. Heat gently, shaking the pan occasionally, until the cranberries are tender and the liquid has evaporated. Leave the cranberries to cool.

Arrange a little cheese in each pastry case. Just before serving, place the pastry boats in the oven for 2-3 minutes until the cheese has just melted. Remove them from the oven and arrange a few cranberries on each barquette. Serve immediately.

GOATS' CHEESE AND HERB TARTLETS

MAKES 4

FOR THE PASTRY
115 g/4 oz flour
½ tsp salt and ¼ tsp freshly ground black pepper
85 g/3 oz butter, cut into small pieces
1 egg yolk
FOR THE FILLING
100 g/3 ½ oz full-fat soft goats' cheese
*2 tbsp chopped mixed herbs,
including basil, marjoram and parsley*
2 tbsp finely chopped spring onions
1 egg
150 ml/¼ pt single cream
½ tsp freshly ground black pepper

To make the pastry: sift the flour, salt and pepper into a bowl. Add the butter and rub it in finely with the fingertips. Stir in the egg yolk and mix together with a fork to form a firm dough.

Knead the dough on a lightly floured surface until smooth. Roll it out thinly and use to line four 11 cm/4½ in diameter loose-based fluted tart tins. Chill for 30 minutes.

Preheat the oven to 200C/400F/gas 6.

Bake the cases blind for 10 minutes, or until lightly browned at the edges and cooked at their bases. Reduce the oven temperature to 190C/375F/gas 5.

While they are baking make the filling: place the cheese, herbs and spring onions in a bowl and beat together until well blended. Add the egg, cream and pepper and beat again until well blended.

Pour the mixture into the pastry cases and return them to the cooler oven for 10-15 minutes, until the filling has just set. Serve warm or cold.

GRUYÈRE AND PROSCIUTTO BARQUETTES

MAKES 6

FOR THE PASTRY
115 g/4 oz flour
½ tsp salt and ¼ tsp freshly ground pepper
85 g/3 oz butter, cut into small pieces
1 egg yolk
1 tbsp freshly chopped basil
FOR THE FILLING
85 g/3 oz Gruyère cheese, thinly sliced
35 g/2 oz prosciutto, cut into strips
150 ml ¼ pt single cream
1 egg
½ tsp French mustard
¼ tsp freshly ground pepper

To make the pastry: sift the flour, salt and pepper into a bowl, add the butter and rub it in finely with the fingertips. Stir in the egg yolk and basil and mix together with a fork to form a firm dough.

Knead the dough on a lightly floured surface until smooth. Roll it out thinly and use to line six 15 cm/ 6 in barquette moulds. Chill for 30 minutes.

Preheat the oven to 200C/400F/gas 6.

Bake the cases blind for 10 minutes, or until lightly browned at the edges and cooked at their bases. Reduce the oven temperature to 190C/375F/gas 5.

While they are baking make the filling: arrange the cheese slices in the pastry cases with the strips of prosciutto on top. In a bowl, whisk together the cream, egg, mustard and pepper.

Spoon the egg mixture into the pastry cases and return them to the cooler oven for 15 minutes, or until the filling has just set. Serve warm or cold.

POT STICKER
DUMPLINGS *are a
popular Chinese
snack often included
in the 'dim sum'
menus traditional to
family Sunday
lunches, which
feature dumplings of
all types - steamed,
grilled and fried.*

SESAME PRAWN TOASTS

MAKES 24

*225 g/8 oz raw prawns in their shells, heads removed
30 g/1 oz canned Chinese water chestnuts, drained
30 g/1 oz streaky bacon, chopped
½ tsp salt
1 tsp cornflour
white of 1 small egg
6 slices of white bread, crusts removed
4 tbsp sesame seeds
vegetable oil, for frying*

Remove the shells from the prawns. Using a sharp knife, make an incision along the length of the back of each prawn (the outside curve). Remove and discard any dark thread, or gut.

Place the prawn meat, water chestnuts, bacon, salt, cornflour and egg white in the bowl of a blender or food processor and reduce to a smooth purée.

Alternatively, reduce the ingredients to a purée in a large mortar with a pestle, or simply chop them as finely as possible with a sharp knife.

Spread the purée evenly over the slices of bread.

Spread an even layer of sesame seeds on a large plate and then press the spread sides of the bread on them to coat them evenly with seeds.

Fill a frying pan or wok with oil to a depth of about 2.5 cm/1 in. Heat until nice and hot, then fry the toasts, coated side down, for about 1 minute or so, until the seeds are crisp and golden. Turn and fry on the other side until the bread is crisp and golden. Drain on paper towels.

Cut each slice into 4 even strips and serve as soon as possible.

POT STICKER DUMPLINGS

MAKES 16

*170 g/6 oz flour
2 tbsp vegetable oil
150 ml/¼ pt chicken or vegetable stock
sweet chilli sauce or other dipping sauce, to serve*
FOR THE FILLING
*85 g/3 oz white crab meat
30 g/1 oz white cabbage, finely chopped
1 small spring onion, finely chopped
2.5 cm/1 in cube of peeled fresh root ginger, finely
chopped
1 tbsp dry sherry
1 tbsp soy sauce
¼ tsp salt
1 tsp sesame oil
½ tsp sugar*

In a bowl, mix the flour with 125 ml/4 fl oz of very hot water to make a dough. Knead for 10 minutes, adding a little more water if the dough seems too dry or a little more flour if it seems too sticky. Cover with a damp cloth and leave to rest for 30 minutes.

Meanwhile, make the filling: mix all the ingredients together in a bowl.

Knead the rested dough again for 5 minutes and divide it into 16 equal balls. On a floured surface, roll the balls out to make circles of dough with a diameter of about 7.5 cm/3 in. Keep the balls and circles of dough covered with a damp cloth while working to prevent them drying out.

Place a small teaspoon of stuffing in the centre of each circle of dough. Moisten the edges with water. Fold each circle over in half to make a semi-circle and pinch the edges to seal. Using the thumb and forefinger, 'frill' the edges to make each dumpling into a small Cornish pasty shape, with a frilly seam on top and a flat bottom.

Heat the oil in a frying or sauté pan which is large enough to take the dumplings snugly in one layer and preferably has a tight-fitting lid. Fry the dumplings over a very low heat until their flat bottoms are crisp and golden.

Pour over the stock, cover and simmer over a very low heat for 12-15 minutes, or until all the liquid has been absorbed. Remove the lid and cook for a further 2 minutes.

Serve hot, accompanied by sweet chilli sauce or another dipping sauce.

THAI FISH CAKES

MAKES 8

225 g/8 oz skinless white fish fillets, coarsely chopped
1 ½ tsp Thai red curry paste
1 tbsp cornflour
1 tbsp fish sauce
1 small egg, beaten
1 large red or green chilli pepper, deseeded and chopped
2 shallots, finely chopped
85 g/3 oz thin French beans, finely chopped
2 tbsp vegetable oil
Cucumber and Carrot Relish (see page 11) or a dipping sauce, to serve

In a blender or food processor, blend the fish until just smooth. Add the curry paste, cornflour, fish sauce and egg and process briefly until mixed. Be careful not to over-process, or the fish will lose all texture! Transfer to a small bowl and mix in the chilli pepper, shallots and beans.

Divide the mixture into 8 portions and shape them into round cakes about 6 mm/¼ in thick.

Heat the oil in a frying pan over a moderate heat and fry the cakes for 3-4 minutes on each side, until uniformly golden.

Serve immediately with Cucumber and Carrot Relish or a dipping sauce.

DEEP-FRIED 'SEAWEED'

225 g/8 oz cabbage greens, very finely shredded
vegetable oil, for deep frying
sugar, for sprinkling

Heat the oil in a wok until just beginning to smoke, then deep-fry the shredded cabbage in small batches for a few seconds only, until it turns dark and crispy.

Remove each batch with a slotted spoon, drain on paper towels and keep warm while the remaining batches are being cooked.

Serve sprinkled with a little sugar as soon as all the greens are cooked.

THAI RED CURRY PASTE *is flavoured with lime zest, lemon grass, galangal and trassi – the South-east Asian condiment made from fermented shrimp – and is available from Oriental suppliers.*

As here, the DEEP-FRIED 'SEAWEED' *served in many Chinese restaurants is not seaweed at all but shredded greens. Use a food processor to shred them very finely.*

Popular in Singapore, Malaysia and Indonesia, SATAY *dishes consist of tiny 'kebabs' and may contain meat, poultry or fish.*

Japanese TERIYAKI SAUCE, *made from soy beans and wine and used as a marinade and basting sauce, is available bottled from Oriental shops, as are small wooden skewers.*

CHICKEN SATAY

MAKES 8 SMALL SKEWERS

225 g/8 oz skinless chicken breast, cut into
2 cm/¾ in cubes
FOR THE MARINADE
1 tbsp brown sugar
2 tbsp soy sauce
juice of ½ lemon
1 tbsp vegetable oil
FOR THE DIPPING SAUCE
1 tbsp vegetable oil
1 small onion, finely chopped
1 garlic clove, crushed
1 tbsp crunchy peanut butter
1 tbsp sweet chilli sauce
1 tsp soy sauce
3 tbsp boiling water

First make the marinade: in a small bowl, dissolve the sugar in 1 tablespoon of hot water and then add the remaining ingredients and mix well. Add the chicken pieces and stir until well coated, then leave for at least 1 hour or up to 24 hours in the refrigerator.

Meanwhile make the dipping sauce: in a small pan, heat the oil over a moderate heat and cook the onion until softened. Then add the remaining ingredients and simmer for 3 minutes. Transfer to a serving bowl and allow to cool.

Soak 8 small wooden skewers in water for 30 minutes or more, to prevent them scorching too much during cooking. Preheat a hot grill or barbecue.

Thread the marinated meat on the prepared skewers and cook them under the grill or on the barbecue for 4-5 minutes, turning once.

Serve accompanied by the dipping sauce.

NOTE: for an unusual and attractive presentation use bay twigs instead of skewers.

TERIYAKI CHICKEN

MAKES 12 SKEWERS

2 tbsp vegetable oil
5 tbsp Teriyaki sauce
1 tbsp dry sherry
1 tbsp brown sugar
1 garlic clove, crushed
2.5 cm/1 in cube of peeled fresh root ginger, crushed in a garlic press or very finely chopped
½ small red sweet pepper, deseeded and cut into 1 cm/½ in squares
225 g/8 oz skinned chicken breast, cut into 1 cm/½ in cubes
strips of spring onion and cucumber, to serve

Soak 12 small wooden skewers in water for 30 minutes or more, to prevent them from scorching too much under the hot grill.

Place all the ingredients except the chicken, spring onion and cucumber in a bowl and mix them well to combine.

Drop the pieces of chicken into the marinade and toss them well in the mixture to ensure that they are coated on all sides. Cover and leave for at least 30 minutes, or up to 3 hours, shaking the bowl occasionally.

Preheat a hot grill or barbecue.

Thread the pieces of chicken and pepper onto the skewers and grill or barbecue for about 5 minutes, or until cooked through, turning 2 or 3 times and brushing each time with marinade.

Serve immediately, accompanied by the spring onion and cucumber.

SPRING ROLLS

MAKES 12

12 spring roll wrappers
vegetable oil, for deep-frying
FOR THE FILLING
5 dried Chinese mushrooms
1 tbsp vegetable oil
½ tsp Oriental sesame oil
225 g/8 oz minced pork
2 spring onions, finely chopped
2 garlic cloves, crushed
1 small carrot, grated
6 canned Chinese water chestnuts, drained and chopped
75 g/2 ½ oz peeled cooked prawns, chopped
1 tbsp soy sauce
1 egg, beaten

Soak the dried mushrooms in warm water for 30 minutes. Drain, remove and discard the stalks and slice the caps thinly.

Make the filling: heat the oils in a wok or frying pan over a moderate heat and stir-fry the pork for 5 minutes. Add the onions, garlic, carrot, mushrooms and water chestnuts and continue to stir-fry for 2 minutes. Allow the mixture to cool.

Add the prawns, soy sauce and most of the egg to the mixture, saving a little egg to seal the wrappers.

Divide the mixture into 12 portions and place one on the edge of each pastry wrapper. Fold in the sides of each and roll it up, brushing the join with a little of the reserved egg to seal.

Deep-fry the rolls in batches in hot oil in a wok for about 4-5 minutes each, or until golden and crispy. Be careful not to have the fat too hot or the skins will burn before the filling is cooked through. Drain on paper towels and keep warm while the rest are being cooked. Serve as soon as all are cooked.

NOTE: serve with a dipping sauce made from equal parts soy sauce and wine vinegar.

WATER CHESTNUTS IN CRISPY BACON

200 g/7 oz smoked streaky bacon, rinds removed
225 g/8 oz canned Chinese water chestnuts, drained

Soak some wooden toothpicks in water for 30 minutes or more to prevent them from burning during cooking. Preheat a hot grill.

Using the back of a knife, scrape each slice of bacon to stretch it a little and then cut it across into 2 even lengths.

Wrap each water chestnut in a length of bacon and secure with one of the toothpicks.

Grill the parcels for 5-7 minutes, turning once, until the bacon is crispy.

Serve immediately.

SPRING ROLL *wrappers are available fresh or frozen from Oriental suppliers, as are* CHINESE DRIED MUSHROOMS.

ORIENTAL SESAME OIL *differs from the sesame oil sold in health food shops as it is made from toasted sesame seeds to give much greater flavour.*

THAI STUFFED CHICKEN WINGS

MAKES 12

12 chicken wings (see below)
115 g/4 oz minced pork
55 g/2 oz canned bamboo shoots, drained
55 g/2 oz canned Chinese water chestnuts, drained
30 g/1 oz button mushrooms
2 garlic cloves, crushed
2 tsp dark soy sauce
1 tsp sugar
1 egg, lightly beaten
4 tbsp flour
salt and freshly ground black pepper
vegetable oil, for deep-frying and greasing
Plum Sauce (see page 11), to serve

Try to buy wings with 2 joints. Cut off the bits furthest from the tip, skin them and take the flesh from the bones. Mince this flesh and add it to the pork in a large bowl. If wings with only the wing tip and 1 joint are available, buy another 115 g/4 oz minced chicken and add this to the pork.

Chop the bamboo shoots, water chestnuts and mushrooms very finely in a food processor and add to the meat mixture, together with the garlic, soy sauce, sugar and a good seasoning of salt and pepper. Mix very well together and then add the egg to bind and mix well again.

Using a small sharp pointed knife, bone the wings, working from the cut end. There are two bones, one bigger than the other, which will be joined together at that cut end. Separate them first with the point of the knife. The bigger bone will also be firmly attached to the flesh on the side opposite to the small bone - carefully detach this with the knife.

Now using the edge of the knife, scrape the flesh

Sesame Beef Balls; bottom: Thai Stuffed Chicken Wings.

downward from the bones, being careful not to cut the skin. Work down to the joint, then twist and snap each bone off in turn. Discard these bones or reserve them for stock. This will leave wing tips with a hollow pocket of skin and meat attached.

Using a teaspoon and fingers, fill the cavities with the minced meat mixture. They should be filled until they are almost overflowing.

Place the stuffed wings in the lightly oiled upper part of a steamer and steam over boiling water for 20 minutes, or until firm. Allow to cool.

Season the flour with salt and pepper. Coat the cooled wings in it and deep-fry them in batches in hot oil in a wok until the skin is golden brown and nicely crisp. Drain on paper towels and keep warm while the rest are being cooked.

Serve immediately with Plum Sauce.

SESAME BEEF BALLS

350 g/12 oz very lean minced beef
45 g/1 ½ oz rindless streaky bacon, chopped
1 tbsp chopped celery
1 tbsp chopped carrot
1 tbsp finely chopped mushroom
2 spring onions, chopped
1 tbsp cornflour
1 tbsp soy sauce
1 tbsp sherry
½ tsp salt
1 egg, beaten
2 tbsp bottled hoi-sin sauce
2 tsp sugar
1 tbsp sesame seeds
freshly ground black pepper
flour, for dusting
vegetable oil, for deep-frying
hoi-sin sauce, Plum Sauce (see page 11) or other dipping
sauce, to serve

Put the minced beef, bacon, chopped vegetables, mushrooms, spring onions, cornflour, two-thirds of the soy sauce, the sherry, salt and some pepper in a blender or food processor and process until well mixed. Be careful not to over-process.

Using floured hands, form the paste into walnut-sized balls. Coat these thoroughly and evenly in the beaten egg.

Deep-fry the coated balls in hot oil in a wok until well browned all over. Drain the cooked balls on paper towels.

Remove all but 2 tablespoons of the oil from the pan and add the remaining soy sauce, the hoi-sin sauce, sugar and sesame seeds.

Heat the pan over a moderate heat, add the beef balls and cook for a few minutes, shaking the pan occasionally until the balls are coated with the sauces and sesame seeds and turn a deep mahogany brown all over.

Serve immediately with more hoi-sin sauce, Plum Sauce or other dipping sauce.

Fresh CHINESE WATER CHESTNUTS *are occasionally available from Chinese markets.*

HOI-SIN SAUCE, *one of the most popular dipping sauces in China, is available in bottles from most better supermarkets.*

RICE, GRAINS AND PASTA

One of the greatest changes in our eating habits in the last few years has been the increasing displacement of the potato by rice and pasta in our meal-making. As much as being a matter of convenience, this reflects our new interest in the foods of other cultures, especially India, the Orient and the Mediterranean. Perhaps the peak of creativity in Mediterranean cooking is reached in their cunning uses of rice and grains. Scarcely ever served as mere accompaniments, they are cooked slowly with flavouring ingredients to make such dishes as risotto, paella and lasagne. Less common grains such as couscous, polenta and bulghar wheat are also cooked with rich sauces or made into refreshing salads. The myriad different pasta shapes available can be combined with literally innumerable sauces to make anything from light snacks to substantial meals – and even interesting desserts.

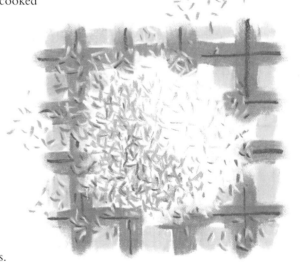

Saffron Paella (page 56) with an array of rice, pasta, pulses and flavouring ingredients.

There are endless variations on the Spanish rice dish PAELLA – only rice, oil and saffron are essential. Other ingredients may include green beans, shelled peas and artichoke hearts, lobster, duck and rabbit.

SAFFRON PAELLA

SERVES 6-8

*1 chicken, dressed weight about 1.35 kg/3 lb, cut into 12
pieces, backbone and giblets retained
4 onions
3 large garlic cloves, chopped
white of 1 leek, chopped
1 celery stalk, thinly sliced
bouquet garni
12 black peppercorns
350 g/12 oz squid, sliced into rings
about 18 mussels
4 tbsp olive oil
250 g/9 oz chorizo sausage, sliced
1 large red sweet pepper, deseeded and cut into thick strips
1 large green sweet pepper, deseeded and cut into thick
strips
few strands of saffron
6 large tomatoes, peeled and chopped
350 g/12 oz long-grain rice
6-8 langoustines or Dublin Bay prawns (optional)
salt and freshly ground black pepper
cayenne pepper
lemon wedges, to serve*

Put the chicken giblets and backbone in a pan with 2 of the onions coarsely chopped, the garlic, leek, celery, bouquet garni, peppercorns and a large pinch of salt. Barely cover with water and bring to the boil. Skim and then simmer for about 1 hour.

Meanwhile, put the squid in a pan and cover with cold water. Bring to the boil and simmer for 5 minutes, drain and set aside. Scrub the mussel shells well, discarding any open ones which do not close when tapped. Finely chop the remaining onions.

Heat the oil in a large deep frying or paella pan over a moderate heat and brown the chicken pieces. Remove them with a slotted spoon and set aside.

In the same oil, cook the chorizo, squid, pepper strips and chopped onions gently for a few minutes. Stir in the saffron and cook for another 5 minutes. Add the tomatoes, and bring to the boil. Season well and add a good pinch or two of cayenne.

Stir in the rice. Place the chicken pieces, mussels and langoustines, if using, on top. Pour over the strained chicken stock and bring to the boil.

Cover and simmer gently for about 20 minutes, or until the rice is tender. Keep checking the rice; if it looks too dry at any time, add a little water. Serve with lemon wedges.

SALAMI AND BLUE CHEESE RISOTTO

*45 g/1½ oz butter
2 tbsp olive oil
1 large onion, finely chopped
2 large garlic cloves, finely chopped
350 g/12 oz risotto rice, preferably arborio
850 ml/1½ pt hot chicken or veal stock
225 g/8 oz Italian salami, peeled and cubed
225 g/8 oz Gorgonzola or other blue cheese
2 celery stalks, chopped
1 large red pepper, deseeded and cut into thin strips
large pinch of dried sage
2 tbsp finely chopped flat-leaf parsley
salt and freshly ground black pepper
cayenne pepper
chopped chives, to garnish*

In a large heavy-based pan which has a tight-fitting lid, melt the butter with the oil over a moderate heat. Add the onion and garlic. Cook gently for 1 or 2 minutes until soft and just beginning to colour.

Add the rice and sauté over a fairly high heat for 2 minutes. Add 300 ml/½ pt of stock, stir well and bring to the boil. Reduce the heat and simmer gently for about 5 minutes, until the stock is absorbed.

Continue to add the remaining stock, one-quarter at a time, stirring well and waiting until it has all been absorbed before adding more. The whole process should take about 30 minutes and the final result should be rice that is richly creamy and slightly sticky - but not mushy.

About half-way through, add half the salami and cheese with the celery, red pepper and sage.

With the final addition of stock, add the remainder of the salami and cheese and the parsley. Adjust the seasoning with salt, pepper and cayenne. Serve garnished with chives.

CHICKEN AND LAMB COUSCOS

SERVES 6-8

2 tbsp oil
1 large chicken, cut into 12 pieces, backbone retained
250 g/8½ oz lean stewing lamb, cut into large cubes
3 onions, chopped
4 garlic cloves, crushed
3 turnips, cut into chunks
3 large carrots, chopped
few strands of saffron
½ tsp each of ground cumin, ginger and turmeric
4 large ripe tomatoes, chopped
4 courgettes, chopped
85 g/3 oz seedless raisins
bunch of flat-leaf parsley, finely chopped
bunch of coriander, finely chopped
200 g/7 oz canned cooked chickpeas, drained
450 g/1 lb pre-cooked couscous
2 tsp harissa paste
30 g/1 oz butter
2 or 3 tbsp rose water
55 g/2 oz stoned dates, cut into shards
salt and freshly ground black pepper
more harissa paste, to serve

In the bottom part of a couscoussier or a large heavy-based saucepan, heat the oil over a fairly high heat and brown the pieces of chicken and lamb.

Add the onions, garlic, turnips, carrots and the chicken backbone. Cover with water, season and stir in the saffron and other spices. Bring to the boil and simmer for about 1 hour, skimming as necessary.

Remove and discard the backbone. Add the tomatoes, courgettes, raisins, most of the herbs and two-thirds of the chickpeas. Simmer for 30 minutes more.

Either prepare the couscous by simply pouring boiling water over it, leaving it to steep for about 10 minutes and draining it, or by steaming it for about 20 minutes in the top part of the couscoussier.

Ladle out 2 cupfuls of the broth and season it with a little of the harissa. When the couscous is fluffed up and ready, stir in one-third of this seasoned broth along with the butter, the remaining chickpeas, rose water and dates.

Serve the couscous on a large warmed serving dish with the pieces of meat and vegetables piled in the centre and some of the broth poured over. Sprinkle with the reserved herbs and serve the remaining seasoned broth and more harissa separately.

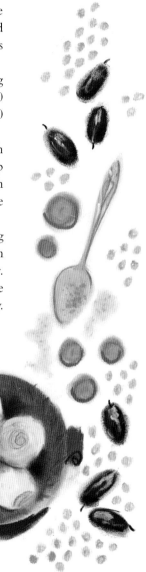

LENTIL AND BULGHAR PILAF WITH YOGURT

225 g/8 oz green lentils, preferably le Puy
bay leaf
1 tsp cumin seeds, finely crushed
1 tsp coriander seeds, finely crushed
225 g/8 oz bulghar wheat
pinch of cayenne
6 tbsp olive oil
2 onions, thinly sliced
2 garlic cloves, finely chopped
2 tbsp finely chopped coriander leaves
juice of ½ lemon
150 ml/¼ pt Greek yogurt
salt and freshly ground black pepper

Soak the lentils in cold water for about 1 hour, drain and put them in a pan. Pour in 1.1 litre/2 pt of fresh water and add the bay leaf and spices. Bring to the boil, boil for 10 minutes, then simmer for about 20 minutes until just tender.

Remove the bay leaf and add the bulghar wheat with a pinch of cayenne and seasoning to taste. Stir well, cover and turn off the heat. Leave to sit for about 20 minutes, or until the bulghar is tender. Check from time to time to see if it has become too dry and add a little more water as necessary.

Meanwhile, heat one-third of the oil in a frying pan over a moderate heat and cook the onion and the garlic until brown and just beginning to caramelize.

Transfer the lentil and bulghar mixture to a warmed serving dish. Dribble over the remaining oil and top with the onion and garlic mixture. Stir the lemon juice into the yogurt and pour it over the middle. Sprinkle the dish with the coriander.

Serve hot, warm or cold, with a green salad.

Top: Chicken and Lamb Couscous (page 57); bottom: Lentil and Bulghar Pilaf with Yogurt

GAME LASAGNE

SERVES 4-6

2 large partridges
400 g/14 oz desert apples, peeled, cored and thickly sliced
300 ml/½ pt dry cider
300 ml/½ pt game consommé
125 g/4½ oz butter
4 tbsp flour
400 ml/14 fl oz milk
150 ml/¼ pt single cream
225 g/8 oz mature farmhouse Cheddar cheese, grated
1 level tsp ground allspice
1 tbsp oil
400 g/14 oz fresh lasagne, preferably a mixture of colours
30 g/1 oz grated Parmesan cheese
salt and freshly ground black pepper

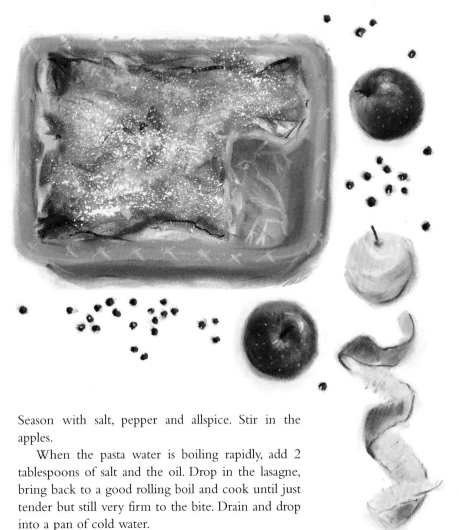

Preheat the oven to 190C/375F/gas 5.

Put the partridges in a baking dish with the apples, cider and consommé. Cover with foil and bake for 20 minutes. Remove from the oven and allow to cool.

When the birds are cool enough to handle, slice the flesh thinly. Using a slotted spoon, transfer the apples to a bowl and reserve the cooking liquid.

Put a large pan of water to heat for the lasagne.

Melt 55 g/2 oz of the butter in a saucepan over moderate heat. Sprinkle in 2 tablespoons of flour and cook for 1 or 2 minutes, stirring continuously. Gradually add the milk to make a smooth liquid. Bring to just below the boil, still stirring continuously, and simmer gently until it thickens. Stir in the cream and cheese and continue to stir until the cheese has all melted. Season.

In another pan make another sauce as above, starting with 55 g/2 oz of the remaining butter and the remaining flour, but adding about 350 ml/12 fl oz of the reserved game cooking liquid instead of milk.

Season with salt, pepper and allspice. Stir in the apples.

When the pasta water is boiling rapidly, add 2 tablespoons of salt and the oil. Drop in the lasagne, bring back to a good rolling boil and cook until just tender but still very firm to the bite. Drain and drop into a pan of cold water.

Grease a large ovenproof casserole with the remaining butter. Spoon some cheese sauce over the bottom and arrange some of the drained lasagne over that. Layer some partridge flesh over the lasagne and spoon some game sauce and apples over that. Continue layering in this way, finishing with some cheese sauce.

Sprinkle with Parmesan and bake for 30 minutes, until bubbling and well browned on top.

TAGLIATELLE WITH ROAST GARLIC

*about 30 large garlic cloves, preferably the fresh summer
variety, unpeeled
bay leaf
6 tbsp olive oil
55 g/2 oz pine kernels
450 g/1 lb dried tagliatelle
small bunch of basil leaves
1 tbsp balsamic vinegar
salt and freshly ground black pepper
grated Parmesan cheese, to serve*

Preheat the oven to 220C/425F/gas 7.

Put the garlic cloves and bay leaf in the centre of
a large sheet of foil. Add 2 tablespoons of oil, wrap in
a loose parcel and put in a baking dish.

Bake for 20 minutes, or until the garlic is tender
but not mushy. About half-way through, add the pine
kernels to the oven, scattered on a baking tray.

Meanwhile, put about 4.5 litre/8 pt of water in a
pasta pan or a large saucepan. Add 2 tablespoons of
salt and 1 tablespoon of oil and bring to the boil.

When the water is boiling rapidly, put the pasta in
and bring it back to a rolling boil as quickly as
possible. Boil rapidly, uncovered, until the pasta is
tender but still firm, testing regularly.

Remove the foil parcel and toasted pine kernels
from the oven. Take the garlic from the parcel and
allow to cool slightly. Squeeze the cloves out of their
skins, first snipping off one end if necessary. Keep the
pine kernels and garlic cloves warm. Finely chop most
of the basil, reserving 12 small leaves.

As soon as the pasta is ready, drain well and stir in
the remaining oil, together with most of the garlic
and pine kernels, the chopped basil, vinegar and
seasonings. Dot the remaining garlic, pine kernels and
basil leaves over the top as garnish.

Serve accompanied by grated Parmesan.

*The delicious Italian
fresh double-cream
cheese
MASCARPONE is
now quite widely
available over here.
More usually served
with sugar or fruit at
the end of a meal,
its subtle flavour and
buttery texture are
also incomparable in
some savoury dishes.*

PASTA SHELLS WITH MASCARPONE AND NUTS

*170 g/6 oz Mascarpone cheese
30 g/1 oz butter
1 tbsp balsamic vinegar
½ tsp freshly grated nutmeg
450 g/1 lb pasta shells
1 tbsp olive oil
2 egg yolks
55 g/2 oz Parmesan cheese
85 g/3 oz shelled walnuts, coarsely chopped
salt and freshly ground black pepper*

Put the mascarpone in a large serving bowl and stir in
the butter, vinegar, a pinch of the nutmeg and
seasonings. Place in a warm place in the kitchen.

Cook the pasta in boiling salted and oiled water as
described for the tagliatelle. While the pasta is
cooking, in another large bowl lightly beat the egg
yolks with half the Parmesan and some seasoning.

Drain the pasta quite quickly so that some water
still clings to it and immediately stir it well into the
egg mixture. The egg should cook on contact.

While the pasta is still very hot, add it to the
cheese mixture together with two-thirds of the
walnuts and toss to coat uniformly.

Sprinkle over the remaining walnuts, Parmesan
and nutmeg to serve.

*Clockwise from the top: Tagliatelle with Roast Garlic; Pasta
Shells with Mascarpone and Nuts; Spaghettini with Chicken
and Aubergine (page 62)*

Throughout Italy many types of PASTICCIO, or pasta pies, are served on special occasions like Sunday lunch. Usually topped with a pastry lid, they may be filled with a wide variety of types of pasta and other ingredients, including aubergines, Ricotta cheese and pigeon.

SPAGHETTINI WITH CHICKEN AND AUBERGINE

1 large aubergine, cut into 1 cm/½ in cubes
6 tbsp olive oil
1 onion, finely chopped
4 garlic cloves, finely chopped
115 g/4 oz chicken breast, cut into 1 cm/½ in cubes
about 30 stoned black olives
400 g/14 oz canned chopped plum tomatoes
pinch of sugar
1 or 2 tbsp tomato paste
450 g/1 lb dried spaghettini
salt and freshly ground black pepper
chopped basil, parsley or tarragon, to garnish

First make the sauce: sprinkle the aubergine with salt and leave to drain in a colander for about 20 minutes. Rinse well and pat dry.

Heat 2 tablespoons of oil in a sauté pan over a moderate heat and cook the onion for 1 or 2 minutes. Add the garlic and cook for 1 minute more. Using a slotted spoon, transfer the onion and garlic to a bowl.

Add the pieces of chicken to the pan and sauté them briskly for a minute or two, until beginning to brown. Transfer to the bowl.

Add 2 more tablespoons of oil to the pan and sauté the aubergine until gently browned.

Halve some olives for garnish and chop the rest.

Return the chicken, garlic and onion to the pan

along with the chopped olives and the tomatoes with their liquid. Season and add a pinch of sugar. Simmer gently for about 10 minutes. It should be a good thick sauce: adjust the consistency with some tomato paste, as necessary.

Meanwhile, cook the pasta in boiling salted and oiled water until just tender but still firm to the bite, as described for tagliatelle.

Stir a tablespoon of oil into the cooked and drained pasta and pour the sauce over it. Garnish with the reserved olives and the herbs.

NOTES: add some chopped ham or bacon or a spoonful of brandy when sautéing the chicken for more flavour. This dish is also good for vegetarians without the chicken. Sprinkle with some strips of Mozzarella cheese to make it more substantial.

OPEN PASTICCIO WITH CHICKEN LIVERS

SERVES 6

FOR THE PASTRY
285 g/10 oz flour
140 g/5 oz butter, softened, plus more for greasing
salt and freshly ground black pepper
FOR THE FILLING
*450 g/1 lb tagliatelle, preferably a mixture of colours -
white, green, red and black as available*
7 tbsp olive oil
1 large onion, finely chopped
3 garlic cloves, finely chopped
85 g/3 oz chicken livers, trimmed
3 tbsp Marsala or sweet sherry
150 ml/¼ pt crème fraîche
115 g/4 oz frozen spinach leaves, defrosted
2 or 3 pinches of freshly ground nutmeg
1 buffalo Mozzarella cheese
2 tbsp finely grated Parmesan cheese

First make the pastry: sift the flour with a pinch of salt and rub the butter into it gently with the fingertips. When it has a crumb-like consistency, add 200 ml/7 fl oz of cold water, a little at a time, to make a smooth dough. Roll into a ball and leave in a cool place for 1 hour.

Roll the rested pastry out to a thickness of about 1 cm/½ in and fold it in three. Roll out and repeat this process twice more and then roll back into a ball and leave to rest for 30 minutes more.

Preheat the oven to 220C/425F/gas 7 and generously grease a 23 cm/9 in pie dish with butter. Roll out the pastry and use to line the dish.

Make the filling: cook the pasta in boiling salted and oiled water as in the tagliatelle recipe, but stop cooking when just slightly underdone. Drain thoroughly. Stir in 2 tablespoons of oil and season.

While the pasta is cooking, heat 2 tablespoons of the remaining oil in a sauté pan over a moderate heat and sauté the onion for 2 or 3 minutes. Add the garlic and cook for 1 minute more. Then add the chicken livers, and as soon as these change colour, add the Marsala or sherry. Sauté for 1 minute more, stir in the cream and then season. Set aside.

Season the spinach with salt, pepper and nutmeg.

Arrange a layer of half the tagliatelle in the bottom of the pastry case, so that there is a depression in the middle. Pour the chicken liver mixture into the centre. Arrange half the Mozzarella slices on top and then cover these with half the spinach. Put half the remaining tagliatelle on top of this, followed by layers of the remaining Mozzarella, spinach and tagliatelle. Sprinkle over the remaining oil and the Parmesan.

Bake for about 30-35 minutes, until the pastry is firm and the top golden. Leave to cool for 2 or 3 minutes before removing from the pie dish.

Top: Open Pasticcio with Chicken Livers; bottom: Mozzarella and Tomato Salad with Avocado (page 174)

RISOTTOS *of all types are found in Italian cuisine, from those simply flavoured with cheese or herbs to those containing rich assortments of fish, shellfish, meat or poultry. It is important to use a good stock and the right type of rice, such as arborio, which absorbs a great deal of liquid and gives the desired sticky texture.*

HERB AND WILD MUSHROOM RISOTTO

30 g/1 oz dried ceps (porcini)
115 g/4 oz fresh mushrooms, preferably wild
115 g/4 oz butter
1 small onion, finely chopped
350 g/12 oz risotto rice, preferably arborio
150 ml/¼ pt dry white wine
1.1 litre/2 pt hot chicken stock
2 tbsp chopped parsley
2 tbsp chopped sage
3 tbsp freshly grated Parmesan cheese
salt and freshly ground black pepper

Put the dried ceps in a small bowl and cover with warm water. Leave to soak for 20 minutes, then rinse thoroughly, drain and chop, reserving a few for garnish. Halve, slice or quarter the fresh mushrooms, according to their size.

Melt half of the butter in a heavy-based saucepan over a moderate heat. Add the onion and cook for 5 minutes to soften.

Stir in the rice and the fresh mushrooms and cook for 2-3 minutes until the rice is translucent. Add the wine and chopped ceps and cook for 3 minutes until all the liquid is absorbed. Add 575ml/1 pt of the stock to the pan, lower the heat, cover and simmer for 10 minutes, until the stock is absorbed. Add a further 300 ml/½ pt of stock and continue cooking as before.

Keep checking and adding stock until the rice is tender. Total cooking time will be 20-30 minutes.

Stir in the chopped herbs with the remaining butter, seasonings and half the Parmesan, grated.

Serve, garnished with the reserved ceps and the remaining Parmesan thinly shaved.

PASTA WITH OVEN-BAKED TOMATOES, CHICKEN LIVERS AND WATERCRESS

2 tbsp extra virgin olive oil, plus more for greasing
55 g/2 oz whole hazelnuts
450 g/1 lb large cherry tomatoes, or other flavoursome variety, halved
1 tsp herbes de Provence
350 g/12 oz pasta shapes
1 onion, chopped
1 garlic clove, crushed
450 g/1 lb chicken livers, cut into bite-sized pieces
½ bunch (about 75 g/2½ oz) watercress, coarsely chopped
salt and pepper
fresh basil leaves, to garnish

Preheat the oven to 200C/400F/gas 6 and lightly grease a baking tray with oil.

In a dry frying pan, dry-fry the hazelnuts for 1-2 minutes. Allow them to cool slightly and then rub off and discard the skins.

Arrange the tomato halves, cut side up, on the baking tray. Sprinkle with salt, pepper and herbs and bake for 15 minutes, or until hot and bubbling.

Meanwhile, cook the pasta in plenty of boiling salted water until just tender but still firm. Drain well, return to the pan and keep warm.

While the pasta is cooking, heat the oil in a frying pan or wok over a moderate heat and cook the onion for about 5 minutes, stirring frequently, until soft and translucent. Add the garlic and livers and stir-fry for 3-4 minutes, or until the livers are just cooked. Add the chopped watercress and stir-fry for a few seconds longer or until it just begins to wilt.

Add the tomatoes, chicken liver mixture and the nuts to the pan of pasta. Toss gently but thoroughly and divide between 4 warmed plates or soup dishes. Serve immediately garnished with basil leaves.

VINE LEAVES STUFFED WITH CORIANDER RICE

225 g/8 oz preserved vine leaves or 40 fresh leaves
400 g/14 oz cooked brown rice
2 tbsp tomato paste
2 onions, diced
2 garlic cloves, crushed
1 tsp ground cinnamon
2 tbsp finely chopped coriander
1 tbsp currants
1 tbsp flaked almonds
2 tbsp walnut oil
juice of 2 limes
450 ml/¾ pt vegetable stock
salt and freshly ground black pepper

Place the fresh vine leaves in a large bowl and scald them thoroughly with boiling water. If using preserved leaves, allow them to soak for 10 minutes

Drain the leaves, refresh under cold water and separate out on paper towels, dull side up.

In a bowl, combine the rice, tomato paste, onions, garlic, cinnamon, coriander, currants, almonds and salt and pepper.

Place 10 leaves in the base of a flameproof casserole. Cut any stems from the other leaves and place a scant tablespoon of the filling in the centre of each leaf. Fold the stem end of each leaf over the filling, then fold in the sides and continue to roll up the leaf carefully from the stem end to form a firm package about 5 cm/2 in long.

Place these side by side, seam side down in the casserole. Sprinkle with the walnut oil and lime juice, and add just enough vegetable stock to cover them. If necessary, add a little water.

Cover the casserole and bring it to a gentle simmer. Simmer over a low heat for 1 hour. Throughout this time check that the vine leaves remain moist.

Transfer to a warmed serving dish and serve any excess liquid as a sauce.

If serving cold, leave to cool in the covered casserole dish, then transfer to a serving dish.

If VINE LEAVES *are difficult to obtain, use large spinach or Swiss chard leaves. The rice stuffing may also be flavoured with minced lamb or chicken.*

Translucent CELLOPHANE NOODLES *are made from rice flour rather than wheat and have a very delicate flavour. Bottled* CHINESE BLACK BEAN SAUCE, *made from fermented beans, is a widely used condiment in Chinese kitchens and is available from Oriental shops and better supermarkets.*

CELLOPHANE NOODLES WITH BLACK BEAN SAUCE

170 g/6 oz cellophane noodles
1 tbsp vegetable oil
1 large onion, thinly sliced
2 garlic cloves, crushed
300 ml/½ pt chicken stock
1 heaped tbsp Chinese black bean sauce
4 tsp light soy sauce
½ tsp chilli powder
1 scant tsp Oriental sesame oil

Soak the noodles in hot water for 10 minutes and then drain them well.

Heat the oil in a wok or large frying pan and stir-fry the onion for 2 minutes. Add the garlic, stock, sauces and chilli powder and simmer for 5 minutes.

Add the noodles and cook for 2 minutes, stirring constantly. (They will absorb most of the liquid.)

Sprinkle over the sesame oil, toss well and serve at once.

SPICY COCONUT RICE

SERVES 4-6

450 g/1 lb basmati rice
1 tbsp vegetable oil
1 large onion, chopped
2 garlic cloves, chopped
2 tsp dried coriander
1 tsp cumin
¼ tsp chilli powder
1½ tsp salt
450 ml/1 pt thin coconut milk
chopped fresh coriander or other herbs, to garnish

Wash the rice thoroughly and dry well.

In a large heavy-based saucepan which has a tight-fitting lid, heat the oil over a moderate heat and fry the onion until softened. Add the garlic, spices and salt and stir well. Add the rice and mix well until every grain is coated.

Add the coconut milk and bring to the boil. Turn the heat down to the lowest possible setting, put the lid tightly on the pan and cook undisturbed for 15 minutes.

Without removing the lid, take the pan off the heat to allow the rice to finish cooking in the steam for a further 30 minutes.

Transfer to a serving dish and serve garnished with herbs.

Top: Spicy Coconut Rice; bottom: Cellophane Noodles with Black Bean Sauce

MEAT, POULTRY AND GAME

Until quite recently the usual treatment we gave meat, poultry or game was roasting, grilling or casseroling. The influence of other cuisines has had an effect on even this bastion of our culinary traditions. Perhaps because of its expense, people are generally now much more inventive with meat – using it more as a flavouring ingredient. With current concerns for health there has also been a general move away from red meat – with its high saturated fat and cholesterol content – towards white meat. At the same time, worries about the effects of intensive rearing of both meat and poultry have helped restore the popularity of game.

In the spirit of these movements, we again look for our influence towards the cooking of the Orient, Middle-east and the Mediterranean, where small amounts of meat and poultry are used to such good effect in combination with rice, pasta and vegetables to produce memorable dishes such as kofta, kebabs or moussaka. There is also much to be learned from our own country traditions in the range of hot-pots or stews flavoured with lamb or pork chops and, of course, the delights of the savoury pastry – from Raised Poultry Pie and Steak and Mushroom Pudding to the glories of Game Pie.

Left: Steak and Mushroom Pudding (page 71); right: Beef and Guinness Pie (page 70)

BEEF FILLET IN BACON WITH MUSTARD SAUCE

SERVES 6

30 g/1 oz butter
2 shallots, finely chopped
1 garlic clove, crushed
450 g/1 lb mushrooms, finely chopped
1 tbsp chopped parsley
115 g/4 oz smooth liver pâté
10 slices of rindless back bacon
900 g/2 lb piece of beef fillet, trimmed of fat
1 onion, chopped
2 carrots, chopped
1 celery stalk, chopped
1 tbsp flour
2 tbsp Dijon mustard
150 ml/¼ pt red wine
150 ml/¼ pt beef stock
salt and freshly ground black pepper

Preheat the oven to 200C/400F/gas 6.

Melt the butter in a heavy-based saucepan over a moderate heat. Add the shallots and garlic and cook for 3 minutes, until translucent.

Add the mushrooms and season with salt and pepper. Continue cooking, stirring, for a few minutes. Increase the heat and cook rapidly to evaporate the liquid, until the contents of the pan are fairly dry.

Remove from the heat and add the parsley and pâté to the pan. Mix thoroughly and leave to cool.

Lay the bacon slices, overlapping slightly, on a board. Spread the mushroom pâté mixture over the bacon, then place the beef fillet on top. Season with a little more pepper and wrap the bacon up and around the beef, securing it in place with wooden cocktail sticks or string.

Put the chopped onion, carrot and celery in the base of a roasting pan and place the wrapped beef on top. Cook the beef in the oven for 40 minutes for rare, 50 minutes for medium.

Make the sauce: strain the cooking juices into a small saucepan. Add the flour and mix until smooth. Cook over a moderate heat for 2 minutes, stirring. Stir in the mustard followed by the wine and stock. Bring to the boil, stirring, and simmer for 5 minutes.

Season the sauce to taste and serve with the beef.

BEEF AND GUINNESS PIE

2 tbsp flour, plus more for dusting
½ tsp mustard powder
675 g/1½ lb braising steak, cubed
4 tbsp olive oil
12 baby onions, peeled
250 ml/8 fl oz Guinness stout
250 ml/8 fl oz beef stock
sprig of thyme
2 tbsp Worcestershire sauce
450 g/1 lb Quick Puff Pastry (see page 94)
1 egg, beaten
milk, to glaze
salt and freshly ground black pepper

Mix the flour and mustard powder in a large bowl together with some salt and pepper. Add the meat and toss to coat it well in the seasoned flour.

Heat the oil in a flameproof casserole or large heavy-based pan over a high heat. Add the onions and cook for 3-4 minutes to brown them. Using a slotted spoon, remove the onions and set aside.

Add the cubes of meat to the pan, in batches if necessary, and brown them on all sides.

Stir in the Guinness, stock, thyme and the Worcestershire sauce. Bring to the boil then lower the heat, cover and simmer for about 2 hours, until the meat is tender. After 1½ hours, stir in the reserved onions and remove the thyme.

Preheat the oven to 220C/425F/gas 7. Transfer the filling to a pie dish, piling the meat in the centre to prevent the pastry from sinking during cooking.

On a floured surface, roll out the pastry to a round big enough to cover the pie generously. Dampen the rim of the pie dish with water and cut a long strip of pastry to fit around it. Once this is firmly in place, dampen its top with a little more water. Use the remaining pastry to cover the pie, trim the edges and crimp to seal.

Make a slit in the centre to allow the steam to escape and brush with a mixture of the beaten egg and some milk to glaze. Use the pastry trimmings to decorate the pie and glaze again.

Bake in the oven for 25-30 minutes, until the pastry is well risen and golden brown.

STEAK AND MUSHROOM PUDDING

4 tbsp oil
675 g/1½ lb braising steak
1 onion, chopped
2 tbsp flour
sprig of thyme
sprig of marjoram
1 tbsp Worcestershire sauce
150 ml/¼ pt beef stock
5 tbsp port
115 g/4 oz small button mushrooms
salt and freshly ground black pepper
FOR THE SUET-CRUST PASTRY
350 g/12 oz self-raising flour
1 tsp salt
170 g/6 oz shredded suet

Heat the oil in a large heavy-based saucepan over a high heat. Brown the meat, in batches if necessary, stirring to colour on all sides. Transfer to a plate.

Add the onion to the pan and cook for 5 minutes over a moderate heat until softened. Stir in the flour and cook for a further minute. Add the herbs and Worcestershire sauce to the pan and gradually stir in the stock and port. Heat until thickened.

Return the meat to the pan and bring to the boil. Season, cover and simmer gently for 45 minutes.

Meanwhile, prepare the suet-crust pastry: sieve the flour and salt into a large mixing bowl and stir in the suet. Gradually stir in 250-300 ml/8-10 fl oz of cold water to form a soft, but not sticky, dough.

Grease a 1.1 litre/2 pt pudding basin. Turn the dough out on a lightly floured surface and knead gently. Roll it out to form a large circle about 6 mm/¼ in thick. Cut a quarter wedge from the dough and set it aside to be used for the lid.

Use the remaining dough to line the prepared pudding basin, pressing the edges to form a seal. Spoon alternate layers of the filling and the mushrooms into the basin.

Re-roll the remaining pastry and use it to cover the pudding. Crimp the edges to seal and trim away any excess pastry. Cover with a pleated piece of greaseproof paper and the same of foil and secure tightly with string.

Put the pudding in a large saucepan which has a tight-fitting lid. Pour in enough hot water to come about three-quarters of the way up the basin, cover and steam the pudding for about 2 hours, topping up the water level occasionally to prevent it boiling dry.

THE BEEF AND GUINNESS PIE *may be made with any stout or dark beer. Try adding some canned oysters for a traditional treat.*

GREEN GINGER WINE, *available from good supermarkets and most wine merchants, was once popular added to glasses of wine and is now most often mixed with whisky. It is a useful flavouring as it retains much of the original warmth of the ginger root. The steaks marinated in green ginger wine are also good served with a garlic or orange butter, made respectively with 2 or 3 crushed garlic cloves or the grated rind and juice of 1 large unwaxed orange in place of the crushed root ginger.*

MARINATED STEAKS WITH GINGER BUTTER

½ tsp salt
½ tsp pepper
1 garlic clove, crushed
juice of ½ lime
125 ml/4 fl oz green ginger wine
4 sirloin steaks, each about 170-200 g/6-7 oz
FOR THE GINGER BUTTER
juice from 2.5 cm/1 in cube of fresh root ginger, crushed
through a garlic press
55 g/2 oz butter, softened

In a bowl, mix together the salt, pepper, garlic, lime juice and ginger wine. Add the steaks and toss thoroughly so that they are well coated. Cover the bowl with film and leave to marinate for about 1 hour at room temperature, or up to 3 hours in the refrigerator, shaking from time to time.

Meanwhile, mix the ginger juice with the softened butter and put this on a small piece of kitchen film. Wrap tightly, forming into a small fat log shape. Chill in the refrigerator for about 30 minutes.

Preheat the grill until quite hot.

Remove the steaks from the marinade and cook to the required degree, basting frequently with the marinade. Exact cooking times will depend on how thick the steaks are and the temperature of the grill. Start by cooking them for 2-3 minutes on each side, then cut a little piece off. If it isn't cooked enough simply return it to the grill for another minute or two.

Just before serving, remove the chilled ginger butter from the film and cut the log across to form 4 circular pats. Serve the steaks on hot plates with a pat of ginger butter on top of each.

Top: Marinated Steaks with Ginger Butter; bottom: Spatchcocked Quails with a Tomato Salsa (page 93)

A classic of
Neapolitan cuisine,
PIZZAIOLA *is a rich
and highly flavoured
tomato sauce used
with meat and pasta.*

KOFTA, *or
meatballs, are
ubiquitous in Arab
cooking, although
they vary widely
from place to place
in their exact
ingredients. They
may even be shaped
into fingers or flat
cakes, like
hamburgers. For the
right melting texture
the meat must be
minced at least two or
three times, or pulsed
in a food processor
until smooth.*

NEAPOLITAN STEAKS WITH PIZZAIOLA SAUCE

4 thick rump or sirloin steaks
2 tbsp olive oil
salt and freshly ground black pepper
FOR THE PIZZAIOLA SAUCE
2 tbsp olive oil
2 onions, finely chopped
4 garlic cloves, finely chopped
1 small red pepper, deseeded and finely chopped
675 g/1½ lb very ripe tomatoes, chopped
large pinch of oregano
3 tbsp coarsely chopped flat-leaf parsley
dash of Tabasco sauce

First make the sauce: heat the oil in a saucepan and sauté the onions for 2 or 3 minutes, until lightly coloured. Add the garlic and chopped red pepper and cook for a minute or so more.

Add the tomatoes, oregano and most of the parsley. Season with salt and pepper and Tabasco. Cover and simmer gently for about 15 minutes, stirring from time to time. The tomatoes should not be allowed to become too pulpy.

Towards the end of this time, over a fairly high heat put the oil in a large sauté pan which has a lid. Season the steaks and brown them rapidly on both sides.

Once the steaks are browned on both sides, reduce the heat to very low and pour the sauce over them. Cover and cook for 3-7 minutes, depending on how well done the steaks are to be. Adjust the seasoning, if necessary.

Serve the steaks with their cooking sauce poured over them and sprinkled with the reserved parsley.

NOTE: try adding some chopped mushrooms to the sauce for extra flavour.

FRUIT AND NUT KOFTA

1 kg/2¼ lb minced lean steak or lamb, or a mixture
30 g/1 oz butter
2 onions, finely chopped
2 garlic cloves, crushed
55 g/2 oz pine kernels
3 or 4 dried apricots, finely chopped
55 g/2 oz seedless raisins
2 eggs, lightly beaten
pinch of allspice
2 tbsp flour
2 tbsp grated Parmesan cheese
2 tbsp olive oil
salt and freshly ground black pepper
chopped flat-leaf parsley, to garnish
lemon slices, to serve

Ask the butcher to pass the meat through the mincer 2 or 3 times to get the right consistency.

Melt the butter in a large sauté pan over a moderate heat and sauté the onion, garlic and pine kernels briefly until just beginning to colour.

Transfer these to a large bowl and knead together with the meat, fruit, eggs, allspice and salt and pepper. Form into walnut-sized meatballs.

In a shallow plate, mix the flour and cheese and season well. Roll the meatballs in the mixture.

Add the oil to the pan and sauté the meatballs quite gently until golden brown and cooked right through.

Arrange in concentric circles on a warmed serving plate, garnish with parsley and serve with lemon slices.

These meatballs are delicious served hot with a lemony yogurt or spicy tomato sauce and accompanied by rice or potatoes. They are equally good cold with salad or as part of a buffet or picnic.

SPICY LAMB MEATBALLS ON SKEWERS

MAKES 16

350 g/12 oz minced lamb
30 g/1 oz fresh white breadcrumbs
½ small onion, very finely chopped or grated
1 tbsp finely chopped parsley
30 g/1 oz pine kernels
30 g/1 oz raisins, chopped
½ tsp cinnamon
1 egg, lightly beaten
salt and pepper
TO SERVE
1 small mild onion, sliced and separated into rings
4 tbsp Greek-style yogurt

In a bowl, combine all the ingredients thoroughly (easiest in a food processor) and season well. With wetted hands, form the mixture into 16 walnut-sized balls. Chill for 2-3 hours, or up to 24, to firm them up.

If using wooden skewers, soak 4 of them in water for 1 hour beforehand to prevent them from burning during cooking.

Preheat the grill until quite hot.

Thread the meatballs carefully on 4 skewers and grill, turning them occasionally (handle them carefully as they are quite fragile), for 15-20 minutes until the outsides are crispy and brown. The exact time will depend on the heat of the grill.

Serve immediately, accompanied by the onion rings and yogurt.

PROVENÇAL BROCHETTES D'AGNEAU

3 garlic cloves, crushed
juice of 1 lemon
2 tbsp extra virgin olive oil
1 tbsp herbes de Provence
900 g/2 lb lean lamb, such as leg or neck 'fillets', cut into about 2.5 cm/1 in cubes
2 onions, cut into about 2.5 cm/1 in chunks
salt and pepper

Mix the garlic, lemon juice, oil, herbs and seasoning in a bowl and then thoroughly mix in the lamb cubes. Cover the bowl with film and leave the meat to marinate, stirring occasionally, for at least 1 hour at room temperature or up to 12 hours in the refrigerator.

If using wooden skewers, soak 8 of them in water for 1 hour beforehand to prevent them from burning during cooking. Preheat the grill until quite hot.

Thread the meat on 8 skewers, alternating the pieces with chunks of onion.

Cook under the grill for about 4-5 minutes on each side, until cooked through.

YOGURT MOUSSAKA

SERVES 6-8

2 aubergines, thinly sliced
about 100 ml/3½ fl oz olive oil
350 g/12 oz lean minced lamb or steak
4 large onions, thinly sliced
3 large garlic cloves, finely chopped
3 tbsp finely chopped flat-leaf parsley
400 g/14 oz canned chopped plum tomatoes, drained
5 tbsp tomato paste
2 eggs
450 ml/¾ pt Greek yogurt
2 tbsp lemon juice
pinch of freshly grated nutmeg
55 g/2 oz Parmesan cheese
salt and freshly ground black pepper

The Greeks claim MOUSSAKA *as their own dish, although the Turks adopted it and spread it throughout the Islamic world. This version uses yogurt and eggs instead of the more usual white sauce.*

Put the aubergine slices in a colander and sprinkle them generously with salt. Leave to drain for about 30 minutes and then rinse thoroughly. Pat dry.

Heat 2 tablespoons of the oil in a large frying pan over a moderate heat and brown the aubergine slices in batches, draining them on paper towels as they are ready and adding more oil to the pan as needed.

Add 1 or 2 more tablespoons of the oil to the pan, increase the heat to high and brown the meat by spreading it out into a flat cake and cooking this rapidly, undisturbed, until the underside is well coloured. Then break up the cake, stir the meat well and form it into a flat cake yet again. Cook in the same way. Repeat this process until the meat is a good uniform colour. Transfer to a bowl.

Heat 1 or 2 more tablespoons of the oil in the pan over a moderate heat and cook the onions for 2 or 3 minutes until soft. Add the garlic and parsley and cook for a minute or so more. Add the tomatoes, browned meat and tomato paste and simmer for about 30 minutes. Season well.

Preheat the oven to 180C/350F/gas 4 and grease a deep baking dish generously with 1 tablespoon of the remaining oil.

Put a layer of one-third of the aubergine slices in the bottom of the prepared dish. Spoon over half the meat mixture and then repeat the layers, finishing with a layer of aubergine slices.

Mix the eggs into the yogurt and season with salt, pepper, lemon juice and nutmeg. Pour this over the contents of the dish. Sprinkle Parmesan over the top and bake for about 45 minutes, until golden brown.

NOTE: try adding layers of sautéed mushrooms or courgettes, par-boiled potatoes or spinach, or slices of Gruyère cheese for extra interest. (You can then even omit the meat to make a vegetarian moussaka.) Add some red wine or 1 or 2 spoonfuls of brandy to the onions for extra flavour.

HONEYED LAMB KEBABS

900 g/2 lb boned leg of lamb, cut into 2.5 cm/1 in cubes
4 onions, cut into quarters
4 tomatoes, quartered
2 red sweet peppers, quartered and deseeded
2 green sweet peppers, quartered and deseeded
8 bay leaves
chopped oregano or flat-leaf parsley, to garnish
lemon wedges, to serve
FOR THE HONEY MARINADE
1 unwaxed lemon
4 tbsp honey
6 tbsp olive oil
2 garlic cloves, crushed
2 tbsp chopped oregano
2 tsp crushed black peppercorns

First make the honey marinade: finely grate 1 teaspoon of lemon zest and extract the lemon juice. Mix these with the remaining ingredients in a bowl. Add the pieces of lamb and onion quarters and stir well to coat them thoroughly. Cover and leave in a cool place for a few hours, stirring occasionally.

Preheat a hot grill or barbecue. Drain the pieces of lamb and onion well and thread them on skewers interleaved with pieces of tomato, pepper and bay leaves.

Grill until well browned on all sides, basting with the marinade from time to time.

Garnish with chopped oregano and serve with lemon wedges and accompanied by a green, mixed or tomato and onion salad.

NOTE: add rolled bacon slices or quartered mushrooms to the kebabs for extra interest. Try replacing the oregano with mint, rosemary or basil.

Clockwise from the top: Fruit and Nut Kofta (page 74) with a lemon-yogurt sauce, Honeyed Lamb Kebabs with a spicy tomato sauce, and Chicken Drumsticks with Garlic and Lime (page 90)

LEG OF LAMB WITH WHOLE ROAST GARLIC

SERVES 4-6

1 leg of lamb, weighing about 1.5 kg/3½ lb
1 tsp mustard powder
3 large rosemary sprigs
3 whole heads of garlic
1 tbsp olive oil
175 ml/6 fl oz port
4 tbsp redcurrant jelly
1 tsp cornflour
salt and freshly ground black pepper
rosemary sprigs, to garnish (optional)
redcurrant sprigs, to garnish (optional)

Preheat the oven to 230C/450F/gas 8. Sprinkle the lamb with salt, pepper and mustard and rub in well.

Cut 2 of the rosemary sprigs into 3.5 cm/1½ in pieces. Using a pointed knife, make incisions deep into the lamb and insert the rosemary pieces into them.

Place the remaining rosemary sprig in a roasting pan and place the lamb on top. Roast in the oven for 20 minutes, then lower the oven temperature to 180C/350F/gas 4 and continue cooking for a further 1½ hours. The lamb should still be a little pink inside.

About 40 minutes before the end of the cooking time, brush the heads of garlic with the olive oil and add them to the roasting pan.

Transfer the cooked lamb and garlic to a warmed serving platter and leave to rest for 12-15 minutes before carving the lamb and serving.

Meanwhile, prepare the sauce: pour off any excess fat in the roasting pan. Add the port to the pan together with 100 ml/3½ fl oz of water. Bring to the boil and cook over a moderate to high heat for 2 minutes, stirring and scraping up the sediment with a wooden spoon.

Add the redcurrant jelly and stir until dissolved. Cook for 1 minute. Blend the cornflour with 2 tablespoons of cold water and add to the sauce. Stir until thickened.

Season the sauce to taste and serve with the lamb, garnished with rosemary and redcurrants if using, and the roast garlic.

IRISH HOT-POT

8-12 lamb chops from the middle neck
2 onions, thinly sliced
225 g/8 oz carrots, thinly sliced
675 g/1½ lb potatoes, thinly sliced
1 tbsp rosemary spikes (optional)
300 ml/½ pt well-flavoured beef or lamb stock
30 g/1 oz butter
salt and freshly ground black pepper
chopped parsley, to garnish

Preheat the oven to 160C/325F/gas 3.

Trim any excess fat from the chops and layer them in a large casserole dish with the onions, carrots, potatoes and rosemary, if using. Season each layer with salt and pepper and finish with a layer of overlapping slices of potato.

Bring the stock to the boil and pour it over the casserole. Dot the butter over the surface. Cover tightly with a lid or foil and bake in the oven for 2 hours.

Remove the lid from the casserole and increase the oven temperature to 220C/425F/gas 7 for 15-20 minutes, until the potatoes are browned.

Serve the hot-pot in soup plates, sprinkled with chopped parsley.

Left: Leg of Lamb with Whole Roast Garlic; right: Gratin Dauphinois (page 162)

HERBED LEG OF LAMB WITH TOMATO SAUCE

SERVES 6-8

boned leg of lamb, weighing about 1.35 kg/3 lb
3 small sprigs of rosemary
½ tsp each snipped basil, thyme and oregano
rock salt and freshly ground black pepper
FOR THE SAUCE
1 tsp olive oil
2 onions, coarsely chopped
2 garlic cloves, crushed
1 green sweet pepper, deseeded and thinly sliced
1 red sweet pepper, deseeded and thinly sliced
400 g/14 oz canned peeled tomatoes, drained
1 tbsp tomato paste
115 g/4 oz oyster mushrooms, coarsely chopped
150 ml/¼ pt dry white wine

Preheat the oven to 230C/450F/gas 8.

Lay the meat out flat and sprinkle it with the herbs, rock salt and freshly ground black pepper. Roll up as tightly as possible, then tie with string.

Place in a roasting pan and roast for 25 minutes. Reduce the temperature to 220C/425F/gas 7 and cook for a further 45-50 minutes. Transfer to a warmed serving plate and keep warm.

Make the sauce: put the olive oil in a heavy-based pan over a moderate heat, then add the onions and garlic and sauté for 3-5 minutes, until translucent.

Add the peppers and combine thoroughly with the onions. Cook for 2 minutes, then add the tomatoes, tomato paste and the mushrooms. Stir well and cook for 2 minutes.

Season and add the wine. Increase the heat and bring to the boil, stirring constantly. Continue to boil to reduce a little, then serve with the lamb.

NUT OILS, *such as those made by pressing walnuts and hazelnuts, have fine strong nutty flavours. Excellent in moderation in salad dressings, they are available from good food stores and better supermarkets. Buy them in small quantities as a little goes a long way and they do go rancid quickly.*

SAUTÉED LAMB FILLET WITH FENNEL SAUCE

SERVES 6

2 tbsp walnut oil
900 g/2 lb lamb fillet, cut into 1 cm/½ in slices
¼ tsp salt
freshly ground black pepper
FOR THE FENNEL SAUCE
150 ml/¼ pt vegetable stock
2 fennel bulbs, thinly sliced, with the feathery leaves
reserved for garnish
30 g/1 oz butter
1 tbsp flour
300 ml/½ pt single cream
salt and freshly ground black pepper

First make the sauce: put the stock in a pan with the fennel. Cover, bring to the boil and then cook over a moderate heat for 25 minutes. Remove from the heat and allow to cool.

When cool, liquidize the mixture in a blender or food processor and then push through a fine sieve.

Melt the butter in a pan over a moderate heat, add the flour and cook, stirring constantly, for 3 minutes.

Remove from the heat and stir in the sieved fennel purée. Return to the heat and stir constantly for 5 minutes. Gradually add the cream and then season to taste.

Heat the walnut oil in a frying pan over a moderate heat and add the lamb fillet slices. Sprinkle with the salt and some pepper, increase the heat and sauté the fillet, stirring constantly, for 3 minutes.

Transfer the lamb to a warmed serving dish, cover with the fennel sauce and garnish with the reserved fennel fronds to serve.

LAMB AND BEEF WITH ALMONDS

3 tbsp olive oil
45 g/1½ oz blanched almonds
350 g/12 oz lamb, cubed
350 g/12 oz stewing beef, cubed
1 onion, chopped
2 garlic cloves, chopped
2 tsp coriander seeds, lightly crushed
¼ tsp ground allspice
300 ml/½ pt beef stock
115 g/4 oz no-soak dried apricots, halved
salt and freshly ground black pepper
chopped coriander, to garnish

Preheat the oven to 180C/350F/gas 4.

Heat 1 tablespoon of the olive oil in a large heavy-based saucepan over a moderate heat. Add the almonds and cook, stirring, for 2-3 minutes until golden brown. Transfer to a plate and set aside.

Add the remaining oil to the pan, increase the heat slightly and cook the meat, in batches if necessary, until browned on all sides. Using a slotted spoon, transfer the meat to a large ovenproof casserole.

Add the onion, garlic and spices to the pan and cook over a moderate heat for 5 minutes, stirring frequently. Pour in the stock and bring to the boil. Add the contents of the pan to the casserole. Season with salt and pepper. Cover and cook in the oven for 1 hour.

At the end of this time, add the apricots and browned almonds to the casserole and mix well. Cover again and return the casserole to the oven for a further 45-60 minutes, until the meat is tender.

Adjust the seasoning, if necessary. Serve sprinkled with chopped fresh coriander and accompanied by basmati rice.

NAVARIN OF LAMB

4 tbsp olive oil
675 g/1½ lb lamb fillet from the shoulder, diced
12 baby onions
8-12 baby carrots
6 small baby turnips
2 garlic cloves, chopped
1 tbsp flour
575 ml/1 pt well-flavoured stock
300 ml/½ pt red wine
bouquet garni
8 small new potatoes
salt and freshly ground black pepper
chopped parsley, to garnish
FOR THE CROUTONS
4 large slices of white bread, crusts removed
3 tbsp light olive oil

Heat 2 tablespoons of the oil in a large heavy-based saucepan over a high heat. Add the meat and cook, stirring, until the pieces are browned on all sides. Using a slotted spoon, transfer the meat to a plate.

Put the remaining oil in the pan. Add the onions, carrots and turnips and cook for 5 minutes, stirring, over a medium to high heat. Using a slotted spoon, transfer the vegetables to a plate and reserve.

Add the garlic to the pan and cook for 1 minute. Stir in the flour and cook, stirring, for 2 minutes. Then gradually stir in the stock and wine. Bring to the boil, then return the meat to the pan. Add the bouquet garni and season with salt and pepper. Bring back to the boil. Then lower the heat, cover and simmer for 45 minutes, stirring occasionally.

Add the reserved vegetables and the potatoes to the pan. Cover and continue to simmer for 30 minutes. Then remove the lid and cook uncovered for a further 10-15 minutes to allow the sauce to reduce slightly.

While the sauce is reducing, make the croutons: cut the slices of bread into triangles or use a pastry

NAVARIN OF LAMB *is a traditional French lamb stew and derives its name from* navet, *the French term for the turnip. When made this way with spring vegetables, the dish is also known as 'Navarin printanier'.*

*The region of
NORMANDY
produces most of
France's apple crop
and for this reason it
is a centre of the
manufacture of cider
and Calvados, the
cider brandy. It is
also the province
most associated with
dairy products.
Hence dishes with
apples, cider,
Calvados or lashings
of butter and cream
characterize the
cooking of
Normandy.*

cutter to cut out circles or other shapes. Heat the oil in a frying pan over a moderate to high heat. When the oil is really hot, add the bread, a few pieces at a time, and cook for a few seconds on each side until golden and crisp. Drain on paper towels.

Adjust the seasoning of the navarin, sprinkle with parsley and serve with the croutons.

PORK WITH JUNIPER, CELERY AND PRUNES

3 tbsp oil
675 g/1½ lb pork tenderloin, cut into 3.5 cm/1½ in pieces
2 shallots, finely chopped
2 celery stalks, cut into matchstick strips
2 tsp juniper berries, lightly crushed
250 ml/8 fl oz dry white wine
3 tbsp sherry
1 bay leaf
4 fresh sage leaves, shredded
12 no-soak prunes
salt and freshly ground black pepper
fresh sage leaves, to garnish

Heat the oil in a large saucepan over a high heat. Add the pork and brown it on all sides. Using a slotted spoon, transfer to a plate and set aside.

Add the shallots to the pan and cook over a moderate heat for 4-5 minutes to soften. Add the celery and juniper and cook for 2 minutes.

Add the wine, sherry and herbs and bring to the boil. Return the meat to the pan, cover and simmer for 20 minutes.

Add the prunes and continue cooking, uncovered,

for 10 minutes until the sauce is reduced by about half and the pork is tender. Adjust the seasoning, if necessary, and serve immediately garnished with fresh sage leaves.

NORMANDY PORK CHOPS

3 tbsp oil
4 pork or veal chops, about 2.5 cm/1 in thick
4 tbsp brandy, preferably Calvados
FOR THE SAUCE
300 ml/½ pt double cream
30 g/1 oz butter
1 tbsp chopped parsley
salt and freshly ground black pepper
FOR THE GLAZED APPLES
2 dessert apples
1 tbsp lemon juice
30 g/1 oz butter
large pinch of sugar

Heat the oil in a large heavy-based frying pan over a high heat. Add the chops and brown them on both sides. Add the brandy to the pan and carefully set it aflame. Allow the flames to subside and season with salt and pepper.

Lower the heat and cook the chops for about 3-4 minutes on each side, until done. Transfer the chops to a warmed serving plate and keep warm.

Make the sauce: add the cream and butter to the pan, stirring well to scrape up all the sediment. Stir in the parsley and cook for 3-4 minutes, until the sauce begins to thicken. Season and keep warm.

Make the glazed apples: peel, core and cut the apples into thick wedges and toss these in the lemon juice. Melt the butter in a frying pan over a moderate heat and add the apples. Sprinkle with the sugar and fry for 2-3 minutes to brown.

Serve the chops accompanied by the glazed apples and the sauce.

PAPRIKA AND CARAWAY ROAST PORK WITH APPLE SAUCE

SERVES 6-8

1 pork neck joint, weighing about 1.8 kg/4 lb, trimmed
of fat and neatly tied
2 tbsp olive oil
2 tsp paprika
2 tsp caraway seeds
2 large cooking apples, peeled, cored and cut into even-
sized pieces
1 tbsp flour
450-575 ml/¾-1 pt chicken stock or water from
cooking potatoes or vegetables
salt and pepper

Preheat the oven to 180C/350F/gas 4.

Place the pork on a rack or trivet set in a roasting pan. Dribble the oil over it and season it generously with salt and pepper. Roast for 3 hours, basting occasionally. After 2 hours, baste thoroughly and sprinkle over the paprika and caraway seeds.

Towards the end of the cooking time, make the apple sauce: cook the apples together with 2 tablespoons of water in a saucepan which has a tight-fitting lid over a moderate heat, shaking the pan occasionally until the apples dissolve into a light mush. The exact cooking time will depend on the apples. Watch them continuously to ensure that they do not burn. Stir in a pinch of salt to bring out the flavour and then keep the apple sauce warm.

When the meat is done, transfer it to a warmed serving plate and leave it to rest while making the gravy. Remove the fat from the roasting tin, leaving about 1 tablespoon (there might not be much more than that if the meat was really lean) and place the roasting pan over a moderate heat. Stir in the flour and mix it well into the fat, stirring up the dark sediment on the base of the pan (a wire balloon whisk is useful for this job).

Pour in about 450 ml/¾ pt of stock or vegetable water and bring to the boil, whisking all the time to make sure no lumps form. Simmer for 2-3 minutes. Adjust the seasoning and add more stock if necessary to give a good pouring consistency. (The gravy should not be too thick.) Strain into a warmed gravy boat.

To serve: slice the meat as thinly as possible and serve with the gravy and the apple sauce.

Previous page, left: Paprika and Caraway Roast Pork with Apple
Sauce; bottom right: Provençal Gratin of Courgettes (page 165)

SPICED CHICKEN TART

SERVES 6

170 g/6 oz frozen puff pastry, defrosted
FOR THE FILLING
30 g/1 oz butter or margarine
1 leek, thinly sliced
1 garlic clove, crushed
½ tsp ground turmeric
2 tsp ground cumin
2 tsp garam masala
225 g/8 oz chicken breast, diced
1 potato, peeled, diced and cooked
1 tbsp chopped coriander
grated zest and juice of 1 unwaxed lime
½ tsp salt and ¼ tsp freshly ground black pepper
1 tbsp mango chutney
150 ml/¼ pt single cream
2 eggs
TO GARNISH
sprigs of coriander

Roll the pastry out thinly on a lightly floured surface and use it to line a 23 cm/9 in ovenproof pie plate. Flute the edges and chill for 30 minutes.

Preheat the oven to 200C/400F/gas 6.

Bake the pastry case blind for 10-15 minutes, until lightly browned at the edge.

While the case is baking make the filling: melt the butter or margarine in a saucepan over a moderate heat. Add the leek and garlic and fry quickly for 1 minute. Stir in the spices, chicken and potato. Cook, stirring frequently, until the chicken has turned white. Add the coriander, lime zest, juice, salt, pepper and chutney. Remove from the heat.

Beat together the cream and eggs and stir into the chicken mixture. Pour into the case and return to the oven for 15-20 minutes, until the filling has set.

Serve hot or cold, garnished with coriander.

CHICKEN BREASTS WITH COCONUT TARRAGON CREAM

45 g/1½ oz butter
1 tbsp hazelnut oil
2 tbsp chopped tarragon
4 large fresh skinned chicken breasts
2 tbsp coconut cream
salt and freshly ground black pepper

Melt the butter with the oil in a heavy-based pan over a moderate heat. Add half the tarragon, followed by the chicken breasts. Cover and cook for about 5 minutes.

Remove the lid and turn the chicken breasts over. Season, increase the heat a little and cook for a further 5 minutes.

Reduce the heat to moderate and add the coconut cream. Baste the chicken and adjust the seasoning, if necessary.

Increase the heat again, turn the breasts once more and cook for a further 2 minutes.

Transfer the chicken and its sauce to a warmed serving dish and garnish with the remaining tarragon.

NOTE: this dish works equally well with more economical pieces of chicken such as drumsticks, thighs or wings.

GARAM MASALA, *meaning hot spice mixture, is an intensely aromatic blend of ground spices used in making some Indian recipes. It is available commercially but it is possible to grind your own Garam Masala. There are many different blends, but most use coriander, cumin, cardamom, ginger, cloves and black pepper.*

RAISED POULTRY PIE

SERVES 6

FOR THE FILLING
*675 g/1½ lb boneless chicken or turkey meat, cut
into thin strips
225 g/8 oz chicken or turkey livers, chopped
225 g/8 oz streaky bacon, chopped
1 tbsp green peppercorns in brine, drained
2 garlic cloves, chopped
3 tbsp sherry
salt and freshly ground black pepper*
FOR THE HOT WATER CRUST PASTRY
*140 g/5 oz lard, diced, plus more for greasing
450 g/1 lb flour
1 tsp salt
1 egg, beaten
milk, to glaze*

First make the filling: mix all the ingredients well in a large bowl and set aside.

Preheat the oven to 200C/400F/gas 6. Grease a raised pie mould or 15 cm/6 in loose-bottomed cake tin with some lard.

Make the pastry: sieve the flour and salt into a large bowl. In a small saucepan, heat the lard and 125 ml/4 fl oz of water until melted. Bring to the boil then pour over the flour. Mix thoroughly to a soft dough.

Turn out on a lightly floured surface and knead until just smooth. While still warm, roll out three-quarters and use to line the prepared mould or tin.

Fill the pie with the prepared mixture and roll out the remaining pastry to make a lid. Crimp the edges of the pastry to seal and make a few steam holes in the lid. Use pastry trimmings to decorate the top of the pie. Mix the beaten egg and some milk and brush the top with this glaze.

Bake for 30 minutes, then lower the temperature to 180C/350F/gas 4 and cook for another 1 ¼ hours. Allow to cool in the tin and serve cold.

CHICKEN WITH GARLIC AND OLIVES

*8 small chicken portions (preferably legs and
thighs), skinned
sprig of thyme
sprig of rosemary
1 bay leaf
3 tbsp olive oil
1 large onion, thinly sliced
5 garlic cloves, halved
200 ml/7 fl oz dry white wine
12 stoned black olives
12 stoned green olives, sliced
salt and freshly ground black pepper
chopped fresh parsley, to garnish*

Rinse the chicken pieces, pat them dry and season. Tie the herbs into a bundle with string.

Heat the oil in a large heavy-based saucepan over a moderate to high heat. Add the chicken portions and brown them on all sides.

Add the herbs, onion and garlic and cook for a further 5 minutes. Stir in the wine and bring to the boil. Then lower the heat, cover and cook for 30 minutes.

Using a slotted spoon, transfer the chicken to a warmed serving platter. Stir the juices in the pan thoroughly to blend the garlic.

Add the olives to the pan and cook, uncovered, for about 5 minutes to reduce the sauce by about one-third. Discard the herbs, adjust the seasoning to taste and pour the sauce over the chicken pieces.

Serve sprinkled with chopped fresh parsley to garnish.

*Left: Raised Poultry Pie; right: Celeriac and Swede Purée
and Carrot and Parsnip Purée from the Trio of Vegetable Purées
(page 162)*

MOROCCAN LEMON CHICKEN

4 unwaxed lemons
1 large corn-fed or free-range chicken, dressed weight about
1.5 kg/3½ lb, but giblets retained
2 onions
bay leaf
1 tsp black peppercorns
3 tbsp finely chopped flat-leaf parsley
1 tbsp olive oil
1 tsp finely chopped fresh root ginger
pinch of cinnamon
3 tbsp finely chopped coriander leaves
salt and freshly ground black pepper

Preheat the oven to 220C/425F/gas 7.

Grate 1 tablespoon of zest from the lemons and pare off 2 or 3 thin strips of rind. Quarter 2 of the other lemons.

Trim the giblets, removing any gall taint and put in a small pan with 1 of the onions, the bay leaf, peppercorns, the strips of lemon rind and any stalks from the parsley. Cover with water, bring to the boil and simmer gently for about 1 hour. Strain.

Finely chop the remaining onion. Heat the oil in a sauté pan over a moderate heat and sauté it briefly, together with the grated lemon zest, ginger, cinnamon and seasonings, until the onion is soft.

Transfer to a bowl and mix in most of the herbs. Stuff the chicken with this mixture and the lemon quarters, squashing them lightly as you insert them.

Place the chicken in a roasting pan, breast downwards. Add just enough water to cover the base and cook for about 50-60 minutes, turning over half-way through and basting regularly, until well browned all over and the juices run clear when the thickest part of the thigh is pierced.

Transfer the chicken to a warmed serving plate, tipping it so that any liquid inside the bird drains back into the pan. Garnish with one of the remaining lemons, cut into wedges, and the remaining herbs.

Deglaze the roasting pan with the juice from the last of the lemons, scraping up any sediment with a wooden spoon, and boil briefly to reduce to a sticky liquid. Add the giblet stock and boil to reduce to a sauce-like consistency. Adjust the seasoning and serve this sauce separately, adding any juices that run from the chicken during carving.

In North Africa this dish would be made using lemons which have been dried or preserved in oil, giving a much more pungent flavour.

The ancient Persian FAISINJAN *sauce of pomegranates and walnuts was used mostly for wild duck and other game birds, but suits chicken and domesticated duck. If fresh pomegranates are unavailable, use 2 or 3 tablespoons of pomegranate syrup made up with 300 ml/½ pt of water instead of the sieved juice, but do not add sugar.*

CHICKEN DRUMSTICKS WITH GARLIC AND LIME

3 garlic cloves, crushed
2 tbsp olive oil
4 limes
12 chicken drumsticks, preferably from corn-fed or
free-range birds
salt and freshly ground black pepper
cayenne pepper, to garnish

Mix together the garlic, olive oil and the juice of 3 of the limes in a large bowl and season well. Add the chicken pieces and mix them in so that they are well coated. Cover and leave to marinate in the refrigerator for several hours, turning from time to time.

Preheat the oven to 200C/400F/gas 6.

Drain the drumsticks well and arrange in a baking dish. Bake for about 30 minutes, or until well browned and the juices run clear when the thickest part is pierced.

While the chicken is cooking, transfer the marinade to a saucepan and boil it until reduced to a thick sticky sauce-like consistency. Adjust the seasoning (according to preference, the bitterness may also be cut slightly with a little sugar).

Serve the drumsticks dusted lightly with cayenne, with the remaining lime cut into wedges and the sauce in a bowl for dipping.

DUCK BREAST FAISINJAN

4 pomegranates
juice of 1 large lemon
1 tbsp brown sugar or honey
4 boned duck breasts or 2 large French magrets
1 tbsp olive oil
1 onion, finely chopped
85 g/3 oz walnuts, chopped
salt and freshly ground black pepper

Halve the pomegranates and scoop the seeds out into a food processor, reserving 2 or 3 tablespoons. Blend briefly and then press through a sieve.

Put the juice obtained into a saucepan and add half its volume of water, the lemon juice, sugar and seasoning. Bring to the boil and simmer gently for about 20 minutes. Allow to cool.

Prepare the duck breasts by scoring the fat with diagonal cuts down to the flesh along its length.

Put the duck breasts in a bowl and pour over the cooled pomegranate mixture. Stir well, cover and leave to marinate for 2 or 3 hours.

Preheat a hot grill. Drain the duck breasts, reserving the marinade. Pat them dry and grill fat side up for 5-8 minutes, until well browned. Turn and cook the other side in the same way. (Duck is best served fairly pink; if you prefer it well done, reduce the heat and cook for another 10 minutes or so.)

While the duck is cooking, heat the oil in a saucepan over a moderate heat and add the onion and walnuts. Cook gently for 2 or 3 minutes until the onion is soft. Add the pomegranate mixture to the saucepan, bring to the boil and simmer for about 5 minutes. Adjust the seasoning and the sweet-and-sour balance with more lemon juice or sugar.

Serve the duck thickly sliced, sprinkled with the reserved seeds and with the sauce served separately.

Duck Breast Faisinjan garnished with watercress

Ready-made PESTO SAUCE *is sold by most delicatessens and good supermarkets. However, you can easily make your own by crushing a handful of basil leaves with 1 garlic clove, 1 heaped teaspoon of pine kernels and 2 tablespoons of freshly grated Parmesan in a mortar. Then work in enough olive oil to produce a thick paste. Any left over from this recipe would make a wonderful pasta sauce.*

CHICKEN BAKED WITH SAVORY AND ORANGE

1 tbsp freshly grated peeled root ginger
½ tsp ground cloves
¾ level tbsp flaked rock salt
1 tsp coarsely ground black pepper
½ tsp ground coriander seeds
8 sprigs of winter savory
45 g/1½ oz butter, softened
1 large fresh oven-ready chicken, cut into quarters
1½ tbsp juice and the thinly pared rind from 1 unwaxed orange, cut into julienne strips
170 g/6 oz dry white wine

Preheat the oven to 200C/400F/gas 6.

Place the ginger, cloves, salt, black pepper, coriander seeds and 2 sprigs of winter savory in a blender or food processor and pulse gently until reduced to a fine powder. In a bowl, blend the mixture into the softened butter.

Lift the skin gently from the chicken quarters and make several incisions into the flesh. Fill the incisions with the butter mixture, then cover over with the skin, securing with cocktail sticks.

Line a baking dish with foil and place the remaining winter savory sprigs on the base of the pan. Put the chicken on top of the savory, then pour over the orange juice.

Cook in the oven for 40-50 minutes, until tender and the juices run clear when a skewer is inserted in the thickest part of the thigh. Transfer the chicken to a warmed serving dish and keep warm.

Place the orange rind strips in the base of a small pan and add the wine. Cover and simmer gently for 3 minutes. Add the pan juices and the savory from the pan and bring to the boil. Boil rapidly for 2 minutes to reduce slightly.

Strain the sauce into a warmed jug and serve with the chicken.

BRIE AND BASIL CHICKEN

1 oven-ready chicken, weighing about 1.35-1.8 kg/
3-4 lb, with giblets
115 g/4 oz Brie, mashed
1 tbsp ready-made pesto sauce
1 tbsp extra virgin olive oil
salt and pepper
FOR THE STOCK
1 onion, chopped
1 bay leaf
sliver of rind from an unwaxed lemon
couple of parsley sprigs

First make the stock by putting all the ingredients in a small pan together with the chicken giblets and 450 ml/¾ pt of water. Bring to the boil and then simmer gently for 1 hour. Strain and discard the solids. There should be about 300 ml/½ pt stock left. Make up to that quantity with water, if necessary.

Preheat the oven to 200C/400F/gas 6.

Prepare the chicken: starting at the end with the large cavity, carefully ease a hand under the skin to release it from the flesh. The skin will stay attached at the breastbone. Now ease the fingers under the skin of the drumsticks to loosen this too. (This is easier than it sounds and only takes a second or two.)

Mix the mashed cheese with the pesto and, using the fingers, work this paste all over the breast and legs under the skin. Pull the skin back to cover the flesh and secure with skewers, if necessary.

Place the prepared chicken in a small roasting pan or shallow ovenproof dish. Brush it all over with the oil and season with salt and pepper. Pour the stock around the chicken and roast for 1½ hours, basting every 20 minutes or so. If the stock dries up before the bird is cooked, add a little water. At the end of cooking there should just be a few spoonfuls of flavoursome juice in the pan.

Carve the chicken and serve with these pan juices and plainly cooked fresh vegetables.

RABBIT WITH PRUNES, OLIVES AND BACON

1 large dressed rabbit, cut into pieces
115 g/4 oz stoned prunes, halved
2 tbsp oil
1 tbsp flour
300 ml/½ pt red wine
300 ml/½ pt chicken stock
2 garlic cloves, finely chopped
bouquet garni
140 g/5 oz streaky bacon, rinded and cut into strips
85 g/3 oz stoned black olives, halved
salt and fresh ground black pepper
FOR THE MARINADE
300 ml/½ pt red wine
2 tbsp oil
1 large onion, coarsely chopped
1 large carrot, coarsely chopped
12 peppercorns
bay leaf

Mix the marinade ingredients in a bowl and add the rabbit and prunes. Stir well, cover and leave in a cool place for 2-3 hours or overnight, stirring occasionally.

Using a slotted spoon, remove the rabbit, prunes and vegetables from the marinade and pat dry.

Heat the oil in a large flameproof casserole over a moderate heat and brown the rabbit pieces in it.

Remove the rabbit and brown the vegetables. Sprinkle over the flour and sauté for a minute or so.

Stir in the marinade, wine and stock together with the garlic, bouquet garni and seasoning. Return the rabbit pieces to the casserole. Bring to the boil, cover and simmer gently for about 30 minutes.

Towards the end of this time, dry-fry the bacon until browned. Add this, the olives and prunes to the casserole and cook for a further 15 minutes.

Transfer rabbit and vegetables to a serving dish. Boil the juices rapidly to reduce them to a sauce.

SPATCHCOCKED QUAILS WITH A TOMATO SALSA

4 dressed quails
4 tbsp extra virgin olive oil
salt and pepper
FOR THE SALSA
225 g/8 oz tomatoes, finely chopped
1 small mild onion, finely chopped
1 garlic clove, crushed
3 tbsp finely chopped parsley
grated zest and juice of ½ unwaxed lemon
2 tsp sugar

If using wooden skewers, soak 8 of them in water for 1 hour beforehand to prevent them from burning during cooking.

First make the salsa: combine all the ingredients in a bowl together with 1 tablespoon of the olive oil and chill for 30-60 minutes to allow the flavours to develop. Preheat the grill until quite hot.

Place the quails, breast side down, on a work surface. Using a sharp knife or a pair of kitchen scissors, cut along either side of the backbone and remove it. (This is much easier than it sounds and only takes a few seconds.) Flatten each bird by turning it over, placing the palm of the hand on the breast and pressing down firmly. (Again easier than it sounds.)

Thread 2 skewers diagonally through each bird, each from one wing to the opposite leg. This will hold them flat and neat for cooking. Brush all over with some of the remaining olive oil and season with salt and pepper.

Grill for 25-30 minutes, turning occasionally and brushing with a little more oil as necessary. Make sure the birds are cooked through (pierce the thickest part of the thigh with a knife or skewer; the juices should run clear).

Serve immediately with the cold salsa.

SPATCHCOCKING *is a means of preparing any bird for the rapid process of grilling, as it flattens the bird while leaving it whole and on the bone.*

ROAST DUCK WITH BABY TURNIPS

1 oven-ready duckling, weighing about 1.8 kg/4 lb
45 g/1½ oz butter
675 g/1½ lb small baby turnips
2-3 tsp soft light brown sugar
salt and freshly ground black pepper
FOR THE SAUCE
2 shallots, finely chopped
1 tsp grated zest from an unwaxed lemon
150 ml/¼ pt dry white wine
150 ml/¼ pt chicken stock
5 tbsp Marsala
2 tsp cornflour

Preheat the oven to 200C/400F/gas 6.

Using a needle or skewer, prick the skin of the duck all over to let the fat run. Season the duck well with salt and pepper, rubbing it well into the skin. Place the bird on a rack in a roasting pan and cover loosely with foil.

Roast for 1-1¼ hours, removing the foil halfway through cooking to allow the skin to brown and crisp. As the foil is removed, take 3 tablespoons of duck fat from the roasting pan and reserve.

Make the sauce: heat the reserved duck fat in a small heavy-based saucepan over a low heat. Add the shallots and cook gently for 5-7 minutes, until soft and just beginning to brown.

Stir in the lemon zest, wine and stock. Bring to the boil, cover and simmer for 10 minutes. Stir in the Marsala. Blend the cornflour with 2 tablespoons of cold water, add this to the sauce and stir until thickened. Season to taste, then cover and set aside.

Melt the butter in a large heavy-based pan. Add the turnips and cook, stirring, over a medium heat for 2 minutes. Add 150 ml/¼ pt of water to the pan together with the sugar, salt and pepper. Bring to the

If BABY TURNIPS *are unavailable, glaze some baby onions in the same way and serve the duck garnished wit these and some fresh green peas.*

boil. Cook, uncovered and stirring frequently, for about 15 minutes until the turnips are just tender and the liquid has evaporated to a caramelized glaze.

Serve the duck on a warmed platter, surrounded by the glazed baby turnips and garnished with sprigs of herbs. Gently reheat the sauce to accompany it.

GAME PIE

SERVES 6

2-4 game birds, depending on size (about 1.35 kg/3 lb)
6 black peppercorns
bouquet garni
2 onions
55 g/2 oz butter
225 g/8 oz small-cap mushrooms, thickly sliced
115 g/4 oz streaky bacon, chopped
1 tbsp flour
3 hard-boiled eggs, shelled and quartered
1 tbsp chopped parsley
salt and freshly ground black pepper
FOR THE QUICK PUFF PASTRY
(makes about 450 g/1 lb)
225 g/8 oz strong white flour
170 g/6 oz chilled butter, cut into small dice
1 tsp lemon juice
about 150 ml/¼ pt iced water
1 egg, beaten
milk, to glaze

Make the pastry: sieve the flour with a pinch of salt into a mixing bowl. Stir in the butter, add the lemon juice and mix in sufficient iced water to form a firm dough. Do not break up the butter pieces. Turn the dough out on a floured surface and form into a brick shape. Wrap in film and chill for 10 minutes.

On a well-floured surface, lightly roll out the pastry to a long rectangle about 6 mm/¼ in thick. It should be about three times longer than it is wide.

Fold the bottom third up and the top third down. Press the edges lightly with the rolling pin. Cover with film and chill again for 10 minutes.

Return the pastry to the floured surface, but giving it a quarter turn clockwise. Roll out to a rectangle again and fold and chill as before. Repeat this turning, rolling and chilling process twice more. Wrap in film and chill for at least 30 minutes.

While the pastry is chilling put the birds, peppercorns and bouquet garni in a large pan. Quarter one of the onions and slice the other. Add the quartered onion to the pan. Add just enough water to cover and bring to the boil. Lower the heat, cover and simmer for 45-60 minutes, until the meat is easily separated from the bone. Transfer the birds to a plate and allow to cool. Strain the stock.

Preheat the oven to 220C/425F/gas 7.

When the birds are cool enough to handle, pull the meat from the carcasses, keeping it in fairly large pieces. Arrange these in the bottom of a pie dish.

Melt the butter in a heavy-based saucepan over a moderate heat. Add the sliced onion, the mushrooms and bacon and cook, stirring, for 5 minutes. Stir in the flour and cook for a further minute. Gradually stir in 300 ml/½ pt of the reserved stock and bring to the boil. Simmer gently for 5 minutes to give a rich sauce.

Add the egg quarters to the pie dish, piling them slightly in the centre. Sprinkle with the parsley and season with salt and pepper. Cover with the sauce.

Roll out the pastry to a round large enough to cover the pie dish generously. Dampen the rim of the pie dish with water and cut a long strip of pastry to fit around it. Once in place, dampen this and use the remaining pastry to cover the pie. Crimp the edges.

Brush the pastry with egg and milk mixture to glaze. Lightly mark a lattice pattern in the pastry.

Bake in the oven for about 30 minutes, until the pastry is well risen and golden brown. Serve hot.

Roast Duck with Baby Turnips

VENISON, or deer meat, is available from good butchers and many supermarkets. The meat of genuine wild deer has an incomparable flavour and is very healthy, having fed on grass and heather and being free from additives. Nowadays, however, most venison is farm-reared and as a result is much less expensive - but considerably inferior in flavour.

RABBIT CASSEROLE WITH MUSTARD AND MARJORAM

SERVES 6

125 ml/4 fl oz vegetable oil
1 oven-ready rabbit, weighing about 1-1.35 kg/2¼-3 lb, cut into pieces
2 tbsp Dijon mustard
4 tbsp flour
2 tbsp tomato paste
3 bay leaves
1 tsp dried marjoram
300 ml/½ pt vegetable stock
300 ml/½ pt red wine
2 garlic cloves, crushed
1 tsp salt
225 g/8 oz slices of back bacon, rinds removed
freshly ground black pepper
4 slices of brown bread, to garnish

Preheat the oven to 180C/350F/gas 4.

Heat half the oil in a deep sauté pan over a moderate heat and brown the pieces of rabbit on all sides.

Using a slotted spoon, transfer the browned rabbit pieces to a large ovenproof casserole. Using a spatula, spread them with the Dijon mustard.

Add the flour and tomato paste to the oil in the sauté pan and cook for 2 minutes, stirring constantly. Add the herbs, stock and wine, followed by the garlic. Season with the 1 teaspoon of salt and some pepper. Bring to the boil and cook for a further 2 minutes.

Pour the sauce over the rabbit, cover the casserole and cook in the oven for 2½ hours.

Roll the bacon rashers up, then halve these rolls. Skewer them with cocktail sticks and dry-fry them until well browned. Add them to the casserole 30 minutes before the end of cooking time.

About 10 minutes before the end of cooking time, cut each slice of bread into 4 triangles. Heat the remaining oil in a frying pan until very hot and then fry the bread triangles until golden brown.

Adjust the seasoning of the casserole, if necessary and serve garnished with the bread croûtes.

VENISON AND SAGE PATTIES WITH PEARS

SERVES 6

675 g/1½ lb minced venison
1 tbsp grated zest and 3 tbsp juice from an unwaxed lemon
½ tbsp finely chopped sage
1 bay leaf, crushed
½ tbsp chopped parsley
12 slices of streaky bacon, rinds removed
6 fresh pears, peeled, sliced and warmed
salt and freshly ground black pepper

Mix the venison, lemon zest and juice, sage, bay leaf and parsley in a bowl. Cover and leave to marinate for 24 hours.

Preheat a hot grill.

Season the marinated mixture and form it into 6 patties. Wrap 2 slices of bacon around each one and secure with wooden cocktail sticks. Grill for 6 minutes on each side.

Place on a warmed serving dish and arrange the warmed pear slices decoratively on top to serve.

ROAST PHEASANT WITH THYME BRANDY CREAM

SERVES 4-6

2 large oven-ready pheasants
2 unwaxed oranges, quartered
2 unwaxed lemons, quartered
75 g/2½ oz butter
55 g/2 oz slices of streaky bacon
1 tbsp hazelnut oil
4 onions, chopped
4 bay leaves
2 large sprigs of thyme
2 tbsp brandy
300 ml/½ pt double cream
salt and freshly ground black pepper
large bunch of watercress, to garnish

Preheat the oven to 230C/450F/gas 8.

Wipe the pheasants thoroughly inside and out and stuff the cavities with alternating orange and lemon quarters.

Place the birds in a roasting pan and smooth 30 g/1 oz of the butter over each pheasant, using a spatula. Cover the breasts with the bacon. Season and pour 150 ml/¼ pt of water into the pan.

Place on the middle shelf of the oven and cook for 45 minutes, basting frequently with the pan juices.

Towards the end of this time, melt the remaining butter with the hazelnut oil in a saucepan over a moderate heat. Add the onions and sauté gently until translucent. Add the bay leaves and sprinkle the thyme into the onions. Cover and simmer for 5 minutes.

When the pheasants are cooked, use a spoon to squash the oranges and lemons into the birds' cavities, then tip the juice into the pan. Remove and discard the citrus quarters, place the pheasants on a warmed serving platter and keep hot.

Add the roasting pan juices to the onion mixture and increase the heat. Warm the brandy in a small pan over a very low heat and add it to the sauce. Remove the bay leaves. Then gently stir in the cream, taking care that it does not boil. Adjust the seasoning, if necessary, and transfer to a warmed jug.

Serve the carved birds garnished with the watercress and the pieces of roast bacon bard, and accompanied by the sauce.

WILD BOAR CUTLETS WITH APPLE AND JUNIPER

8 wild boar cutlets or large pork chops
575 ml/1 pt buttermilk
8 juniper berries, crushed
6 crab apples or red Cox's, unpeeled, cored and sliced
½ tbsp cornflour
salt and freshly ground black pepper

In a shallow pan, marinate the cutlets or chops in the buttermilk for 36 hours.

Preheat a hot grill.

Remove the cutlets or chops and reserve the buttermilk. Pat the meat dry. Season the juniper berries with salt and pepper and press this mixture on both sides of the pieces of meat. Grill for 5-10 minutes on each side, until cooked as desired.

While the cutlets or chops are cooking, put the buttermilk in a heavy-based pan and add the apple slices. Bring to the boil and then simmer gently for 5 minutes.

In a small bowl, add 2 tablespoons of the buttermilk to the cornflour and mix thoroughly. Add this back to the buttermilk and apple mixture and bring to the boil, stirring continuously. Reduce the heat and simmer gently for 3 minutes, still stirring. Season.

Serve the sauce immediately to accompany the cooked cutlets or chops.

Although increasingly rare, WILD BOAR is still found in many parts of Europe. It is available in this country occasionally from better butchers. The dark red meat is low in fat and has a rich gamy flavour. Something approaching this may be produced using well-aged pork in a juniper berry marinade or sauce.

FISH AND SHELLFISH

Nowadays shellfish like scallops, mussels and oysters – even some fish – are thought of as rather sophisticated ingredients that are the preserve of grand restaurants. In the old days, of course, their abundance made them poor men's food. This is reflected in the traditional ways in which they were cooked – unadorned by rich creamy sauces flavoured with brandy and truffles. Instead their delicate flavour was brought out by plain cooking or the addition of readily obtained ingredients like herbs, cheese, nuts and fruit.

Even dishes like the classic Bouillabaisse of France started as a means whereby the local fishermen made the best use of what they hadn't managed to sell.

In our new health-conscious mood we are turning more to fish dishes, especially those involving the nutritious and health-giving oily fish like mackerel, sardines and tuna.

In this chapter you will also find interesting new slants on old favourites, like Baked Cod in Cheese Sauce, Fragrant Kedgeree with Coriander Seeds and Salmon Fish Cakes with Dill and Egg Sauce.

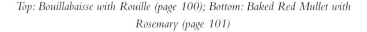

Top: Bouillabaisse with Rouille (page 100); Bottom: Baked Red Mullet with Rosemary (page 101)

Conger eel, gurnard and the Mediterranean rascasse, or scorpion fish, are essential for an authentic version of the Provençal fish soup BOUILLABAISSE, *but any good selection of white and firm-fleshed fish will do. The soup must boil vigorously as this emulsifies the oil.*

The spicy mayonnaise ROUILLE *is a popular accompaniment to many fish dishes, especially soups. Traditionally, slices of bread are spread with a little rouille, placed in the bottom of deep bowls and the broth poured over.*

BOUILLABAISSE WITH ROUILLE

SERVES 6–8

1 kg/2¼ lb mixed whole white fish, such as whiting, bass, haddock, cod, red mullet, monkfish and red snapper
675 g/1½ lb whole rich fish, such as striped bass, mackerel and eel
225 g/8 oz mussels
3 onions
3 leeks
3 celery stalks
2 pinches of saffron
450 g/1 lb canned chopped plum tomatoes
4 garlic cloves, crushed
bouquet garni
½ small fennel bulb, finely chopped
thin strip of orange rind
bunch of flat-leaf parsley
175 ml/6 fl oz olive oil
1 bay leaf
juice of ½ lemon
1 tbsp tomato paste
salt and freshly ground black pepper
thick slices of country bread, toasted, to serve
FOR THE ROUILLE
4 garlic cloves, chopped
2 egg yolks
1 tsp cayenne pepper
6 tbsp olive oil
1 or 2 tbsp tomato paste

Buy the fish whole but make sure that the fishmonger has scaled them thoroughly. Cut all the fish into large chunks, reserving the heads and tails. Place the pieces in a large bowl, keeping the white and rich fishes separate. Scrub the mussel shells well, discarding any which do not close on being tapped.

Cut one each of the onions, leeks and celery stalks into large pieces and chop the rest of them.

Soak the saffron in a few spoonfuls of warm water and add half of it to the bowl of fish along with the chopped onions, leeks and celery, the tomatoes, garlic, bouquet garni, fennel, orange rind and two-thirds of the parsley, finely chopped. Pour over the oil and season well. Cover and leave to marinate for an hour or two in a cool place.

Meanwhile, place all the fish trimmings in a large pan. Add the vegetables which have been cut into large pieces, most of the remaining bunch of parsley, the bay leaf and lemon juice and just cover with water. Season and bring to a simmer. Simmer for 20 minutes and then strain through a sieve.

Remove the pieces of fish from the marinade and set aside. Tip the remaining contents of the bowl into a large saucepan. Add the strained fish stock and the remaining saffron and its water. Bring to the boil and simmer for about 30 minutes.

While this cooks, make the rouille: put the garlic and eggs in a food processor along with the cayenne and a tiny pinch of salt. Blend to a thick paste and, with the machine still running, add the oil in a thin steady stream as if making mayonnaise. The sauce should have a thick creamy consistency. Colour it with tomato paste and season with more salt and cayenne as necessary (it should be quite spicy).

Bring the simmering liquid to a rapid boil and add the chunks of rich fish and the prepared mussels. Continue to boil as rapidly as possible for about 6 minutes and then add the white fish chunks. Continue to cook in the same way for another 5 minutes, or until the flesh of the white fish flakes readily. Transfer the fish and shellfish to a warmed serving dish, discarding any mussels which have failed to open. Remove the bouquet garni and orange rind from the broth and pour it into a warmed tureen. Add just enough tomato paste to give a good colour and adjust its seasoning. Snip the remaining parsley over the fish and the broth to garnish.

BAKED RED MULLET WITH ROSEMARY

4 tbsp olive oil
85 g/3 oz shallots, finely chopped
2 garlic cloves, crushed
6 sprigs of rosemary
250 ml/8 fl oz dry white wine
4 small red mullet, scaled and gutted, but with their livers retained
juice of 1 lemon
2 tbsp finely chopped flat-leaf parsley
salt and freshly ground black pepper
lemon wedges, to serve

Preheat the oven to 230C/450F/gas 8 and grease a baking dish with some of the oil.

Put the shallots and garlic in a saucepan with 2 rosemary sprigs, cut in half. Add all but 6 tablespoons of the wine and boil until reduced by about three-quarters, to leave the softened shallots and a sticky liquid. Discard the rosemary.

With a sharp knife, make some shallow cuts into the back of the fish to allow the heat to permeate. Slip a rosemary sprig and some seasoning into the cavity of each fish.

Spread the shallot mixture in the bottom of the baking dish, season and arrange the fish on top, alternating heads and tails. Dribble over the remaining oil and wine and bake for 15 minutes, basting from time to time.

Sprinkle with the lemon juice and parsley to serve, accompanied by lemon wedges.

MARINATED SARDINES

8 fresh sardines, cleaned and filleted
300 ml/½ pt olive oil
1 large onion, thinly sliced
3 garlic cloves, finely chopped
strip of unwaxed orange rind
2 or 3 sprigs of thyme
2 or 3 sprigs of rosemary
1 bay leaf
juice of 2 lemons
salt and freshly ground black pepper
cayenne pepper
2 tbsp finely chopped flat-leaf parsley, to garnish
lemon wedges, to serve

Put the sardine fillets in a large sauté pan and add half the oil. Heat to a gentle simmer and cook until golden. Turn and cook the other sides in the same way. Transfer the sardines to a deep dish.

Mix the onion, garlic, orange rind, herbs and lemon juice into the oil in the pan together with the remaining oil and 3 tablespoons of water. Season with salt, pepper and a large pinch of cayenne.

Bring to the boil and simmer for about 15 minutes. Leave to cool slightly, then pour the cooled mixture over the sardines and leave to marinate overnight.

To serve, sprinkle with the chopped parsley and garnish with lemon wedges.

Serve the MARINATED SARDINES *with crusty bread and a green salad.*

BACCALÀ IN GOLDEN BREAD CROÛTES

450 g/1 lb salt cod
4 thick slices from a square white loaf
45 g/1½ oz butter, melted
200 ml/7 fl oz olive oil
2 garlic cloves
about 150 ml/¼ pt single cream, warmed
2 tsp walnut oil
1 tbsp lemon juice
pinch of nutmeg
salt and freshly ground black pepper
1 tbsp finely chopped flat-leaf parsley, to garnish
lemon wedges, to serve

Soak the salt cod for 1 or 2 days, ideally under cold running water, to remove excess saltiness.

Drain the fish and put it in a large pan with cold water to cover. Cover, bring to the boil and simmer very gently for 6 or 7 minutes, until just tender.

Drain and leave to cool until it can be safely handled. Remove and discard all skin and bones and flake the flesh into a large bowl.

Preheat the oven to 180C/350F/gas 4.

Trim out a deep hollow on one side of each slice of bread, taking care not to tear all the way through. Using a pastry brush, paint the pieces of hollowed-out bread all over with melted butter.

Bake the croûtes for 15-20 minutes, or until a good uniform golden colour. Remove from the oven and, while still warm, carefully rub them all over with one of the garlic cloves. Keep warm.

While the croûtes are baking, warm 150 ml/¼ pt of the oil in a heavy-based pan. When very hot, reduce the heat and add the fish. Using a wooden spoon, beat in the fish over a very gentle heat.

When the mixture begins to be really mushy, crush in the remaining garlic and stir it in. Transfer to a large mortar or food processor. Start adding the remaining oil and the warmed cream in alternating small amounts, pounding or blending in each addition thoroughly before adding any more. Be careful not to over-process or the mixture will lose its texture.

The resulting purée should be smooth and stiff enough to hold a shape. Stir in the walnut oil, lemon juice and nutmeg and season to taste.

Spoon the mixture into and around the croûtes and sprinkle with the parsley to serve, accompanied by lemon wedges and a tomato salad.

GRILLED SOLE WITH LEMON AND PARMESAN

2 unwaxed lemons
8 Dover sole fillets, skinned
45 g/1½ oz butter, melted
3 tbsp grated Parmesan cheese
salt and freshly ground black pepper
lemon wedges, to serve

Finely grate 1 tablespoon of zest from 1 of the lemons and extract the juice from them both.

Rinse the sole fillets, pat them dry and lay them in a shallow baking dish. Mix the lemon zest into the juice and season with a little salt and some pepper. Pour this over the fish and leave to marinate for about 30 minutes, turning the fillets from time to time.

Preheat a moderate grill.

Remove the fish from the marinade. Arrange the fillets in the grill pan and brush the tops with some butter. Grill for 5-7 minutes, until just done. Then turn the fillets, brush the other sides with butter and sprinkle with the Parmesan. Grill for another 5-7 minutes until the cheese is melted and golden.

Serve the sole immediately with the pan juices poured over them and with lemon wedges.

BACCALÀ, or salt cod, is popular in the cooking of many Mediterranean countries, from Spain and Portugal to Greece. The French have their own celebrated version of the fish, puréed with oil and milk, known as brandade de morue. Thorough soaking of the fish to remove excess saltiness is essential.

FRAGRANT KEDGEREE WITH CORIANDER SEEDS

225 g/8 oz basmati rice
450 g/1 lb smoked cod or haddock
2 bay leaves
1 small onion, halved
1 tbsp coriander seeds, lightly crushed
½ tsp turmeric
300 ml/½ pt milk
30 g/1 oz butter
3 hard-boiled eggs, shelled
freshly ground black pepper
chopped fresh parsley, to garnish (optional)
lemon wedges, to garnish

Cook the rice in 575 ml/1 pt of simmering salted water in a covered pan for 8-10 minutes, until all the water is absorbed. Set aside and keep hot.

Put the fish in a large shallow pan together with the bay leaves, onion and spices. Pour over the milk, bring to the boil and poach gently for 5 minutes.

Remove and discard the onion. Lift out the fish and transfer it to a plate. When it is cool enough to handle, skin and flake the fish, removing any bones. Add the fish flesh to the rice.

Add the butter to the contents of the pan, bring to the boil and cook rapidly for 3 minutes to reduce slightly.

Coarsely chop 2 of the hard-boiled eggs and add these to the pan. Warm through for a minute or so, then add to the reserved rice and fish mixture. Toss lightly to mix.

Season with pepper and serve immediately, sprinkled with chopped fresh parsley, if using, and garnished with lemon wedges and the remaining hard-boiled egg, cut in slices or quarters.

SKATE WITH CAPERS AND BLACK BUTTER

4 pieces of skate, each weighing 225-285 g/8-10 oz, skinned
1 small onion, sliced
1 bay leaf
1 tbsp chopped parsley plus a few parsley stalks
300 ml/½ pt dry white wine (optional)
1½ tbsp capers
55 g/2 oz butter
1 tsp black peppercorns, lightly crushed
2 tbsp white wine vinegar
salt

Place the skate in a large pan with the onion, bay leaf and the parsley stalks. Pour over the white wine, if using, or water to cover. Bring to the boil, then lower the heat and simmer for 12-15 minutes, until the fish is just cooked firm.

Using a fish slice, transfer the fish to a large warmed dish. Sprinkle with the chopped parsley and capers and season with the salt. Cover loosely with foil and keep hot.

Melt the butter in a pan with the peppercorns, allowing the butter to foam and brown slightly. Pour this mixture over the fish. Add the vinegar to the pan and bring to the boil, swirling it around.

Pour the contents of the pan over the fish and serve at once.

SKATE *are related to rays and sharks. They are so large that only skinned pieces of the 'wings' are seen in the shops. Thicker pieces give the best value, as the proportion of flesh to skeleton is higher. Skate is the only fish which is better for being a day or two out of the water. It may smell faintly of ammonia, but this is actually a sign of freshness and will go on cooking.*

KEDGEREE *originated in British India and quickly became a favourite breakfast dish in Britain. The original Indian dish consisted simply of rice with onions and eggs and the British added fish.*

BAKED COD IN CHEESE SAUCE

30 g/1 oz butter
4 cod steaks, each about 2.5 cm/1 in thick
juice of ½ lemon
salt and freshly ground black pepper
FOR THE CHEESE SAUCE
450 ml/¾ pt milk
1 bay leaf
1 small onion, quartered
2 cloves (optional)
30 g/1 oz butter
30 g/1 oz flour
1 tsp Dijon mustard
85 g/3 oz mature farmhouse Cheddar cheese
3 tbsp double cream
large pinch of freshly grated nutmeg
15 g/½ oz fresh white breadcrumbs

Preheat the oven to 180C/350F/gas 4 and use a little of the butter to grease a shallow ovenproof dish large enough to hold the cod steaks in one layer.

Arrange the fish in the dish and sprinkle with the lemon juice, salt and pepper. Dot with the remaining butter. Cover loosely with foil and bake in the oven for about 30 minutes, removing the foil after 20 minutes.

Meanwhile, prepare the cheese sauce: put the milk in a small saucepan with the bay leaf, onion and cloves, if using. Bring to the boil, then cover and leave to infuse for 15-20 minutes. Strain.

Melt the butter in another small heavy-based saucepan. Stir in the flour and cook, stirring, for 1-2 minutes. Stir in the mustard. Gradually add the strained milk, stirring constantly. Bring to the boil, still stirring, and cook until thick and smooth.

Left: one of the Salmon Fish Cakes with Dill and Egg Sauce (page 107); right: Baked Cod in Cheese Sauce

Add 55 g/2 oz of the cheese to the sauce and stir until smooth again. Stir in the cream and season with nutmeg, salt and pepper.

Pour the hot sauce over and around the cod steaks. Sprinkle with the breadcrumbs and the remaining cheese. Return to the oven and bake for a further 8-10 minutes until browned.

TROUT WITH ALMONDS

4 whole trout, cleaned
2 tbsp light olive oil
1 shallot, finely chopped
1 garlic clove, crushed
55 g/2 oz flaked almonds
85 g/3 oz butter
grated zest and juice of ½ unwaxed lemon
1 tbsp chopped parsley
salt and freshly ground black pepper
lemon wedges, to garnish
parsley sprigs, to garnish

Preheat a hot grill.

Using a sharp knife, make 2 or 3 diagonal slits into the flesh of each side of the fish. Season the fish inside and out with salt and pepper.

Cook the fish under the grill for about 3 minutes on each side, until the flesh flakes easily from the bone. Do not allow it to overcook or it will be dry.

Meanwhile, heat the oil in a frying pan over a moderate heat. Add the shallot and garlic and cook for 2-3 minutes until soft. Stir in the almonds and cook until they are pale golden in colour.

Add the butter and allow it to sizzle, but take care that it does not burn. Stir in the lemon zest and juice and the chopped parsley. Season to taste.

Transfer the cooked fish to warmed serving plates and spoon over the almond butter mixture. Serve at once, garnished with lemon and parsley.

The TROUT WITH ALMONDS *may be made with any type of trout. Farmed rainbow trout are more common and economical, but wild brown trout — when available — are much tastier.*

The simple old-fashioned Edwardian SALMON SHAPE recipe is perfect for picnics as it may be transported in the mould and then turned out on a serving plate at the site. It can be made with fresh salmon, but canned salmon actually gives a better flavour.

FISHERMEN'S PASTIES

85 g/3 oz cucumber, diced finely
85 g/3 oz cream cheese
2 tbsp double cream
1 tbsp finely chopped dill or parsley
285 g/10 oz puff pastry, defrosted if frozen
115 g/4 oz cooked fresh salmon, skin and bones removed
1 egg yolk
2-3 tbsp milk
salt and pepper
butter, for greasing

Sprinkle the cucumber with a little salt and leave it in a colander for 1 hour to drain. Rinse well and dry thoroughly on a clean tea towel.

Preheat the oven to 220C/425F/gas 7 and grease a baking sheet with butter. Thoroughly mix the cheese with the cream and the herbs. Season.

Roll out the pastry thinly. Using the top of a suitable bowl as a guide, cut out 4 rounds with a diameter of about 18 cm/7 in. Leaving a clear border around their edges, divide the cheese mixture between the rounds. Then pile the flaked salmon and cucumber on top to make neat mounds.

Dampen the clear pastry borders lightly with water. Fold each circle in half over the filling to make semi-circles. Seal the edges well with a fork, pressing in a little ridge all the way to make a decorative seam.

Now turn the parcels so that there is a flat part underneath and the seams are standing up. Flute these to give them the look of Cornish pasties.

Mix the egg and milk and brush the pasties with this glaze. Arrange on the baking sheet and bake for about 15-20 minutes, or until evenly browned. After about 7-8 minutes' cooking, prick each pasty in a couple of places to allow any steam to escape.

Once they are cooked, remove them from the oven and leave to cool.

SALMON SHAPE WITH DILL AND MUSTARD SAUCE

SERVES 4-6

450 g/1 lb canned red salmon, drained
45 g/1 ½ oz breadcrumbs, preferably white
juice of ½ lemon
5½ tbsp milk
2 eggs, beaten
scrape of nutmeg
salt and pepper
FOR THE SAUCE
2 tbsp sugar
2 tbsp white wine vinegar
2 tbsp chopped dill
2 tbsp Dijon mustard
1 tsp salt
150 ml/¼ pt vegetable oil, plus more for greasing

Preheat the oven to 200C/400F/gas 6 and grease an ovenproof bowl or mould with oil.

Either mash the salmon and mix it well with all the other ingredients, or whizz them all in a food processor.

Season the mixture generously, pack it into the prepared bowl or mould and cover tightly with foil.

Place in a bain-marie, or roasting pan half-filled with boiling water, and bake for 45 minutes or until firm. Remove from the oven and allow to cool completely.

Make the sauce: mix together the sugar, vinegar, dill, mustard and salt. Whisking all the time, pour in the oil in a thin steady stream until the mixture emulsifies.

Turn out the salmon shape and serve cut in slices accompanied by the sauce.

SALMON FISH CAKES WITH DILL AND EGG SAUCE

450 g/1 lb salmon (tail piece)
150 ml/¼ pt milk
6 black peppercorns
1 bay leaf
225 g/8 oz potatoes, peeled
30 g/1 oz butter
1 egg yolk
1 tsp finely grated zest from an unwaxed lemon
1 tbsp finely chopped parsley
salt and freshly ground black pepper
flour, for dusting
vegetable oil, for frying
FOR THE DILL AND EGG SAUCE
30 g/1 oz butter
150 ml/¼ pt single cream
2 hard-boiled eggs, shelled and chopped
2 tbsp chopped dill
2 tsp lemon juice

Put the salmon, milk, peppercorns and bay leaf in a saucepan. Bring to the boil, cover and then simmer gently for 15 minutes.

Transfer the fish to a plate, reserving the cooking liquid. When cool enough to handle remove and discard the skin. Flake the flesh into a large bowl, removing any bones. Mash lightly with a fork.

While the fish is cooking, cut the potatoes into 3.5 cm/1½ in chunks and cook them in boiling salted water for 12-15 minutes until soft. Drain well and return to the heat for a few seconds to dry. Add the butter and 1 tablespoon of the reserved cooking liquid from the fish. Mash until smooth.

Add the potato to the fish together with the egg yolk, lemon zest and parsley. Season with salt and pepper. Mix together lightly, then divide the mixture into 4 equal portions and shape these into flat cakes on a floured surface. Chill until required.

Meanwhile prepare the sauce: melt the butter in a small pan. Add the cream, hard-boiled eggs and dill and bring to the boil. Cook, stirring, for 2-3 minutes until creamy. Stir in the lemon juice, season and keep warm while cooking the fish cakes.

Heat the oil in a frying pan over a moderate heat. When the oil is quite hot, cook the fish cakes for 6-8 minutes until golden brown, turning once or twice.

Serve the cooked fish cakes with the sauce.

GRILLED SALMON WITH PICKLE BERRY SAUCE

4 salmon steaks
2 tbsp extra virgin olive oil
salt and pepper
FOR THE SAUCE
450 g/1 lb mixed soft fruits, such as strawberries (sliced if large), raspberries, blackberries, blueberries, redcurrants, etc.
2 tbsp sugar
½ tsp salt
1 tbsp wine vinegar, preferably balsamic
1 small garlic clove, crushed
1-2 green or red chilli peppers, deseeded and finely chopped
2 tbsp chopped coriander leaves

Preheat the grill until quite hot.

First make the sauce by putting all the ingredients except the coriander in a saucepan. Bring to the boil, cover and simmer over the lowest possible heat for 5 minutes. Stir in the coriander and keep warm if serving hot (see below).

Brush the salmon with olive oil and season with salt and pepper on both sides. Grill for about 5-10 minutes on each side until cooked, brushing occasionally with extra oil. The exact time will vary very much depending on the thickness of the steaks and the heat of the grill. Keep testing to see when the fish is cooked (it will flake readily when forked). Do not overcook as salmon becomes dry and tasteless if overdone.

Serve immediately, with a little of the sauce, which may be served hot or cold. This recipe makes more sauce than will probably be needed as it is not worth making a smaller quantity. However, any leftover sauce will keep for several days in the refrigerator and is excellent with plainly roasted duck or other poultry or grilled meat.

The TUNA AND SWEETCORN FISH CAKES *may be made with ordinary potatoes and can also be simply fried in a little oil.*

TUNA AND SWEETCORN FISH CAKES

MAKES 8

1 sweet potato
140 g/5 oz canned tuna, drained and mashed
115 g/4 oz canned or frozen sweetcorn, drained or defrosted
55 g/2 oz fresh white breadcrumbs
1 egg, lightly beaten
1 tbsp melted butter
¼ tsp chilli powder
salt and pepper
flour, for coating
dill pickles, to serve

Preheat the oven to 200C/400F/gas 6.

Bake the sweet potato for 30-40 minutes, until tender. Allow to cool slightly and then scoop out 225 g/8 oz of the flesh.

In a bowl, thoroughly mix together the measured sweet potato with all the other ingredients, seasoning well. Form this mixture into 8 flat round patties about 1 cm/½ in thick.

Coat the patties in flour, shake off the excess and chill for at least 1 hour (or up to 12) to allow them to firm up.

Preheat the grill until quite hot.

Cook the fish cakes under the hot grill for 5-10 minutes on each side, or until crispy and brown on both sides.

Serve immediately with dill pickles.

TUNA ROULADE WITH DILL AND CAPERS

SERVES 6-8

200 g/7 oz canned tuna in oil
4 eggs, separated
2 tbsp freshly grated Parmesan cheese
FOR THE FILLING
300 ml/½ pt milk
1 onion, quartered
2 large sprigs of parsley, finely chopped
1 bay leaf
30 g/1 oz butter
30 g/1 oz flour
4 hard-boiled eggs, shelled and coarsely chopped
1 tsp grated zest and 1 tsp juice for an unwaxed lemon
2 tbsp finely chopped dill leaves
1 tsp capers
salt and freshly ground black pepper

Preheat the oven to 200C/400F/gas 6 and line a 33 x 23 cm/13 x 9 in Swiss roll tin with waxed paper.

Prepare the filling: pour the milk into a small pan and add the onion, parsley and bay leaf. Bring quickly to the boil. Cover and leave to infuse off the heat for at least 20 minutes.

Meanwhile, in a mixing bowl, mash the tuna with its oil to a purée using a hand blender or fork.

Beat the egg yolks lightly, then beat them into the mixture in the bowl. Season. Beat the egg whites to stiff peaks and gently fold them into the mixture.

Pour the mixture into the prepared tin and level with a spatula. Bake on the top shelf of the oven for 10-15 minutes, until well risen, firm and light golden in colour. Leave to cool in the tin.

Finish the filling: melt the butter in a saucepan over a moderate heat. Add the flour, stirring constantly for 2 minutes. Add the strained milk, stirring constantly, and gently bring to the boil. Reduce the heat and simmer for 3 minutes. Add the eggs, lemon zest and juice, the dill and the capers. Season.

Sprinkle a piece of waxed paper slightly larger than the Swiss roll tin with the Parmesan cheese. Turn the cooled roulade out on the paper and peel off the original waxed paper from the upturned base.

Re-heat the filling, if necessary, and spread the mixture over the roulade with a spatula, leaving a 2.5 cm/1 in margin all the way around.

By lifting one short end of the paper, roll up the roulade like a Swiss roll. Transfer to a serving dish, sprinkle any remaining Parmesan on the top and serve immediately, cut in thick slices.

ROULADE is the French term for rolled and stuffed items, especially used for meats and omelette mixtures, as with this TUNA ROULADE. Canned red salmon makes a good alternative to tuna.

SOUSED HERRINGS

SERVES 6

12 fresh herrings, cleaned
blade of mace
1 bay leaf
6 black peppercorns
2 cloves
1 onion, sliced
125 ml/4 fl oz white wine vinegar
salt and freshly ground black pepper

Preheat the oven to 200C/400F/gas 6.

Remove and discard the heads of the herrings. Cut the fish along the opening made from cleaning them, down to the tail. Lay them skin side up and press firmly along the backbones to loosen them. Turn them over and lift away the bones.

Season the filleted fish with salt and pepper and roll them up to the tail. Secure each rolled herring with a wooden cocktail stick.

Arrange the rolled herrings in a baking dish or roasting pan and add the mace, bay leaf, peppercorns and cloves. Scatter the onion slices over and around the fish. Mix the vinegar with 125 ml/4 fl oz of water and pour this over the fish.

Cover the dish with foil and bake in the oven for about 40 minutes, removing the foil for the last 15 minutes of cooking.

Serve hot with buttered new potatoes, or leave to cool in the baking dish and serve cold with salad and rye bread.

These two recipes are good examples of how oily fish such as mackerel, herrings, sardines – and even salmon – suit sharp dressings that offset their fattiness.

BAKED MACKEREL WITH GOOSEBERRY SAUCE

15 g/½ oz butter
4 whole mackerel, cleaned
4 sprigs rosemary
1 large onion, thinly sliced
100 ml/3½ fl oz dry white wine
salt and freshly ground black pepper
FOR THE GOOSEBERRY SAUCE
30 g/1 oz butter
1 shallot, finely chopped
450 g/1 lb gooseberries, halved
25 g/¾ oz caster sugar

Preheat the oven to 200C/400F/gas 6 and use the butter to grease a shallow ovenproof dish large enough to take the fish in one layer.

Cut the heads from the mackerel, if preferred. Using a sharp knife, make 2 or 3 deep slits into the flesh on each side. Tuck a rosemary sprig into the cavity of each fish and season them inside and out with salt and pepper.

Arrange the onion slices in the base of the baking dish and place the mackerel on top. Pour over the wine and bake for 30 minutes, until the fish is tender and the flesh flakes easily from the bone.

Meanwhile, prepare the gooseberry sauce: melt the butter in a small heavy-based saucepan over a moderate heat. Add the shallot and cook for 4-5 minutes, until soft but not coloured.

Add the gooseberries, sugar and 2 tablespoons of water. Season with salt and pepper. Cover and cook for 10 minutes, stirring frequently, until soft.

Purée the sauce in a blender or food processor and then pass this through a sieve. Return the sieved purée to the pan.

When the mackerel is cooked, add 2-3 tablespoons of the cooking liquid to the sauce and warm it through. Adjust the seasoning to serve.

GRILLED MACKEREL WITH HORSERADISH AND YOGURT SAUCE

2 large mackerel, each weighing about 900 g/2 lb (or 4
small mackerel), cleaned
1 lemon, thinly sliced
salt and pepper
FOR THE SAUCE
150 ml/¼ pt low-fat natural yogurt
2 spring onions, finely chopped
1 tbsp finely chopped parsley
2 tbsp ready-made horseradish relish

Preheat the grill until quite hot.

First make the sauce: combine the ingredients in a bowl and chill for 30-60 minutes to allow the flavours to develop.

Season the cavities of the fish with salt and pepper and fill them with the lemon slices.

Put the fish under the grill and cook them for 6-7 minutes on each side, or until cooked through. (Smaller fish will take only 4–5 minutes on each side.)

Serve the fish immediately with the chilled sauce and garnished with more lemon slices and sprigs of herbs if wished.

NOTE: this piquant sauce works well with most oily and smoked fish, such as herring or smoked trout. Try replacing the parsley with dill for a change.

GRILLED KING PRAWNS WITH PASSION FRUIT VINAIGRETTE

3 tbsp extra virgin olive oil
2 garlic cloves, crushed
16-20 whole unpeeled large raw prawns
FOR THE DRESSING
seeds and pulp from 2 passion fruits
1 tbsp lemon juice
2 tbsp sunflower or corn oil
2 tsp sugar
salt and pepper

Mix the oil and garlic in a bowl. Add the prawns and toss until each prawn is well coated. Cover the bowl with film and leave to marinate at room temperature for 30 minutes.

Preheat the grill until quite hot.

Meanwhile, make the dressing by combining the ingredients, seasoning well. Transfer to a serving bowl or small jug.

Remove the prawns from the marinade and grill them for 2-3 minutes on each side, or until they have turned pink and are cooked through. Brush them with any remaining marinade when turning them over. Do not overcook the prawns or they will become tough and tasteless.

Serve immediately, with the vinaigrette as a dipping sauce. As these prawns have to be eaten with the fingers, provide plenty of paper napkins.

For the GRILLED KING PRAWNS WITH PASSION FRUIT VINAIGRETTE *it is imperative that you use uncooked prawns in their shells. These are available fresh and frozen from good supermarkets, fishmongers and Oriental grocers (there they may be called 'Tiger' prawns).*

SEAFOOD IN HERB AND SAFFRON SAUCE

3 tbsp olive oil
1 onion, chopped
1 red sweet pepper, deseeded and sliced
1 green sweet pepper, deseeded and sliced
2 large garlic cloves, crushed
2 tsp paprika
115 g/4 oz prepared squid, coarsely chopped
4 tomatoes, peeled and coarsely chopped
½ tsp ground saffron
2 bay leaves
85 g/3 oz flaked almonds
175 ml/6 fl oz dry white wine
grated zest and juice of 1 unwaxed lime
300 ml/½ pt fish stock
115 g/4 oz peeled cooked prawns
115 g/4 oz shelled mussels
115 g/4 oz shelled scallops, halved if large
3 tbsp brandy
1 tbsp chopped dill
125 ml/4 fl oz single cream
salt and freshly ground black pepper
flat-leaf parsley, to garnish
hot crusty bread, to serve

SAFFRON, *the dried stamens of a type of crocus, is one of the most ancient and valued of spices. As well as imparting a wonderful golden colour, it also gives a subtly strong flavour which works particularly well with fish and seafood, rice and some pastries.*

Heat the oil in a large flameproof casserole over a moderate heat. Add the onion, peppers, garlic, paprika and squid and sauté gently for 10 minutes.

Stir in the tomatoes, saffron, bay leaves, almonds, wine, lime zest and juice and the stock. Bring to the boil and cook for 3 minutes. Season.

Reduce the heat and add the prawns, mussels and scallops. Mix thoroughly, cover and simmer for 5 minutes. Add the brandy and dill and simmer for 3 minutes more. Stir in the cream and adjust the seasoning, if necessary.

Garnish with parsley just before serving with hot crusty bread.

SWEDISH FISH SOUFFLÉ WITH DILL

SERVES 4–6

100 g/3½ oz butter, plus more for greasing
2 tbsp crisp breadcrumbs
4 eggs, separated
100 g/3½ oz flour
575 ml/1 pt milk
225 g/8 oz cooked smoked haddock, flaked
1 tbsp finely chopped dill
salt and freshly ground black pepper

Preheat the oven to 220C/425F/gas 7 and grease an 18 cm/7 in ovenproof soufflé dish carefully with butter, making sure that the rim is also well coated. Then dust this layer of butter with the breadcrumbs, shaking out any excess.

Beat the egg whites to stiff peaks.

Melt the butter in a large heavy-based pan over a moderate heat. Stir in the flour and cook gently for 2 minutes. Slowly add the milk, stirring constantly. Reduce the heat and cook for a further 5 minutes.

Remove from the heat and add the egg yolks, one at a time, followed by the fish. Stir a spoonful of the egg whites into this mixture to loosen it and then carefully fold in the remaining egg whites together with the dill and seasoning to taste.

Fill the prepared dish with the soufflé mixture and tap the dish on a work surface to help the filling settle with a level top and no air pockets.

Stand the dish in another slightly larger dish and pour boiling water into this to about halfway up the sides of the inner soufflé dish.

Bake for 30–40 minutes, until the soufflé is well risen and golden brown. Serve immediately.

Left: Tuna Roulade with Dill and Capers (page 109); right: Seafood in Herb and Saffron Sauce

FISH AND SHELLFISH STEW

SERVES 6

900 g/2 lb assorted prepared whole fish, such as conger eel,
monkfish, red or grey mullet, mackerel, bream, cod or
whiting
350 g/12 oz mussels in their shells
2 crab claws, shells broken
225 g/8 oz crayfish or large prawns in their shells
4 tbsp olive oil
1 onion, chopped
1 large leek, sliced
3 garlic cloves, chopped
1 small fennel bulb, sliced
450 g/1 lb ripe tomatoes, peeled and chopped
1 bay leaf
bouquet garni
large pinch of saffron strands
2 strips of zest from an unwaxed orange
300 ml/½ pt dry white wine
salt and freshly ground black pepper
toasted slices of French bread, to serve
chopped fresh parsley, to garnish

Remove the heads and bones from the fish (or get the fishmonger to do it). Set aside the fish and put the trimmings into a large saucepan. Add water to cover and bring to the boil. Then lower the heat, cover and simmer for 15 minutes. Strain and reserve the stock.

Cut the fish into pieces. Scrub the mussels and remove any 'beards'. Discard any open mussels which do not close on being tapped. Rinse the crab claws and the crayfish or prawns.

Heat the oil in a large saucepan over a moderate heat. Add the onion, leek, garlic and fennel and cook gently for 10 minutes, stirring frequently.

Add the tomatoes, herbs, saffron, orange zest and wine to the pan. Pour in the strained fish stock and bring to the boil. Season. Boil for 10 minutes, then lower the heat to a gentle simmer.

Add the fish in batches, starting with firm-fleshed types, such as conger eel and monkfish, which will need up to 10 minutes cooking, followed by the flaky white fish, such as cod and whiting. Finally add the shellfish, which will require only 2 or 3 minutes cooking. Discard any mussels which do not open.

First serve the broth poured into soup bowls over the toasted slices of French bread. Serve the seafood as a separate course, sprinkled with chopped fresh parsley to garnish.

PRAWN AND SCALLOP PIE

675 g/1 ½ lb potatoes, peeled and quartered
55 g/2 oz butter
6 tbsp single cream
large pinch of freshly grated nutmeg
white parts only of 4 spring onions, chopped
2 tomatoes, peeled, deseeded and quartered
170 g/6 oz oyster mushrooms
450 g/1 lb shelled scallops, halved if large
3 tbsp flour
300 ml/½ pt dry white wine
300 ml/½ pt fish or chicken stock
225 g/8 oz peeled cooked prawns
2 tbsp chopped herbs, such as parsley, tarragon or dill
juice of ½ lemon
salt and freshly ground black pepper

Preheat the oven to 200C/400F/gas 6

Cook the potatoes in boiling salted water for about 12 minutes until soft. Drain well and return to the pan briefly to dry them. Mash with half the butter and half the cream until smooth. Season with some nutmeg, salt and pepper to taste.

Meanwhile, melt the remaining butter in a large heavy-based saucepan over a moderate heat. Add the spring onions and cook for 4-5 minutes until they are soft, but not browned. Stir in the tomatoes, mushrooms and scallops and cook for 3 minutes.

Sprinkle over the flour and cook for 1 further minute, then remove from the heat and gradually stir in the wine and stock. Heat, stirring, until thickened. Cook for 1 minute.

Stir in the remaining cream, the prawns, herbs and lemon juice. Season with salt and pepper. Transfer to a 1.1 litre/2 pt pie dish and either spoon or pipe the potato mixture on top.

Bake in the oven for 25-30 minutes, until the top is browned and the filling is piping hot.

SEAFOOD LASAGNE

SERVES 6

450 g/1 lb mussels
150 ml/¼ pt dry white wine
2 garlic cloves, thinly sliced
170 g/6 oz peeled cooked prawns
225 g/8 oz shelled scallops, sliced
225 g/8 oz skinless fillets of firm white fish, such as cod or whiting, diced
3 tbsp olive oil
1 onion, sliced
1 small green or red sweet pepper, deseeded and chopped
450 g/1 lb tomatoes, deseeded and chopped
1 tbsp chopped parsley
1 tbsp chopped dill
2 tbsp brandy
8 sheets of fresh or dried lasagne verde
45 g/1½ oz Parmesan cheese, grated
salt and freshly ground black pepper
butter, for greasing
FOR THE BECHAMEL SAUCE
30 g/1 oz butter
4 tbsp flour
700 ml/1¼ pt milk
1 bay leaf
large pinch of freshly grated nutmeg

Scrub the mussels and remove any 'beards'. Discard any open mussels that do not close when tapped.

Put the wine and garlic in a large saucepan and bring to the boil. Add the mussels, cover and cook over a high heat for about 3 minutes, until almost all of the mussel shells have opened. Strain, reserving the cooking liquor. Discard any unopened mussels, reserve a few good-looking open whole mussels for garnish and shell the rest. Set aside with the prawns, scallops and fish.

Heat the oil in a large shallow pan over a moderate heat. Add the onion and sweet pepper and cook them for 4-5 minutes until they have just softened.

Stir in the tomatoes and the reserved mussel cooking liquor. Season with salt and pepper. Bring to the boil. Then lower the heat, cover and simmer for 10 minutes. Stir in the scallops, fish, herbs and brandy and cook for a further 2 minutes. Add the prawns and shelled mussels and remove from the heat.

Preheat the oven to 190C/375F/gas 5 and lightly grease a shallow baking dish with butter.

Cook the lasagne in a large pan of rapidly boiling salted water until just tender. Drain well.

Make the bechamel sauce: melt the butter in a small heavy-based saucepan. Add the flour and cook, stirring constantly, for 1-2 minutes. Gradually add the milk, stirring constantly. Still stirring, cook until smooth and thickened.

Add the bay leaf and season with nutmeg, salt and pepper. Cook over a gentle heat for about 5 minutes, then remove the bay leaf.

Fill the prepared dish with alternating layers of seafood mixture, pasta and sauce, finishing with a layer of sauce. Sprinkle with grated Parmesan and bake in the oven for 30-35 minutes, until the top has browned.

Serve hot, garnished with the reserved open mussels still in their shells.

For a more economical version of the SEAFOOD LASAGNE, *omit the scallops and use only 115 g/4 oz of prawns. In their place, add a layer of 285 g/10 oz mixed chopped vegetables, such as celery, courgettes, broccoli and mushrooms, which have been lightly sautéed in butter.*

To be absolutely sure
of the cleanliness of
MUSSELS *and to
remove lingering
grittiness it is a good
idea to soak them in
salted water for a
couple of hours
before further
preparation. Adding
some oatmeal or
flour to the water
can make the
mussels plumper and
tastier.*

MUSSELS WITH CREAM AND BACON

SERVES 4-6

1.35 kg/3 lb mussels
30 g/1 oz butter
2 tbsp olive oil
1 onion, chopped
2 garlic cloves, finely chopped
85 g/3 oz smoked bacon, chopped
1 bay leaf
2 tbsp coarsely chopped oregano
350 g/12 oz tomatoes, peeled, deseeded and quartered
300 ml/½ pt dry white wine
100 ml/3½ fl oz double cream
salt and freshly ground black pepper
sprig of flat-leaf parsley, to garnish

Scrub the mussels and remove any 'beards'. Discard any open mussels that do not close when tapped.

Melt the butter with the olive oil in a large saucepan over a moderate heat. Add the onion, garlic and bacon and cook for 5 minutes, until just beginning to colour.

Stir in the bay leaf, oregano, tomatoes and wine. Bring to the boil. Add the mussels to the pan, cover and cook for 4-5 minutes until almost all of the shells open. Using a slotted spoon, transfer the mussels to a plate, discarding any that do not open. Set aside.

Cook the sauce over a high heat, uncovered, for 5 minutes to reduce the liquid by about one-third. Meanwhile, remove about half of the mussels from their shells. Discard these shells.

Stir the cream and all the mussels into the sauce and season with salt and pepper.

Garnish with the sprigs of parsley to serve, accompanied by warm crusty bread or pasta.

Left: Mussels with Cream and Bacon; right: Prawn and Scallop Pie (page 114)

ORIENTAL DELIGHTS

*T*he Oriental style of eating is quite different from our
traditional concept of 'meat and two veg' main courses.
Instead, an Oriental meal will usually consist of a central dish of
rice or noodles accompanied by a variety of 'made' dishes. These
might be only a couple of stir-fries for a simple family meal, or
there could be a succession of countless elaborate recipes for a
banquet or special occasion. Whatever the type of meal, however,
the balance of ingredients will
invariably tip heavily towards
fresh vegetables, grains and
fruit, with meat, poultry
and fish appearing in much
smaller quantities than is
generally the case in the
West. For this reason alone,
the Oriental diet is a very
healthy one.

   Many of the dishes in this
chapter may be served as
Western-style main courses with
accompanying rice and vegetables.

Dover Sole with Mushrooms and Pork (page 132) served with plainly cooked
white rice

STUFFED BEAN CURD

MAKES 8

block of firm tofu, weighing about 675 g / 1½ lb
3 tbsp vegetable oil
250 ml / 8 fl oz chicken stock
½ tsp salt
1 generous tbsp Chinese oyster sauce
1 tsp cornflour, mixed with a little water, plus more
for dusting
2 thinly sliced spring onions, to garnish
FOR THE STUFFING
115 g / 4 oz minced chicken
1 tbsp finely chopped onion
2 tbsp light soy sauce
1½ tsp cornflour

The SPICED BEEF is also delicious served cold and sliced as part of a picnic or in sandwiches.

First make the stuffing by mixing together the ingredients in a bowl.

Cut the tofu into 4 equal portions which will measure about 10 cm / 4 in square by 3 cm / 1¼ in thick. Now cut these diagonally across to make triangular wedges. Using a sharp knife, cut a slit into the long side of each wedge and scoop out a little of the tofu to make a pocket to take the stuffing. Be careful not to cut too deeply, and work very carefully as the tofu is very fragile.

Dust the insides of each pocket with a little cornflour and carefully fill with the stuffing.

Heat the oil in a pan wide enough to take the pieces of curd in one layer (a sauté pan or deep-frying pan is ideal) over a very low heat. Place them in the pan with the stuffed side down and cook for about 5 minutes, until the stuffing is golden brown.

Pour in the stock, cover the pan and simmer for 3 minutes. Remove the tofu and keep warm.

Add the salt, oyster sauce, and cornflour mixture to the pan and simmer until thickened.

Arrange the tofu on a warmed serving plate, pour over the sauce and garnish with spring onion.

SPICED BEEF

SERVES 4-6

2 tbsp vegetable oil
900 g / 2 lb piece of rolled topside or brisket of beef
2 tbsp soy sauce
4 tbsp sherry
2 garlic cloves, crushed
3 heads of star anise
1 tbsp sugar
3 carrots, thinly sliced
30 g / 1 oz butter
1 tsp Oriental sesame oil
2 tsp lemon juice
1 tsp black mustard seeds
salt and freshly ground black pepper

Heat the vegetable oil in a saucepan which has a tight-fitting lid and is just large enough to fit the piece of meat snugly. Brown the meat on all sides.

Add the soy sauce, sherry, garlic and star anise. Cover the pan tightly and cook over a very low heat, undisturbed, for 1 hour.

Add the sugar and a good grinding of black pepper, replace the lid and continue to cook for 1 more hour.

Lift the meat out of the pan and allow it to rest for 10 minutes. Meanwhile, boil the liquid in the pan rapidly to reduce it to a sticky sauce.

At the same time, steam the carrots until just tender. Melt the butter with the sesame oil in a saucepan over a moderate heat and add the lemon juice, mustard seeds and a pinch of salt. Toss the steamed carrots in this to coat thoroughly.

Cut the meat into slices and arrange them on a warmed serving platter. Drizzle over the sauce and surround the meat with the carrots. Serve accompanied by plainly cooked white rice.

CRUMBED GINGER STEAKS

2 sirloin steaks, each weighing about 170 g/6 oz
1 tbsp soy sauce
1 tbsp sherry or white wine
1 garlic clove, crushed
2.5 cm/1 in cube of peeled fresh root ginger, crushed
through a garlic press
1 egg, beaten
55 g/2 oz fine fresh white breadcrumbs
3 tbsp vegetable oil
flour, for coating
chopped spring onions, to garnish

Cut each steak in half to make 4 equal pieces in all. Place these between 2 sheets of film, and flatten them with a rolling pin until they are as thin as possible. They should at least double in size.

Mix together the soy sauce, sherry or wine, garlic and ginger in a wide bowl and then put the flattened steaks into it. Mix well so that all surfaces of the meat are coated. Cover with film and leave in the refrigerator for at least 6 hours or up to 24.

Drain the marinated steaks well and pat them dry with paper towels.

Put some flour, the beaten egg and the breadcrumbs in 3 separate shallow dishes. Dip the pieces of steak first in the flour, then shake off any excess. Then dip them in the beaten egg and finally the breadcrumbs.

Heat the oil in a frying pan (not a wok) over a moderate to high heat and fry the pieces of steak, in batches if necessary, for 1–2 minutes on each side, or until the crumbs are crisp and golden.

Serve Western-style, with plain rice or potatoes and vegetables, or slice the steaks into strips and serve as part of an Oriental-style meal. Either way, garnish with the chopped spring onions.

STIR-FRIED BEEF WITH CELERY

3 tbsp soy sauce
2 garlic cloves, crushed
2 tsp cornflour
1 tsp sugar
450 g/1 lb sirloin or rump steak, cut into thin
bite-sized strips
3 tbsp vegetable oil
225 g/8 oz celery, cut across at an angle into thin slices
4 cm/1½ in cube of peeled fresh root ginger, thinly sliced

Combine the soy sauce, garlic, cornflour and sugar in a small bowl and then add the beef strips and mix well until each piece is coated. Leave to marinate for 20–30 minutes.

Heat the oil in a wok or frying pan over a moderate heat and add the meat mixture. Stir-fry for 3–4 minutes.

Add the slices of celery and ginger and continue to stir-fry the mixture for 4 minutes more. Serve immediately.

Based on a traditional Japanese dish, CRUMBED GINGER STEAKS is a simple and unusual way to cook steak. It also allows a little expensive meat to go a long way, so it is worth buying the best quality beef.

SWEET-AND-SOUR SPARE RIBS

1.35 kg/3 lb pork spare ribs
2 tbsp soy sauce
3 tbsp tomato ketchup
6 tbsp orange juice
2 tbsp white or red wine vinegar
2 tbsp soft brown sugar
1 tsp salt
2 garlic cloves, crushed
2.5 cm/1 in cube of peeled fresh root ginger, very finely chopped
¼ tsp chilli powder
freshly ground black pepper

Separate the ribs by cutting down between the bones and put the pieces in a wide ovenproof dish or baking tray.

Combine the remaining ingredients, season well with pepper and pour over the ribs. Mix well so that each rib is coated. Cover and leave to marinate for at least 6 hours, or up to 24 in the refrigerator.

Preheat the oven to 180C/350F/gas 4.

Bake the ribs, uncovered, for 1½ hours, basting them every 15-20 minutes. Increase the oven setting to 220C/425F/gas 7 and cook the ribs for another 30 minutes, turning them over after 15 minutes. The liquid will have almost entirely evaporated, leaving the ribs a deep mahogany brown and covered in a delicious sticky glaze.

These ribs are best eaten with the fingers, so supply lots of napkins and finger-bowls.

Left to right: Stir-fried Beef with Celery (page 121), Stuffed Bean Curd (page 120) and Sweet-and-Sour Spare Ribs

PORK WITH NOODLES, MUSHROOMS AND SPINACH

350 g/12 oz Chinese noodles
3 tbsp vegetable oil
½ small onion, finely chopped
2.5 cm/1 in cube of peeled fresh root ginger, finely chopped
2 garlic cloves, finely chopped
2 red or green chilli peppers, deseeded and finely chopped,
plus extra for garnish (optional)
450 g/1 lb lean pork, cut into thin bite-sized strips
170 g/6 oz firm mushrooms, thinly sliced
4 tbsp white wine or pale stock
350 g/12 oz spinach, torn into smallish shreds
salt and freshly ground black pepper

First cook the noodles according to the instructions on the packet. Drain them well and then toss them in 1 tablespoon of the oil to prevent them from sticking together.

Heat the remaining oil in a wok or large saucepan over a high heat and stir-fry the onion for 1 minute. Add the ginger, garlic and chilli peppers and continue to stir-fry for 1 more minute.

Add the pork strips and mushrooms and continue to stir-fry for 3-4 minutes, or until the meat is cooked and the mushrooms are beginning to soften.

Season with salt and pepper, pour in the wine or stock, add the spinach and stir-fry just until the spinach begins to wilt. Do not over-cook: each piece of spinach should retain some shape and stay separate rather than sticking together in a mush.

Add the cooked noodles to the stir-fried mixture and continue to cook for another 1-2 minutes, until the ingredients are well mixed together and the noodles are really hot.

Serve immediately in 4 warmed bowls and garnish with extra chopped chilli peppers, if using.

NOTE: if good fresh spinach is unobtainable, use spring greens or Cos lettuce.

There is a wide variety of very different types of CHINESE NOODLES, *which require varying degrees of cooking. Always check the packet for cooking times.*

BALINESE PORK

2 tbsp vegetable oil
450 g/1 lb pork fillet, cut into 2 cm/¾ in cubes
1 onion, finely chopped
3 garlic cloves, finely chopped
1 chilli pepper or more to taste, deseeded and finely chopped
1 tsp ground coriander
1 tsp turmeric
1 tsp cornflour
300 ml/½ pt coconut cream
1 tsp salt

Heat half the oil in a wok or saucepan which has a tight-fitting lid over a moderate heat and stir-fry the pork for 3-4 minutes or so, until the meat is coloured all over. Using a slotted spoon, remove the pork from the pan and set aside.

Add the remaining oil to the pan and stir-fry the onion for 3-4 minutes or until softened. Add the garlic, chilli, coriander and turmeric and continue to stir-fry for another 2-3 minutes. Return the pork to the pan.

Dissolve the cornflour in 1 tablespoon of water and stir this into the coconut cream. Add this to the pan and bring to the boil. Add the salt and simmer, covered, over the lowest possible heat for about an hour, or until the meat is tender.

Transfer to a warmed dish to serve.

Pork with Noodles, Mushrooms and Spinach

CRISPY DUCK WITH PANCAKES

SERVES 4-6

1 dressed duck, weighing 1.8-2 kg/4-4 ½ lb, giblets
removed
24 small ready-made Chinese pancakes
salt
bottled hoi-sin sauce, to serve
4 spring onions, cut into small sticks, to serve
¼ cucumber, cut into small sticks, to serve

At least 6 hours ahead, pour a large kettle of boiling water over the duck. This will tighten the skin. Then dry the bird thoroughly inside and out, place it on a rack and leave in an airy place for at least 6 hours, but preferably up to 12.

Preheat the oven to 180C/350F/gas 4.

Prick the skin of the duck all over with a skewer to allow the fat to escape during cooking, then rub the skin all over with salt.

Place the bird on a rack over a roasting tin and roast for 2 hours. The flesh will become very tender and the skin very crisp.

To serve: pull the meat off the carcass and shred this and the skin by pulling it apart with two forks. Arrange the meat and skin on a warmed serving plate and keep warm.

Warm the pancakes through for a couple of minutes in a steamer and then serve these on a warmed serving plate. Serve the sauce, the spring onions and cucumber in separate bowls.

Each pancake is spread with a little sauce. A few pieces of spring onion and cucumber are then arranged on top of this, followed by some of the duck flesh and some of the crispy skin. The pancake is then rolled up and eaten with the fingers. Be sure to provide plenty of napkins and finger-bowls.

CHINESE PANCAKES *for this well-loved dish are available ready-made in packets from Chinese supermarkets.*

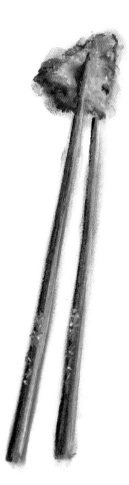

The recipe for BALINESE-STYLE DUCK was given to me by a dance teacher in whose house I stayed on Bali. I have had to adapt it slightly, as not all the spices used are available in the West.

BALINESE-STYLE DUCK

SERVES 6 AS A MAIN COURSE

1 dressed duck, weighing 1.8-2 kg/4-4 ½ lb, with giblets
1½ tsp salt
½ tsp chilli powder
½ tsp ground cumin
½ tsp ground coriander
6 hard-boiled eggs, quartered, to serve
deep-fried onion rings, to garnish (optional)
FOR THE SAUCE
1 tbsp vegetable oil
1 small onion, chopped
1 garlic clove, crushed
2.5 cm/1 in cube of peeled fresh root ginger, crushed through a garlic press or very finely chopped
1 chilli pepper, deseeded and chopped
grated zest and juice of 1 unwaxed lemon
2 tsp brown sugar
300 ml/½ pt coconut cream
2 tsp soy sauce

At least 6 hours ahead, remove the giblets from the duck and set them aside. Pour a large kettle of boiling water over the duck. This will tighten the skin. Then dry the bird thoroughly inside and out, place it on a rack and leave in an airy place for at least 6 hours, but preferably up to 12.

Put the giblets in a small pan, add just enough water to cover and bring to the boil, skimming off any scum which rises to the surface. Cover and simmer for 1 hour. Discard the giblets and boil the stock hard until reduced to about 2 tablespoons of concentrated essence. Set aside.

Preheat the oven to 180C/350F/gas 4.

Prick the skin of the duck all over with a skewer to let the fat run during cooking. Mix 1 teaspoon of the salt with the chilli powder, cumin and coriander and rub this all over the skin. Place the bird on a rack over a roasting tin and roast in the oven for 2 hours.

The skin will become crisp and golden.

Towards the end of this time, make the sauce: heat the oil in a saucepan over a moderate heat and cook the onion until translucent. Add the reduced stock together with the garlic, ginger, chilli, lemon zest and juice, sugar, coconut cream, soy sauce and remaining salt. Bring to the boil, cover the pan and simmer for 30 minutes.

When the duck is cooked, remove from the pan and allow it to rest for 10 minutes. Remove all the skin, cut it into bite-sized pieces and set aside.

Remove the meat and cut into bite-sized pieces. Toss in the sauce to coat thoroughly.

Transfer to a warmed serving dish, surround with the egg quarters, sprinkle over the crispy skin pieces and garnish with the fried onion rings, if using. Serve with plainly cooked white rice.

JAPANESE DEEP-FRIED CHICKEN

450 g/1 lb chicken breast fillet, cut into 3 cm/1¼ in cubes
cornflour, for dusting
vegetable oil, for deep-frying
1 green sweet pepper, deseeded and cut into strips, to garnish
FOR THE MARINADE
2 tbsp soy sauce
1 tbsp sake, sherry or white wine
1 garlic clove, crushed
juice from a 3 cm/1¼ in cube of peeled fresh root ginger, crushed through a garlic press

Make the marinade: mix the ingredients in a bowl. Add the chicken pieces, mix well and leave to marinate for 1 hour, stirring occasionally.

Drain the chicken thoroughly, discarding the marinade. Toss the pieces of chicken in cornflour and shake off any excess. Deep-fry them in batches in hot oil in a wok for 3-4 minutes each, until golden brown and crispy. Drain on paper towels and keep each batch warm while cooking the rest.

When all the chicken is cooked, arrange on a warmed serving plate, surround with the pepper strips and serve immediately.

LEMON CHICKEN

white of 1 egg, lightly beaten
3 tsp cornflour
285 g / 10 oz chicken breast fillet, cut across
into 1 cm / ½ in strips
6 tbsp chicken stock
juice of 1 lemon
2 tsp sugar
2 tsp light soy sauce
2 tsp sherry
1 garlic clove, crushed
pinch of chilli powder
½ small green sweet pepper, deseeded and cut into even
bite-sized pieces
vegetable oil, for frying

Mix the egg white with 2 teaspoons of the cornflour thoroughly in a bowl. Then mix in the chicken strips, making sure they are all well coated. Cover with film and chill for 30 minutes.

Deep-fry the chicken in hot oil in a wok for 1 minute, then drain on paper towels. Keep warm.

In a bowl, mix together the stock, lemon juice, sugar, soy sauce, sherry, garlic and chilli powder.

Leave 1 tablespoon of oil in the wok and stir-fry the pepper for 2 minutes over a moderate heat. Stir in the stock mixture and simmer for 1 minute.

Mix the remaining cornflour with 1 tablespoon of water, add this to the pan and simmer for 1 more minute, stirring. Return the chicken to the pan and stir-fry for about 30 seconds. Serve immediately.

STICKY CHICKEN

8 chicken wings
3 garlic cloves, crushed
4 cm / 1½ in cube of peeled fresh root ginger, crushed
through a garlic press or very finely chopped
juice of 1 lemon
2 tbsp soy sauce
2 tbsp runny honey
½ tsp chilli powder

Divide each chicken wing into pieces by cutting through the joints. Discard any pointed wing tip pieces or use for stock. There should be 16 pieces left.

Combine all the remaining ingredients in a shallow ovenproof dish large enough to accommodate the chicken pieces snugly in 1 layer. Add the chicken and mix to coat thoroughly.

Cover with film and marinate for at least 2 hours in a cool place or up to 24 in the refrigerator.

Preheat the oven to 220C/425F/gas 7.

Remove the film, turn the chicken pieces once more in the marinade and put the dish in the oven. Cook for 20 minutes, turning and basting halfway through. The chicken will be cooked through and coated with a delicious sticky glaze.

These pieces of chicken wing are best eaten with the fingers, so supply plenty of napkins and finger-bowls.

SAKE *is the rice wine of Japan and is much used in their cooking. Sherry makes a good substitute.*

Chicken drumsticks or thighs also work well in the STICKY CHICKEN *recipe.*

CHICKEN WITH STRAW MUSHROOM CURRY

4 skinned chicken breast fillets
2 tbsp vegetable oil
salt and freshly ground black pepper
FOR THE SAUCE
2 tbsp vegetable oil
1 onion, chopped
1 garlic clove, crushed
1 stalk of lemon grass, finely chopped
1 chilli pepper, deseeded and chopped
¼ tsp ground cinnamon
½ tsp ground cardamom
1 heaped tsp curry powder
300 ml/½ pt coconut cream
425 g/15 oz canned straw mushrooms, drained
juice of ½ lemon

If you can't find lemon grass for the CHICKEN WITH STRAW MUSHROOM CURRY, *substitute the grated rind of half a lemon or lime. Small egg-shaped* STRAW MUSHROOMS *are rarely seen fresh in the West, but are readily available canned from Oriental shops.*

First make the sauce: heat the oil in a saucepan over a moderate heat and cook the onion with the garlic and lemon grass, stirring occasionally, for 4–5 minutes, or until the onion has softened.

Add the chilli, dry spices and curry powder. Stir-fry for 1 minute. Add the coconut cream and simmer for another 5 minutes.

Purée the sauce in a blender or food processor and return it to the pan. Add the mushrooms and simmer for 2–3 minutes, or until they are warmed through. Stir in the lemon juice and a pinch of salt.

Meanwhile, season the chicken lightly. Heat the oil in a frying pan over a moderate heat and fry the fillets gently for 3–4 minutes on each side, or until golden brown and cooked through.

Arrange the cooked chicken on a warmed serving platter and spoon over the sauce. If serving as part of a meal to be eaten with chopsticks, slice the chicken across into bite-sized pieces before serving it.

CHICKEN WITH CASHEW NUTS

170 g/6 oz lean skinless chicken, cut into bite-sized pieces
30 g/1 oz carrot, sliced
2 tbsp vegetable oil
55 g/2 oz unsalted cashew nuts
30 g/1 oz canned bamboo shoots, sliced
1 tbsp frozen peas
FOR THE MARINADE
2 tbsp cornflour
1 tsp vegetable oil
FOR THE SAUCE
1 tsp soy sauce
1 tsp dry sherry
½ tsp cornflour
pinch of salt

First make the marinade in a small bowl, mix together the cornflour and oil with 2 tablespoons of water. Add the chicken, mix well and leave to marinate for 10 minutes.

Blanch the carrot slices in boiling salted water for 2 minutes. Drain.

Heat a wok until it is very hot, then add the oil and stir-fry the chicken for 3–4 minutes, until cooked through.

Add the carrot, nuts, bamboo shoots and peas and stir-fry for another minute.

Mix the sauce ingredients together with 4 tablespoons of water. Add this to the pan and cook for another minute or so, until the sauce has thickened. Serve immediately.

Top: Chicken with Straw Mushroom Curry served with plainly cooked noodles; bottom: Chicken with Cashew Nuts

Nuts like almonds or walnuts also work well in place of cashews in the recipe for CHICKEN WITH CASHEW NUTS.

SESAME-CRUMBED
SALMON WITH
GINGER CREAM *is
a particularly fine
East-meets-West
recipe as it provides
a simple and
different way of
cooking salmon to
bring out the best of
its delicate flavour.*

DRIED CHINESE
BLACK
MUSHROOMS *are
very similar to dried
French ceps and
Italian porcini.*

SESAME-CRUMBED SALMON WITH GINGER CREAM

55 g/2 oz sesame seeds
1 egg, beaten
4 skinless salmon fillets, each weighing 115-140 g/4-5 oz
3 tbsp vegetable oil
flour, for coating
salt and freshly ground black pepper
FOR THE SAUCE
300 ml/½ pt single cream
*4 cm/1½ in cube of peeled fresh root ginger, crushed
through a garlic press*
1 tbsp light soy sauce or more to taste

Toast the sesame seeds in a dry frying pan over a low
to moderate heat until lightly coloured and aromatic.
Put the toasted sesame seeds, beaten egg and some
flour in 3 separate shallow dishes.

Season the fish fillets on both sides with salt and
pepper. Dip them first in the flour, shaking off the
excess, then dip them in the egg and finally in the
toasted sesame seeds.

Heat the oil in a frying pan over a moderate to
low heat and fry the coated fish for 2-3 minutes on
each side, until crisp and golden and cooked through.

Meanwhile, make the sauce: combine the cream,
ginger and soy sauce in a small saucepan and simmer
them for 2-3 minutes. Add a little more soy sauce to
taste, if necessary.

Serve accompanied by plainly cooked rice or
noodles and fresh steamed or boiled vegetables.

DOVER SOLE WITH MUSHROOMS AND PORK

45 g/1½ oz dried Chinese black mushrooms
*1 whole Dover sole, weighing about 500 g/1 lb 2 oz,
skinned*
1 tsp cornflour
2 tsp dry sherry
½ tsp Oriental sesame oil, plus more for greasing
¼ tsp soy sauce
1 tsp oyster sauce
45 g/1½ oz shredded lean pork
1 slice of bacon, cut across into thin strips
*1 cm/½ in cube of peeled fresh root ginger, cut into
fine julienne strips*
1 small spring onion, thinly sliced, to garnish
chopped fresh coriander, to garnish

Soak the mushrooms in warm water for 30 minutes.
Drain them thoroughly, cut off and discard the stalks
and thinly slice the caps.

Arrange the fish in a steamer. (First placing 2
strips of lightly oiled foil in a cross shape in the
bottom of the pan will make it easier to remove the
fish when it is cooked.)

Blend the cornflour with a little sherry and then
mix this thoroughly with the remaining sherry,
sesame oil, soy and oyster sauces, pork, bacon and
ginger.

Spoon this mixture on top of the fish and steam it
over boiling water until the fish flakes readily. This
will depend on the fish, but could be anything from
10 to 15 minutes.

Transfer the fish to a warmed serving plate and
garnish with the spring onion and coriander.

CHILLI PRAWNS IN PINEAPPLES

2 small ripe pineapples
1 tbsp vegetable oil
1 onion, chopped
1 garlic clove, crushed
1 large or 2 small stalks of celery, coarsely chopped
2 tbsp chopped sweet pepper (preferably red)
1 tsp chilli powder or more to taste
200 ml/7 fl oz chicken stock
2 heaped tsp arrowroot, dissolved in a little water
350 g/12 oz peeled cooked prawns
115 g/4 oz small seedless grapes (any colour or mixed)
salt and freshly ground black pepper
55 g/2 oz blanched split almonds, grilled or dry-fried until golden, to garnish
4 large or medium cooked prawns in their shells, to garnish

Cut the pineapples in half lengthwise, including the crown of green leaves. Being careful not to cut through the skin, cut out all the flesh and set the shells aside in a warm place. Cut the flesh into bite-sized pieces, discarding any hard core, and set the flesh aside.

Heat the oil in a large saucepan and cook the onion until translucent. Add the garlic, celery, sweet pepper and chilli powder with salt and pepper to taste. Stir-fry the mixture for 2-3 minutes until the vegetables are softened.

Stir in the stock, bring to the boil and simmer for 15 minutes. Add the arrowroot mixture and stir well until the mixture is thickened.

Add the peeled prawns, grapes and pineapple pieces and continue to cook gently until these are just heated through. (The prawns will toughen if cooked too long.)

Pile the cooked prawn mixture into the reserved pineapple half shells and garnish with grilled or fried almonds and the cooked prawns in their shells.

For a striking buffet party dish serve the CHILLI PRAWNS IN PINEAPPLES *in one or two half shells from a large pineapple. A wide variety of seafood suits this treatment: try using scallops or crab meat.*

For the CRISPY SESAME PRAWNS *it is important to keep the tails attached to the prawns when peeling them. They then look much more attractive when cooked and are easier to dip in the sauce and eat.*

CRISPY SESAME PRAWNS

225 g/8 oz raw prawns, peeled
vegetable oil, for deep-frying
sweet chilli sauce or other dipping sauce, to serve
FOR THE BATTER
85 g/3 oz flour
3 tbsp cornflour
1 tsp baking powder
¼ tsp chilli powder
½ tsp salt
1 tbsp vegetable oil
2 tbsp sesame seeds

At least 1 hour ahead, make the batter by thoroughly mixing the flour, cornflour, baking powder and chilli powder with 175 ml/6 fl oz water in a bowl. Leave this batter to rest for at least 1 hour.

Just before using, beat the salt and the oil into the batter until well incorporated and then stir in the sesame seeds.

Dip the prawns in the batter and deep-fry them a few at a time in hot oil in a wok. Drain on paper towels and keep warm while the rest are being cooked.

Serve as soon as all the prawns are cooked, accompanied by a dipping sauce, such as sweet chilli sauce or a mixture of equal parts light soy sauce and malt or white wine vinegar.

INDONESIAN SQUID

1 tbsp vegetable oil
1 small onion, chopped
2 garlic cloves, crushed
2.5 cm/1 in cube of peeled fresh root ginger, finely chopped
½ tsp chilli powder
grated zest and juice of 1 unwaxed lime
1 tbsp soft brown sugar
400 ml/14 fl oz thick coconut milk
12 small prepared squid, sacs sliced into thin rings
salt
chopped coriander, to garnish

Heat the oil in a saucepan or wok over a moderate heat and fry the onion, garlic and ginger for 2-3 minutes.

Add the chilli powder, lime zest and juice, the sugar and some salt to taste. Stir to mix well, then add the coconut milk. Simmer for 10 minutes.

Add the squid tentacles and slices and simmer for 10 minutes. Do not overcook or it will become tough and rubbery.

Serve sprinkled with chopped coriander.

Ready-prepared SQUID *are available fresh from better fishmongers and supermarkets, and frozen from Oriental supermarkets.*

Top: Sesame-crumbed Salmon with Ginger Cream (page 132); bottom: Crispy Sesame Prawns

SPICED CRAB CLAWS

2 tbsp vegetable oil
8 large or 12 medium shelled crab claws, defrosted if frozen
1 small onion, finely chopped
2 garlic cloves, crushed
2 chilli peppers, finely chopped
4 cm/1½ in cube of peeled fresh root ginger, finely chopped
½ tsp ground coriander seeds
1 tsp sugar
1 tbsp soy sauce
2 tsp tomato paste
juice of ½ lime
salt

Shelled crab claws can be bought frozen from Oriental supermarkets.

'MALAYSIAN MILD CURRY PASTE' is sold in many supermarkets. If unavailable, substitute another strong curry paste or a mild Malaysian curry powder.

In a frying pan or wok, heat the oil over a moderate heat and fry the crab claws for 3-4 minutes, or until cooked through. Remove with a slotted spoon and keep warm.

In the oil remaining in the pan, fry the onion, garlic and chilli for 3 minutes. Add the ginger, coriander, sugar, soy sauce, tomato paste and salt to taste with 3 tablespoons of water and simmer for 3 minutes.

Return the crab claws to the pan, add the lime juice, stir to coat thoroughly and simmer for 1-2 minutes, stirring until well heated through.

MUSSELS WITH CURRIED COCONUT NOODLES

1 kg/2¼ lb cleaned mussels in their shells
300 ml/½ pt coconut cream
190 g/6.7 oz jar Sharwood's 'Malaysian mild curry paste'
250 g/8½ oz Chinese noodles
curls of fresh coconut, peeled with a swivel vegetable peeler, to garnish
chopped coriander, to garnish (optional)

Soak the mussels in cold water for at least 1 hour to remove any traces of dirt or sand, changing the water at least 3 times. Drain the mussels and give any which remain open a sharp tap. Those which do not close again are dead and must be thrown away.

Put the coconut cream and the curry paste in a large saucepan which has a tight-fitting lid and place over a moderate heat, stirring gently. Add the mussels, cover the pan and cook for about 5 minutes, shaking the pan occasionally, until all the shells have opened. (Those few which do not should also be discarded.) Do not overcook or the mussels will become tough and rubbery.

Meanwhile, cook the noodles in boiling water, according to the instructions on the packet, and then drain them thoroughly.

To serve: divide the noodles between 6 warmed bowls or dishes and pour over the mussels and sauce. Sprinkle with coconut curls and chopped coriander, if using, and serve immediately.

Top: Mussels with Curried Coconut Noodles; bottom: Spiced Crab Claws

VEGETARIAN MAIN COURSES

*F*ortunately, the old concept of meat being an essential part of a meal is now dying away. As well as the pressure of more and more families now having to accommodate at least one vegetarian in their ranks, greater foreign travel - with a resulting awareness of other cuisines - and the extraordinary range of fresh vegetables, leaves, herbs and fruit now available in our shops have caused even the most conventional cooks to broaden their horizons. Cultures which have traditionally made more of vegetables - or perhaps just used meat and fish more as flavouring ingredients - include the Mediterranean peoples, the Indians, Chinese, Japanese and Latin Americans. Looking towards their heritage gives us myriad wonderful ways of preparing sustaining main-course salads and other dishes based mainly on vegetables.

Top: Bean Stew with Herb Dumplings (page 141); bottom: Vegetable Gratin (page 162)

CURLY ENDIVE LOAF WITH CAPER SAUCE

5 heads of curly endive
75 g/2½ oz butter
55 g/2 oz flour
225 g/8 oz cream
4 eggs, beaten
salt and freshly ground black pepper
FOR THE CAPER SAUCE
30 g/1 oz butter
2 tbsp olive oil
2 onions, sliced
350 g/12 oz tomatoes, peeled, deseeded and coarsely chopped
1½ tbsp capers

Preheat the oven to 180C/350F/gas 4.

Put 3.5 litre/6 pt of water in a large pan and bring it to the boil. Carefully place the endive heads in the water, bring it back to the boil and cook, uncovered, for 15 minutes. Drain and allow to cool. Then squeeze out all remaining liquid and chop the endive coarsely.

Make a béchamel sauce (see page 12), using 55 g/ 2 oz of the butter, the flour and cream. Add the beaten eggs and then the chopped endive. Season.

Grease a 1 litre/1¾ pt charlotte mould with the remaining butter. Fill with the mixture, tapping the mould sharply from time to time to remove air pockets. Allow to settle.

Place the mould in 5 cm/2 in of water in a bain-marie or deep roasting pan filled with hot water. Put this in the oven and cook for 1 hour, until the surface of the loaf is golden brown. The water should not boil at any time during the process.

While the loaf is cooking, make the caper sauce: melt the butter with the oil in a heavy-based pan over a moderate heat. Add the onions and sauté until translucent. Then add the tomatoes and cook thoroughly for about 5-7 minutes, until tender. Season and allow to cool slightly. Then liquidize in a blender or food processor and stir in the capers.

Remove the loaf from the oven. Insert a knife to the bottom of the mould: if it comes out clean the loaf is cooked through; if sticky, return it to the oven for a further 10-15 minutes.

Leave to cool out of the oven for 3 minutes and then unmould on a warmed serving dish and serve with the caper sauce.

LEEK, MOZZARELLA AND PESTO BAKE

8 large leeks, trimmed but leaving as much green as possible
115 g/4 oz fromage frais
2 tbsp ready-made pesto sauce
4 tbsp pine kernels
115 g/4 oz mozzarella cheese, thinly sliced
salt and freshly ground black pepper

Preheat the oven to 200C/400F/gas 6.

Cut each of the leeks into 4 equal lengths. Then place them in a pan of boiling salted water and cook for 5-7 minutes. Remove, refresh under cold running water and place in a colander to drain.

Place the drained leeks in an ovenproof dish. Mix the fromage frais and pesto together and season. Using a spatula, smooth the mixture over the leeks. Sprinkle over the pine kernels and arrange the mozzarella slices over the top of the dish.

Bake in the oven for 20-30 minutes, or until the mozzarella has turned golden brown.

BEAN STEW WITH HERB DUMPLINGS

3 tbsp olive oil
1 onion, chopped
1-2 garlic cloves, crushed
2 celery stalks, chopped
2 carrots, sliced
140 g/5 oz cannellini or black-eye beans, soaked
overnight in cold water
bouquet garni
450 g/1 lb tomatoes, peeled and chopped
850 ml/1½ pt well-flavoured vegetable stock
salt and freshly ground black pepper
FOR THE HERB DUMPLINGS
55 g/2 oz shredded vegetable suet
55 g/2 oz fresh white breadcrumbs
55 g/2 oz self-raising flour
3 tbsp chopped mixed herbs

Heat the oil in a large pan over a moderate heat. Add the onion and garlic and sauté for 4 minutes. Stir in the celery and carrots and cook for 2 more minutes.

Drain the beans, then put in a pan with some fresh water, bring to the boil, and boil fast for 10 minutes. Drain, then add the beans and the remaining ingredients to the vegetable mixture and bring to the boil. Season. Lower the heat, cover and simmer for 45 minutes, stirring occasionally.

Towards the end of this time make the dumplings: mix all the ingredients together with about 5 tablespoons of cold water and seasonings to give a firm dough. Shape into 12 balls.

Arrange the dumplings on top of the stew. Cover and continue simmering for 20 minutes, until the dumplings are light and fluffy. Serve at once.

PUMPKIN STEW WITH HARICOTS OR BARLEY

SERVES 4-6

170 g/6 oz haricot beans or pearl barley, soaked overnight
in cold water
30 g/1 oz butter
2 tbsp olive oil
1 onion, cut into wedges
1 garlic clove, crushed
350 g/12 oz pumpkin, peeled and diced
2 carrots, sliced
1 small fennel bulb, sliced
1 tsp ground turmeric
1 tsp ground coriander seeds
½ tsp ground cinnamon
4 tomatoes, peeled and quartered
1 tbsp chopped mint
1 tbsp chopped coriander leaves
170 g/6 oz French beans
115 g/4 oz small button mushrooms
850 ml/1½ pt vegetable stock
salt and freshly ground black pepper
garlic bread, to serve

Drain the haricot beans or barley and put them in a saucepan. Cover with water and bring to the boil. Boil fast for 10 minutes then simmer for 15 minutes for haricot beans or 5 minutes for barley. Drain and set aside.

Melt the butter with the oil in a large heavy-based saucepan over a moderate heat. Add the onion and garlic and cook for 3 minutes. Stir in the pumpkin, carrots, fennel and spices and continue cooking for 10 minutes, stirring frequently.

Add the beans or barley and all the remaining ingredients to the pan. Season with salt and pepper. Bring to the boil, cover and simmer for 20-25 minutes.

Serve hot with garlic bread.

SPICED WINTER VEGETABLE CASSEROLE

SERVES 6

30 g/1 oz butter
1 onion, chopped
10 garlic cloves
225 g/8 oz small turnips, halved
225 g/8 oz kohlrabi, cut into 2.5 cm/1 in cubes
225 g/8 oz carrots, cut into batons
115 g/4 oz Jerusalem artichokes, diced
½ cinnamon stick
4 cloves
large sprig of thyme
300 ml/½ pt red wine
150 ml/¼ pt well-flavoured vegetable stock
2 tsp cornflour
salt and freshly ground black pepper

Preheat the oven to 200C/400F/gas 6.

Melt the butter in a large heavy-based saucepan over a moderate heat. Add the onion and garlic cloves and cook, stirring, for 5 minutes, until they begin to brown - but do not let them burn.

Stir in all the vegetables and continue cooking for 3 minutes. Transfer to an ovenproof casserole and add the spices and thyme. Pour over the wine and stock and season. Cover and bake for about 1¼ hours, or until all the vegetables are tender.

Blend the cornflour with 2 tablespoons of cold water and stir this into the stew. Return to the oven, uncovered, for 10 minutes to allow the juices to thicken. Remove the cinnamon and adjust the seasoning to serve.

STUFFED MARROW

SERVES 6

5 tbsp olive oil
2 garlic cloves, chopped
1 shallot, finely chopped
2 sprigs of sage or oregano
675 g/1 ½ lb fresh broad beans, shelled
350 g/12 oz ripe tomatoes, peeled and chopped
2 tbsp chopped parsley
1 marrow, weighing 1-1.35 kg/2¼-3 lb
salt and freshly ground black pepper
4 tbsp freshly grated Parmesan cheese, to serve

Preheat the oven to 190C/375F/gas 5.

First prepare the filling: heat 3 tablespoons of the oil in a heavy-based saucepan over a moderate heat. Add the garlic, shallot and herb sprigs and cook for 5 minutes, stirring frequently.

Stir in the beans and tomatoes and season with salt and pepper. Cover and cook for 15 minutes, stirring frequently. Remove the herb sprigs and stir in the chopped parsley.

While the filling is cooking, slice the marrow into six discs. Scoop out the seeds in the centre of each disc together with a little of the inner flesh and arrange the rings that remain in an oiled baking dish.

Brush the marrow flesh with the remaining olive oil. Divide the prepared filling between the marrow rings, cover with foil and bake in the oven for 35 minutes, or until the marrow is tender.

Serve hot, sprinkled with the freshly grated Parmesan cheese.

Top: Red Cabbage with Cloves and Chestnuts (page 163); bottom: Stuffed Marrow

DAIKON, *mooli or Japanese radish is said to aid the digestion and is generally served raw and thinly sliced in salads and fish dishes. It also cooks a little like turnip and may be used in stews.*

RED LENTILS WITH CINNAMON AND COCONUT

SERVES 6

225 g/8 oz split red lentils
850 ml/1½ pt water
3 tbsp extra virgin olive oil
2 large purple garlic cloves, sliced
2 large onions, diced
2 carrots, sliced
2 leeks, cut into 2.5 cm/1 in slices
1 daikon radish, weighing about 115 g/4 oz, diced
½ tsp ground cinnamon
½ tsp mustard seeds
½ tsp ground or crushed cumin seeds
1 tbsp desiccated coconut
15 g/½ oz fresh root ginger, peeled and grated
salt and freshly ground black pepper

Thoroughly wash the lentils in cold water. Drain.

Bring the water to the boil and add the lentils. Bring back to the boil, stirring constantly. Boil fast for 10 minutes, then cover and simmer for 35 minutes, or until the lentils are cooked. Drain and season.

Towards the end of the lentil cooking time, place a large heavy-based pan over a moderate heat. Pour in the olive oil, then add the garlic and sauté it briefly. Add all the vegetables and sauté them for 5 minutes more. Add the cinnamon, mustard seeds, cumin, coconut and fresh ginger. Stir for 2 minutes.

Gently stir the vegetable and spice mixture into the drained lentils. Adjust the seasoning, heat through thoroughly and serve.

STUFFED AUBERGINES

SERVES 6

6 large aubergines
4 tbsp extra virgin olive oil
1 large purple garlic clove, crushed
6 anchovy fillets
1 tsp herbes de Provence
115 g/4 oz tomatoes, peeled, deseeded and coarsely chopped
115 g/4 oz onions, diced
115 g/4 oz stoned Greek olives, finely chopped
170 g/6 oz brown breadcrumbs
salt and freshly ground black pepper

Preheat the oven to 200C/400F/gas 6 and line a baking tray with foil.

Cut the aubergines in half lengthwise. Using a small teaspoon, scoop out the aubergine flesh, leaving about 6 mm/¼ in of flesh under the skin and taking care not to break the skin at any point.

Spread the scooped-out flesh on the prepared baking tray and cook it in the oven for 30 minutes.

Meanwhile, brush the flesh left in the aubergine shells with some of the olive oil and then sprinkle with salt. Place the shells in a baking dish and bake for the last 15 minutes with the scooped-out flesh.

Towards the end of this time, heat the remaining oil in a sauté pan over a moderate heat and add the garlic, anchovies, herbs, tomatoes and onions. Sauté lightly for 3-5 minutes.

Blend these to a smooth purée, then mix this well with the chopped olives and baked aubergine flesh. Season this mixture and use it to stuff the shells. Sprinkle the tops with the breadcrumbs.

Bake the stuffed aubergine halves for 10-15 minutes and then serve immediately.

Left to right: Red Lentils with Cinnamon and Coconut; right: Stuffed Aubergines

TOFU *or bean curd is made from soya beans and is rich in proteins. Rather like fresh cheese in appearance and texture, its gentle flavour lends it to use with a variety of vegetables, herbs and spices. It is particularly tasty when smoked.*

PUMPKIN STUFFED WITH LEEKS AND SMOKED TOFU

SERVES 2

1 orange pumpkin, weighing 900 g-1.35 kg/2-3 lb
1½ tbsp light soy sauce
2 tsp sesame oil
225 g/8 oz smoked tofu, mashed
2 young leeks, thinly sliced or shredded
½ tsp freshly grated nutmeg

Preheat the oven to 200C/400F/gas 6.

Cut off the top of the pumpkin and reserve. Scoop out and discard all the seeds and fibres.

Mix the soy sauce and sesame oil into the tofu together with the leeks and nutmeg. Pack the mixture into the cavity created in the pumpkin and place the top back on. Wrap in foil and bake for 1-1½ hours, depending on size.

Remove the top and halve the pumpkin to serve.

CAULIFLOWER CHEESE WITH NUTS AND OATS

SERVES 4-6

1 large cauliflower
55 g/2 oz unsalted butter
2 onions, finely chopped
300 ml/½ pt milk
85 g/3 oz Gruyère cheese, grated
5 eggs, beaten
85 g/3 oz brown breadcrumbs
30 g/1 oz almonds, toasted
30 g/1 oz hazelnuts, toasted
85 g/3 oz small oat flakes
salt and freshly ground black pepper

Preheat the oven to 180C/350F/gas 4.

Remove all large outer leaves surrounding the cauliflower, but leave the young green ones. Cut the cauliflower lengthwise into 6 parts, complete with core.

Place the cauliflower in a large pan of lightly salted water. Bring to the boil, then reduce the heat and simmer for 5 minutes. Drain thoroughly and place in a 2 litre/3½ pt ovenproof dish.

Melt half the butter in a sauté pan over a moderate heat and sauté the onions in it.

Bring the milk to the boil in a saucepan and stir in the Gruyère cheese and the remaining butter. Season with salt and pepper and stir in the onions. Remove from the heat, then blend in the eggs and one-third of the breadcrumbs.

Cover the drained cauliflower with this sauce and bake the dish on the middle shelf of the oven for 20 minutes.

Remove the cooked dish from the oven and sprinkle with the nuts, oat flakes and remaining breadcrumbs. Return to the oven, turn the heat up to 200C/400F/gas 6 and bake for 10-15 minutes, until the oat flakes are golden.

VEGETARIAN BAKE WITH SAGE HOLLANDAISE

SERVES 6

3 tbsp hazelnut oil, plus more for greasing
2 onions, coarsely chopped
3 beef tomatoes, coarsely chopped
115 g/4 oz oyster mushrooms, coarsely chopped
1 tsp herbes de Provence
1 tbsp light soy sauce
85 g/3 oz buckwheat
30 g/1 oz brown rice
1 egg, beaten
150 ml/¼ pt vegetable stock
1 tbsp crushed hazelnuts
freshly ground black pepper
2 large sage leaves, for garnish

FOR THE GOLDEN SAGE HOLLANDAISE SAUCE

1 tbsp finely snipped golden sage
2 tbsp lemon juice
1 tbsp white wine vinegar
200 g/7 oz unsalted butter
1 tbsp dry white wine
3 egg yolks
salt and freshly ground black pepper

Preheat the oven to 190C/375F/gas 5 and lightly grease an 18 cm/7 in shallow loaf tin with a little hazelnut oil.

Heat the hazelnut oil in a pan over a moderate heat. Add the onions, tomatoes and mushrooms, toss gently to coat evenly and cook for 3 minutes. Add the herbs and the soy sauce and cook for a further 2 minutes. Add the buckwheat and rice and cook for 2 minutes more. Then stir in the egg.

Add the vegetable stock and bring to the boil, stirring constantly. Reduce the heat, cover and simmer for 20-25 minutes or until all the liquid has been absorbed. Season and add the hazelnuts.

Transfer the mixture to the prepared tin and bake for 45 minutes.

While it is baking, make the hollandaise sauce: mix the chopped sage with 1 tablespoon of the lemon juice, the vinegar and 1 tablespoon of water in a small pan and bring them to the boil. Strain off and discard the liquid, reserving the sage. Melt 170 g/6 oz of the butter in a heavy-bottomed pan over a gentle heat. Transfer to a warmed jug.

Place the egg yolks in the same pan and beat them quickly with a whisk. Add half the remaining lemon juice and all the wine together with a pinch of salt. Beat again. Add half the remaining unmelted butter and place the pan in a bain-marie or double boiler.

Whisking steadily, cook gently until the egg yolks are creamy and beginning to thicken. Immediately remove the pan from the heat and stir in the remaining unmelted butter until it dissolves.

Dribble the melted butter into the yolk mixture, whisking fast. Add the butter more rapidly as the sauce thickens. When the sauce is the consistency of double cream, add the remaining lemon juice with the reserved sage and adjust the seasoning.

Serve the sauce with the hot vegetarian bake, garnished with the whole sage leaves.

HERBES DE PROVENCE *consist of mixed bay, thyme, rosemary, basil and savory, usually dried. Ready-made mixtures are available in delicatessens and some supermarkets*

The SAGE HOLLANDAISE *sauce also goes very well with chicken and veal and with rice, cheese and tomato dishes.*

COURGETTE, TOMATO AND GARLIC FLAN

170 g/6 oz shortcrust pastry
350 g/12 oz courgettes
2 eggs, beaten
150 ml/¼ pt milk
150 ml/¼ pt double cream
2 garlic cloves, crushed
1 tsp tomato paste
1 tsp Worcestershire sauce
¼ tsp freshly grated nutmeg
115 g/4 oz tomatoes, sliced
salt and freshly ground black pepper
butter or margarine, for greasing

Preheat the oven to 200C/400F/gas 6 and grease an 18 cm/7 in flan tin with some butter or margarine.

Roll out the pastry and use it to line the flan tin. Line with greaseproof paper and weight with some dried beans. Bake blind for 15 minutes. Leave to cool and then remove the beans and lining paper.

Grate the courgettes and then blanch the shreds for 30 seconds only in boiling salted water. Drain, refresh under cold running water and set aside.

In a bowl, thoroughly mix the eggs, milk, cream, garlic, tomato paste, Worcestershire sauce, nutmeg and seasonings. Add the well-drained courgettes and then spread this mixture evenly in the pastry case. Arrange the tomatoes decoratively on the top.

Bake for 30-40 minutes, until the filling is set and golden in colour.

ASPARAGUS AND DILL TART

SERVES 6

FOR THE PASTRY
170 g/6 oz flour
½ tsp salt and ¼ tsp freshly ground black pepper
¼ tsp mustard powder
85 g/3 oz butter or margarine, cut into small pieces
55 g/2 oz Cheddar cheese, finely grated
1 egg yolk
FOR THE FILLING
170 g/6 oz asparagus tips
1 egg + 1 extra yolk
300 ml/½ pt single cream
½ tsp salt and ¼ tsp finely ground black pepper
3 tbsp chopped dill
2 tsp French mustard

To make the pastry: sift the flour, salt, pepper and mustard powder into a bowl, add the butter or margarine and rub it in finely with the fingertips. Stir in the cheese, egg yolk and 1-2 tablespoons of cold water and mix together to a firm dough.

Knead the dough on a lightly floured surface until smooth. Roll it out thinly and use to line a 35 x 10 cm/14 x 4 in loose-based tranche tart tin. Chill for 30 minutes.

Preheat the oven to 200C/400F/gas 6.

Bake the pastry case blind for 10-15 minutes, until lightly browned at the edges and cooked at the base. Reduce the oven temperature to 180C/350F/gas 4.

While the case is baking make the filling: cook the asparagus in boiling water for 1 minute, then drain well. In a bowl beat together the egg and extra egg yolk, cream, salt, pepper, dill and mustard until well blended. Pour this filling into the pastry case and arrange the asparagus tips over it.

Return to the cooler oven and bake for 20-25 minutes, until the filling has just set.

Allow to cool in the tin, then remove carefully and serve warm or cold.

SPINACH AND RAISIN TART

FOR THE PASTRY
115 g/4 oz flour
½ tsp salt
55 g/2 oz butter or margarine, cut into small pieces
1 tbsp lemon juice
FOR THE FILLING
225 g/8 oz fresh spinach
2 eggs
200 ml/7 fl oz Greek yogurt
½ tsp salt and ¼ tsp finely ground black pepper
1 tsp freshly grated nutmeg
55 g/2 oz raisins

To make the pastry: sift the flour and salt into a bowl, add the butter or margarine and rub it in finely with the fingertips. Stir in the lemon juice and 2-3 tablespoons of cold water and mix together with a fork to form a firm dough.

Knead on a lightly floured surface until smooth. Roll it out thinly and use to line a 20 cm/8 in diameter loose-based fluted tart tin. Chill for 30 minutes.

Preheat the oven to 200C/400F/gas 6.

Bake the pastry case blind for 10-15 minutes, until lightly browned at the edge and cooked at the base. Remove from the oven, and reduce the oven temperature to 180C/350F/gas 4.

While the case is baking, make the filling: plunge the spinach into a saucepan of boiling water for 1 minute. Drain well and chop finely.

Place the eggs, yogurt, salt, pepper and nutmeg in a bowl and beat them together until well blended. Stir in the spinach and raisins and pour the mixture into the pastry case. Return the tart to the cooler oven for 20-25 minutes, until the filling has set.

Leave to cool in the tin, then remove it carefully. Serve warm or cold.

ASPARAGUS is now available throughout the year, although its true season is from June to July. When buying asparagus, look for tightly closed 'buds' or tips and fresh green unwrinkled stems. Nowadays, ready-trimmed tips are available from supermarkets, but you can use the stems for soups and sauces.

FRESH HERB AND GARLIC TART

FOR THE PASTRY
115 g/4 oz flour
1 tbsp Parmesan cheese
¼ tsp mustard powder
½ tsp salt and ¼ tsp freshly ground black pepper
55 g/2 oz butter or margarine, cut into small pieces

FOR THE FILLING
2 garlic cloves, crushed
4 tbsp chopped mixed herbs, including parsley, rosemary, oregano and basil
115 g/4 oz medium-fat soft cheese
4 tbsp Greek yogurt
2 eggs, beaten
½ tsp salt and ¼ tsp freshly ground black pepper

To make the pastry: sift the flour, Parmesan, mustard, salt and pepper into a bowl. Add the margarine or butter and rub it in finely with the fingertips. Stir in 2-3 tablespoons of cold water and mix together with a fork to form a firm dough.

Knead on a lightly floured surface until smooth. Roll out thinly and use to line a 20 cm/8 in diameter loose-based tart tin. Chill for 30 minutes.

Preheat the oven to 200C/400F/gas 6.

Bake the case blind for 10-15 minutes, until lightly browned at the edge and cooked at the base. Reduce the oven temperature to 180C/350F/gas 4.

While the case is baking make the filling: mix the garlic, herbs and soft cheese together in a bowl until well blended. Stir in the yogurt, eggs, salt and pepper and mix well.

Pour the mixture into the pastry case and return it to the cooler oven for 20-25 minutes, until the filling has set. Serve warm or cold.

ONION AND SAGE TART

SERVES 6

FOR THE PASTRY
170 g/6 oz flour
½ tsp salt
55 g/2 oz white fat, cut into small pieces

FOR THE FILLING
350 g/12 oz tiny onions, unpeeled
30 g/1 oz butter
15 cherry tomatoes
2 tbsp chopped sage
1 tbsp flour
150 ml/¼ pt vegetable stock
100 ml/3½ fl oz single cream
2 eggs, beaten
½ tsp salt and ¼ tsp freshly ground black pepper

FOR THE TOPPING
1 tbsp freshly grated Parmesan cheese
1 tbsp chopped sage

To make the pastry: sift the flour and salt into a bowl, add the white fat and butter or margarine and rub them in finely with the fingertips. Stir in 2 tablespoons of cold water and mix together with a fork to form a firm dough.

Knead the dough on a lightly floured surface until smooth. Roll it out thinly and use to line a 23 cm/9 in diameter loose-based tart tin. Chill for 30 minutes.

Preheat the oven to 200C/400F/gas 6.

Bake the pastry case blind for 10-15 minutes, until lightly browned at the edge and cooked in the base.

While the case is baking make the filling: place the onions in a saucepan and cover with cold water. Bring to the boil, cover and cook for 10 minutes, until tender. Drain and cover with cold water. Drain again and then peel off the onion skins.

Melt the butter in a saucepan over a moderate to high heat. Add the peeled onions, the tomatoes and sage and cook quickly for 1-2 minutes, shaking the saucepan continuously. Using a slotted spoon, transfer the tomatoes and onions to a plate. Allow to cool slightly then cut them in half. Arrange them in the pastry case.

Add the flour to the juices in the saucepan and stir well. Add the vegetable stock, bring to the boil and cook for 1 minute. Remove the saucepan from the heat, stir in the cream, eggs, salt and pepper.

Pour the mixture into the pastry case and return it to the oven for 15 minutes. Remove from the oven and give the tart its topping: sprinkle the top with Parmesan cheese and sage and continue to cook for a further 10-15 minutes, until the filling has set and is golden brown. Serve hot or cold.

Left: Fresh Herb and Garlic Tart; right: Onion and Sage Tart

POTATOES WITH WINTER VEGETABLE TRICOLOUR

450g/1 lb thin-skinned potatoes, washed but not peeled
½ tbsp rock salt
1 large head of celeriac, peeled and cut into chunks
675g/1½ lb spinach, stalks removed
3 large carrots, thinly sliced
½ tsp celery salt
1 tbsp single cream
¼ tsp freshly grated nutmeg
salt and freshly ground black pepper

Put the potatoes and salt in a pan of water and place over a moderate heat. Bring to the boil, reduce the heat and cook the potatoes until tender. Drain and place them on a warm plate. The rock salt should dry on the potato skins.

When cool enough to handle, cut the potatoes into thick slices. Keep warm.

Preheat the oven to 230C/450F/gas8.

Cook the celeriac in unsalted boiling water for 15-20 minutes, until tender. Steam the spinach for 10-15 minutes, until tender. Cook the carrots in the celeriac water for 15-20 minutes, until tender.

Blend each vegetable individually to a purée. Season the purées and add the celery salt to the celeriac, the cream to the spinach, and the nutmeg to the carrots.

Spoon the purées decoratively over the potatoes and place them in the oven for 5 minutes to heat them through thoroughly. Serve immediately.

SWISS CHARD AND PINE KERNEL TART

30 g/1 oz butter
1 tbsp olive oil
1 onion, finely chopped
2 large garlic cloves, finely chopped
285 g/10 oz Swiss chard leaves
6 tbsp finely chopped flat-leaf parsley
juice of ½ lemon
250 g/8½ oz frozen shortcrust pastry, defrosted
2 eggs, beaten
45 g/1½ oz pine kernels
150 ml/¼ pt crème fraîche
6 tbsp milk
pinch of freshly grated nutmeg
salt and freshly ground black pepper
flour, for dusting
sun-dried tomatoes in oil, to garnish (optional)

Preheat the oven to 180C/350F/gas 4.

Melt the butter in the oil in a large sauté pan over a moderate heat. Sauté the onion and garlic until translucent and then add the Swiss chard, parsley, lemon juice and some seasoning.

Sauté briefly over a fairly high heat until the chard is softened. Set aside.

Roll the pastry out on a lightly floured surface and use it to line a 25.5 cm/10 in tart pan. Cover the base with foil or baking paper and weight with beans.

Bake blind for about 10 minutes and then remove the weights and paper. Return to the oven for another 10 minutes or so, until the pastry is firm but not yet brown. Brush with a little of the beaten egg and return to the oven for 5 minutes.

While the tart case is baking, toast all but 1 tablespoon of the pine kernels on a baking sheet for 5-10 minutes, until just a good golden brown.

In a bowl, mix the cream, milk, eggs and nutmeg. Season and stir in the chard mixture. At the last minute, stir in the toasted pine kernels.

Pour into the pastry case, scatter over the remaining pine kernels and bake for 20 minutes.

Garnish with chopped sun-dried tomatoes in oil, if wished

NOTES: spinach may be used instead of the Swiss chard. Some chopped bacon or ham may be cooked with the chard for extra flavour.

Alternatively, for a delicious and unusual sweet tart, replace the onion, garlic, parsley and seasoning with sultanas and honey and a pinch of allspice.

VEGETABLES AND SALADS

*E*ven the most adventurous of cooks is quite likely to serve plain boiled, steamed or baked vegetables as side dishes to accompany main meals. Although there is nothing wrong with this no-nonsense approach, there are also many wonderfully easy ways to make vegetable accompaniments little feasts on their own without really spending much more time, money or effort. It may be as simple as tossing in some chopped fresh herbs or a few toasted nuts with the knob of butter just before serving, or an unusual and attractive means of presentation, such as the String Bean Bouquets, or perhaps a novel way of cooking a traditional favourite, like Deep-fried Aubergine with Black Bean Sauce. Many of the recipes which follow, as well as being capable of enlivening the plainest of main courses, are also colourful and interesting enough to be used as starters, snacks or light meals in their own right.

Left to right: Braised Red Onions (page 166); Herby Carrots Tossed in Lemon Mayonnaise (page 167); Sir-fried Courgettes (page 166)

BABY BRUSSELS SPROUTS WITH PINE KERNELS

450 g/1 lb baby Brussels sprouts
½ tbsp hazelnut oil
55 g/2 oz pine kernels
salt and freshly ground black pepper

Steam the sprouts for 3 minutes over boiling water, without removing the lid. Remove from the heat.

Put the hazelnut oil in the base of a warmed serving dish. Add the pine kernels and salt and pepper, followed by the sprouts.

Toss gently until thoroughly coated in oil and then serve immediately.

CABBAGE WITH CARAWAY SEEDS AND SESAME OIL

30 g/1 oz butter
2 tbsp roasted sesame oil
1 tsp caraway seeds
350 g/12 oz white cabbage, thinly sliced
salt and freshly ground black pepper

Melt the butter with the oil in a pan over a moderate heat. Add the caraway seeds and toss gently for 1 minute. Add the cabbage and toss to coat thoroughly in the butter and oil.

Place the lid on the pan and increase the heat. Cook for 2-3 minutes only, shaking the pan constantly.

Season and transfer to a warmed serving dish. Serve immediately.

CABBAGE WITH CARAWAY SEEDS AND SESAME OIL *lends itself to many variations. Try replacing the caraway seeds with poppy seeds, fennel seeds or crushed coriander seeds mixed with blanched strips of zest from an unwaxed orange.*

Left: Cabbage with Caraway Seeds and Sesame Oil; right: Baby Brussels Sprouts with Pine Kernels

BROCCOLI AND CAULIFLOWER WITH FIVE-HERB BUTTER

SERVES 4-6

225 g/8 oz broccoli florets
225 g/8 oz cauliflower florets
salt
FOR THE HERB BUTTER
115 g/4 oz butter
½ tsp each finely chopped marjoram, mint, chives and
tarragon
1 tsp finely chopped parsley
1 tbsp lemon juice

Several hours before, make the herb butter: cream the butter in a bowl until light. Gently work in the herbs and lemon juice. Leave at room temperature for 2 hours to allow the herbs to release their flavours and then chill for 1-2 hours.

Blanch the broccoli and cauliflower florets in boiling salted water for 3-5 minutes, depending on the desired degree of crunchiness.

Using a wire skimmer or slotted spoon, transfer the vegetables to a colander and refresh under cold water. Then return the florets to the boiling water for 1 minute only to re-heat.

Transfer to a warmed serving dish, dot with knobs of the herb butter and serve immediately.

RATATOUILLE

6 courgettes
6 aubergines
2 green sweet peppers
2 red sweet peppers
scant 575 ml / 1 pt extra virgin olive oil
4 large onions, each cut into 6 pieces
6 tomatoes, peeled, deseeded and coarsely chopped
4 purple garlic cloves, finely chopped
large sprig of oregano
juice of ½ large lemon
salt and freshly ground black pepper

Cut the courgettes and aubergines into slices about 2 cm/¾ in thick. Arrange these on a wire rack and sprinkle generously with salt. Leave to drain for half an hour, then rinse and pat dry with paper towel.

While the vegetables are draining, skin the peppers by piercing them with a fork and holding them over a flame or under a hot grill. Turn them so that the skin blisters uniformly. Allow to cool slightly and then the blackened skin comes off with ease. Cut the peppers in half, remove the seeds and slice the flesh in thick strips.

Pour 100 ml/3½ fl oz of the oil into a large frying pan over a moderate heat, then add the courgettes. Raise the heat and cook until the slices are browned on both sides. Using a slotted spoon, transfer the courgettes to a large flameproof casserole. Repeat the process with the aubergines, onions and peppers, adding more oil as necessary.

Add the tomatoes, garlic, oregano and the rest of the oil to the casserole. Add the lemon juice and season with the pepper but not with salt.

Place over a moderate heat and cover. Bring to the boil, then lower the heat and simmer gently for 50-60 minutes, stirring once or twice.

Season with salt. (If there is surplus liquid, drain it off into a pan and boil rapidly to reduce it, then return it to the dish.) Serve hot, warm or cold.

DEEP-FRIED AUBERGINE WITH BLACK BEAN SAUCE

6 small to medium aubergines
2 eggs, beaten
3 tbsp flour
2 tbsp black bean sauce
salt and freshly ground black pepper
corn oil, for deep-frying

Cut the aubergines across into discs about 2 cm/¾ in thick. Lay these flat, sprinkle with salt and leave for half an hour. Rinse and pat dry.

Put the eggs in a small bowl and put the flour on a shallow plate. Season the flour.

Spread both sides of each aubergine slice with a thin coating of black bean sauce. Dip both sides of each slice into the beaten egg, then in the flour. Shake off any excess flour.

Place the aubergine slices in a single layer in the basket of a deep-fryer. Heat the corn oil in the deep-fryer to 180C/360F (a small cube of dry bread browns in 60 seconds). Cook the aubergines, in batches if necessary, for about 2-3 minutes, until well browned.

Drain on paper towels, then place on a warmed serving dish. Serve immediately, or as soon as all are cooked.

Bottled BLACK BEAN SAUCE *is now readily available in better shops and supermarkets. It may be used to give an authentic Cantonese flavour to many dishes, especially stir-fries.*

A bit like a quiche without the pastry, the traditional Italian FRITTATA *is a sort of cross between an omelette and a pancake. A frittata makes ideal picnic food as it may be transported in the pan in which it was made.*

MINTED NEW POTATO AND SUMMER VEGETABLE FRITTATA

450 g/1 lb new potatoes, preferably Jerseys
115 g/4 oz sliced courgettes
115 g/4 oz shelled broad beans or peas
1 tbsp chopped mint
30 g/1 oz freshly grated Parmesan cheese
5 eggs, lightly beaten
30 g/1 oz butter
salt and pepper

Preheat the oven to 180C/350F/gas 4.

In separate pans, steam or boil the vegetables in lightly salted water until just tender but still firm. Drain, refresh in cold running water and then drain well again. Dice the potatoes.

In a small bowl mix the drained vegetables with the mint and Parmesan. Stir in the eggs and season with a little salt (remember that the cheese will be quite salty) and pepper.

Melt the butter in a suitable metal flat tin or dish which can go both over a direct heat and in the oven. Add the egg mixture and cook over the lowest possible heat, undisturbed, for 5 minutes. Transfer to the oven and bake for 10 more minutes.

Allow to cool and serve it cut in wedges.

GRILLED FENNEL AND AUBERGINES

1 aubergine, weighing about 350 g/12 oz, cut across into 1 cm/½ in slices
2 small fennel bulbs, cut lengthwise into quarters
4 tbsp olive oil
salt and pepper
lemon wedges, to serve

Sprinkle the aubergine slices with salt and leave for 3 minutes in a colander to allow the bitter juices to drain out. Rinse thoroughly and pat dry with clean tea towels.

Preheat the grill until quite hot.

Brush the aubergine slices and the pieces of fennel on all sides with olive oil. Season with salt and pepper and arrange in a single layer over the grill pan. Cook until done: it is impossible to give exact cooking times, as these will depend on the size of the vegetable pieces and the heat of the grill. Simply keep turning over the pieces of vegetable, brushing them with a little more oil, if necessary, and wait until they begin to take on a slightly charred look.

Serve immediately with lemon wedges to squeeze over them.

Many firm-textured vegetables – such as courgettes, sweet peppers, plum tomatoes and onions – may be grilled in this manner. Just keep turning the pieces and brushing them with olive oil until suitably charred in appearance.

Left: Minted New Potato and Summer Vegetable Frittata

One of the classics of French cuisine, GRATIN DAUPHINOIS *turns ordinary potatoes into a luxurious treat and may also be enriched by the addition of one or two eggs.*

GRATIN DAUPHINOIS

SERVES 4-6

30 g/1 oz butter
900 g/2 lb potatoes, peeled and very thinly sliced
1 garlic clove, chopped
large pinch of freshly grated nutmeg
300 ml/½ pt double cream
55 g/2 oz Gruyère cheese, grated
salt and freshly ground black pepper

Preheat the oven to 190C/375F/gas 5. Use half of the butter to grease a shallow 1.1 litre/2 pt ovenproof dish.

Layer the potatoes in the dish, dotting the layers with the remaining butter and the garlic and seasoning with nutmeg, salt and pepper.

Pour the cream over and bake in the oven for 1 ¼ hours. Sprinkle with the cheese and return to the oven for 15-20 minutes. Serve hot.

VEGETABLE GRATIN

1 small cauliflower, broken into florets
225 g/8 oz broccoli, broken into florets
white parts only of 4 spring onions, halved
30 g/1 oz butter
30 g/1 oz flour
1 tsp Dijon mustard
450 ml/¾ pt milk
115 g/4 oz mature Cheddar cheese, grated
55 g/2 oz Gruyère cheese, grated
30 g/1 oz hazelnuts, roughly chopped
salt and freshly ground black pepper

Cook the cauliflower, broccoli and spring onions in boiling salted water for 4 minutes. Drain thoroughly and arrange the vegetables in a heatproof serving dish. Keep warm.

Melt the butter in a small heavy-based saucepan,

stir in the flour and cook, stirring, for 1-2 minutes. Stir in the mustard and milk and bring to the boil, stirring constantly, until thickened and smooth. Stir in the Cheddar and season with salt and pepper.

Preheat a medium grill. Pour the sauce over the vegetables and sprinkle with the Gruyère and hazelnuts. Cook under the grill until golden brown. Serve hot.

TRIO OF VEGETABLE PURÉES

SERVES 6

FOR THE JERUSALEM ARTICHOKE PURÉE
285 g/10 oz Jerusalem artichokes, diced
170 g/6 oz potato, diced
knob of butter
2 tbsp single cream
large pinch of freshly grated nutmeg
FOR THE CARROT AND PARSNIP PURÉE
170 g/6 oz carrot, sliced
170 g/6 oz parsnip, sliced
knob of butter
½ garlic clove, crushed
FOR THE CELERIAC AND SWEDE PURÉE
225 g/8 oz celeriac
115 g/4 oz swede
knob of butter
squeeze of lemon juice
1 tbsp chopped parsley
salt and freshly ground black pepper

In 3 separate saucepans, cook the vegetables for each purée in boiling water for 8-10 minutes, until soft. Drain the three vegetable mixtures and return them to their saucepans.

Add a knob of butter to each and season with their respective flavourings, salt and pepper. Using a potato masher, mash each until smooth. Serve hot.

RED CABBAGE WITH CLOVES AND CHESTNUTS

SERVES 6

675 g/1½ lb red cabbage, finely shredded
2 small sharp apples, peeled, cored and sliced
2 tsp juniper berries, crushed
1 tbsp fresh rosemary spikes
30 g/1 oz butter
1 tbsp olive oil
1 onion, finely chopped
½ tsp ground cinnamon
4 cloves
2 tbsp redcurrant jelly
2 tbsp red wine vinegar
150 ml/¼ pt port
225 g/8 oz cooked whole chestnuts
salt and freshly ground black pepper
chopped fresh parsley, to garnish

Preheat the oven to 150C/300F/gas 2.

Arrange the cabbage and apple in layers in a large casserole dish, seasoning each layer with juniper, rosemary, salt and pepper.

Melt the butter with the oil in a heavy-based saucepan over a moderate heat. Add the onion and cook for 4-5 minutes. Stir in the cinnamon, cloves, redcurrant jelly, vinegar and port. Bring to the boil, stirring until the jelly has dissolved.

Pour this over the cabbage and cover the casserole tightly with foil and a lid. Bake in the oven for 2 hours. Check from time to time to see if all the liquid has evaporated, adding a little more port or water as necessary.

Add the chestnuts to the casserole, cover and return to the oven for 15-20 minutes to warm them through. Serve sprinkled with chopped parsley.

GREAT-GRANDMOTHER'S POTATO CAKES

675 g/1½ lb freshly cooked potatoes
1 tbsp butter
1 egg yolk
2 tbsp double cream
1 tsp salt
½ tsp freshly grated nutmeg
6 tbsp brown breadcrumbs
2 tbsp corn oil
freshly ground black pepper

Mash the potato well, then stir in the butter, egg yolk, cream, salt, nutmeg and pepper to taste.

Divide the mixture into 8 and shape these portions into fat cakes. Then roll the cakes in breadcrumbs to coat the outsides evenly.

Put the oil in a frying pan over a moderate heat and fry the cakes until golden brown on both sides.

Drain briefly on paper towels to remove excess oil and serve.

*For good results
with the
PROVENÇAL
GRATIN OF
COURGETTES it is
essential to dry the
courgettes thoroughly
after blanching
them; otherwise any
residual moisture
will thin down the
sauce. A well
preheated oven is
also a key to success.*

ASPARAGUS WITH LIME PEEL BUTTER

*450-900 g/1-2 lb asparagus (depending on appetite)
salt and pepper
FOR THE LIME PEEL BUTTER
115 g/4 oz butter, softened
grated zest of ½ unwaxed lime*

First make the lime peel butter: mix the grated lime zest with the softened butter and put this on a small piece of kitchen film. Wrap tightly, forming the butter into a small fat log shape, and chill until needed (30 minutes in the freezer will do).

Either steam the asparagus or boil in lightly salted water until cooked to taste and then drain well.

While the asparagus is cooking, unwrap the butter and cut the cylinder across into 4 round pats.

Divide the asparagus between 4 warmed plates, season it with salt and pepper and place a pat of flavoured butter on each serving. Garnish with some strips of lime zest, if you wish.

SAUTÉ OF SWEET POTATO AND BACON

*450 g/1 lb orange-fleshed sweet potatoes in their skins
1 tbsp corn or sunflower oil
6 slices of streaky smoked bacon
30 g/1 oz butter
salt and pepper
1 tbsp chopped parsley or chives, to garnish*

Preheat the oven to 180C/350F/gas 4.

Bake the sweet potatoes in their skins for 45 minutes. Remove from the oven and allow to cool slightly. When cool enough to handle, peel off the skins and discard them. Cut the flesh into about 2.5 cm/1 in cubes.

Meanwhile heat the oil in a frying pan over a moderate heat and cook the bacon until really crisp but not burnt. Using a slotted spoon, remove the bacon from the pan, drain it on paper towels and roughly crumble.

Add the butter to the fat in the frying pan and stir-fry the sweet potato cubes for 5-10 minutes, until crisp and golden.

Season with salt and pepper and mix in the bacon pieces. Transfer to a warmed serving dish and sprinkle with chopped herbs,

GRATIN OF POTATOES AND MUSHROOMS

*900 g/2 lb potatoes, peeled and thinly sliced
170 g/6 oz mushrooms, thinly sliced
300 ml/½ pt single cream
1 garlic clove, crushed
salt and pepper
butter, for greasing*

Preheat the oven to 190C/375F/gas 5 and grease an ovenproof dish with some butter.

Arrange the slices of potato and mushroom in alternating layers in the dish, seasoning each layer and finishing with a layer of potatoes.

In a small pan, heat the cream with the garlic until almost boiling. Then pour this over the potatoes.

Bake for about 1½ hours, or until cooked through and golden brown on top.

PROVENÇAL GRATIN OF COURGETTES

55 g/2 oz butter, plus more for greasing
55 g/2 oz flour
500 ml/16 fl oz milk
115 g/4 oz grated Gruyère or Emmenthal cheese
¼ tsp grated nutmeg
450 g/1 lb courgettes, thinly sliced
1 egg, lightly beaten
55 g/2 oz fresh white breadcrumbs
salt and pepper

Preheat the oven to 250C/475F/gas 9 and grease an ovenproof dish with some butter.

In a heavy-based saucepan, melt the butter and add the flour. Cook this roux over a moderate heat for 2–3 minutes, stirring constantly. Remove from the heat. Add the milk gradually, stirring all the time, then return to the heat and simmer for 2–3 minutes, stirring constantly with a balloon whisk to ensure no lumps form.

Add the cheese, season to taste with salt and pepper and mix in the nutmeg. Cook over a gentle heat, stirring constantly, for 5 minutes. Allow to cool for about 10 minutes off the heat.

While the sauce is cooling, blanch the courgette slices in boiling salted water for 2 minutes only. Immediately drain and refresh under cold running water. Drain again and pat dry with paper towels.

Mix the egg thoroughly into the cooked sauce, followed by the well-dried courgettes. Pour the mixture into the prepared dish and scatter the breadcrumbs over the top.

Bake for 15 minutes, or until bubbling and browned on top. Remove from the oven and allow to 'settle' for 10 minutes before serving, as the taste and texture are better if the dish is not too hot.

Sauté of Sweet Potato and Bacon; bottom: Asparagus with Lime Peel Butter

Chinese HOI-SIN *SAUCE is made from soy beans and is flavoured with chilli peppers, garlic and rice vinegar. Its sweet flavour works well with vegetables and meat dishes and is particularly suited to barbecue sauces.*

BRAISED RED ONIONS

*30 g/1 oz butter
4 large red onions, thinly sliced
salt and freshly ground black pepper*

Melt the butter in a heavy-based pan over a moderate heat. Add the onions and cook gently until translucent.

Season, then cover and simmer over a very low heat for 20 minutes.

Stir and transfer to a warmed serving dish.

FLAT MUSHROOMS WITH HOI-SIN SAUCE

*450 g/1 lb flat mushrooms (see below)
30 g/1 oz butter
1 tbsp extra virgin olive oil
juice of ½ lemon
2 tbsp hoi-sin sauce
2 tbsp chopped coriander
salt and freshly ground black pepper*

Try to buy mushrooms which are all about the same size. Clean them well, but do not wash them.

Melt the butter with the oil in a heavy frying pan over a low to moderate heat and toss the mushrooms lightly in it until they are well coated. Cook slowly until tender.

Transfer the mushrooms to a warmed serving plate, leaving the juices in the pan. Season the juices and sir in the lemon juice and hoi-sin sauce.

Pour this over the mushrooms and sprinkle with the coriander to serve.

STIR-FRIED COURGETTES

*30 g/1 oz butter
2 tbsp light soy sauce
8 courgettes, thickly sliced
freshly ground black pepper*

Melt the butter in a large frying pan over a moderate heat. Add the soy sauce and some black pepper, followed by the courgettes.

Stir the courgettes to coat them evenly in the seasoned butter. Cover the pan and shake over a moderate heat for 5 minutes.

Transfer to a warmed serving dish.

HERBY CARROTS TOSSED IN LEMON MAYONNAISE

450 g/1 lb carrots, unpeeled and cut into discs about
1 cm/½ in thick
generous 1½ tsp herbes de Provence
½ tsp zest and 1 tsp juice from an unwaxed lemon
1 tbsp ready-made mayonnaise
salt and freshly ground black pepper

Place the carrots in a pan which has a tight-fitting lid. Barely cover with water and add the herbs.

Cover the pan with its lid and place it over a moderate heat for 15-20 minutes, until the carrots are just tender (adding more water from time to time if necessary).

Drain any remaining water, stir in the other ingredients and season to serve.

POTATOES WITH DANDELION LEAVES AND TOMATO SAUCE

225 g/8 oz potatoes in their skins
225 g/8 oz dandelion leaves
4 tomatoes, thinly sliced
30 g/1 oz stuffed green olives, coarsely chopped
250 ml/8 fl oz warm Quick Tomato Sauce (see page 12)
salt

In a large pan of boiling salted water, cook the potatoes until tender. Drain, leave to cool slightly and then slice. Keep warm.

Blanch the dandelion leaves for 20 seconds only in boiling salted water. Refresh under cold running water, drain and pat dry.

Arrange the leaves in a serving dish and cover with the tomato slices. Sprinkle with olives, arrange the potato slices over that and pour over the sauce.

STUFFED TOMATOES

SERVES 2

2 large beef tomatoes
15 g/½ oz butter
½ tbsp extra virgin olive oil
1 purple garlic clove, crushed
1 large onion, coarsely chopped
1 tbsp chopped parsley
1 tbsp chopped chives
55 g/2 oz Feta cheese, cubed
salt and freshly ground black pepper

Preheat the oven to 190C/375F/gas 5.

Cut the tops from the tomatoes and reserve them.

Scoop out the seeds and pulp to leave an empty cavity in each tomato.

Melt the butter with the oil in a sauté pan over a moderate heat and add the crushed garlic. Sauté for 2 minutes, then add the onion and cook until tender. Season, then sprinkle the parsley and chives into the onions. Stir, then immediately remove from the heat.

Stuff each of the tomatoes with the onion mixture. Then top that filling with the cheese and replace the tops.

Bake in the oven for 30 minutes.

Small tender
DANDELION LEAVES
can be gathered wild
in the early part of
the year and also
grown commercially.
They go well in
salads with chopped
bacon and ham, and
these may be added
to the POTATOES
WITH DANDELION
LEAVES AND
TOMATO SAUCE.

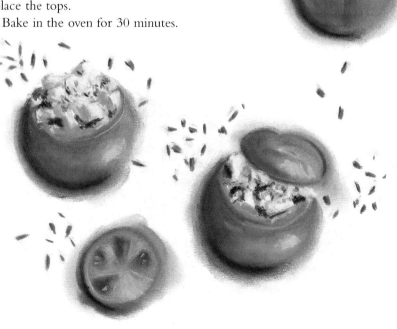

STRING BEAN BOUQUETS

450 g/1 lb fine string beans
bunch of chives
30 g/1 oz canned pimento, drained and cut into long
thin strips
85 g/3 oz butter
½ lemon
rock salt
freshly ground black pepper

Trim all the beans to the same length, leaving the tails on some if necessary.

Plunge the beans into a large pan of boiling salted water and cook for 3-6 minutes, depending on the preferred degree of firmness. Drain and refresh under cold running water. Drain well and pat dry.

In the same water, blanch the chives for 30 seconds only. Refresh, drain and pat dry.

Separate the beans into 6 bundles and tie them together with 2 chives per bundle, securing with two knots. Loop the pimento strips decoratively around the bundles.

Melt the butter in a frying pan over a gentle heat, then carefully roll the bundles in it until they are thoroughly heated through.

Place on a warmed serving plate. Squeeze the lemon juice over the bundles, then sprinkle with rock salt and ground pepper to serve.

NOTE: you can do this sort of ornamental serving with a wide range of vegetables, such as asparagus spears and young leeks. Tying up may also be effected with green spring onion or leek tops which have been cut into long thin strips and blanched. Blanched strips of apple peel or zest from unwaxed oranges, lemons and limes are also effective and provide interesting colour to vegetable side dishes.

JAPANESE PICKLED VEGETABLES

1 cauliflower, separated into florets
1 small daikon radish, peeled and sliced (see p. 144)
2 carrots, sliced
½ large cucumber, peeled and sliced
1 tsp white sugar
pinch of salt
about 450 ml/¾ pt Japanese rice vinegar

Cut the cauliflower florets lengthwise into thin slices.

Arrange the cauliflower slices together with the slices of daikon, carrot and cucumber on a flat serving dish or in a bowl.

Dissolve the sugar and salt in the rice vinegar and pour this over the vegetables. Cover them with film and leave to marinate for 12 hours in the refrigerator.

To serve, drain and spear the pieces of vegetable with cocktail sticks, reserving the marinade for later use with more vegetables.

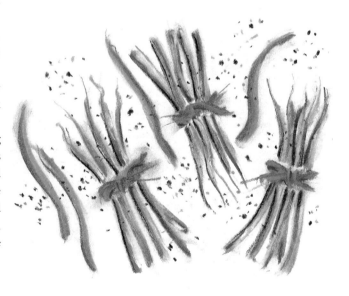

Top: String Bean Bouquets; bottom: Japanese Pickled Vegetables

Stir-frying is the ideal healthy way to cook most vegetables. Use whatever is fresh and in season and try to make the best combination of colours, textures and flavours.

STIR-FRIED VEGETABLES

2 tbsp vegetable oil
1 garlic clove, thinly sliced
2.5 cm/1 in cube of peeled fresh root ginger, finely chopped
1 chilli pepper, deseeded and chopped (optional)
1 small onion, chopped
1 small carrot, cut across at an angle into slices
½ red, green or yellow sweet pepper, deseeded and cut into uniform bite-sized pieces
115 g/4 oz sugar peas or mange-tout peas
55 g/2 oz canned straw mushrooms, drained
1 tsp cornflour
1 tbsp soy sauce
chopped spring onion, chives or fresh coriander, to garnish (optional)

Heat a wok or large frying pan over a moderate heat and add the oil. When it is really hot, add the garlic, ginger and chilli, if using, and stir-fry the mixture for 1 minute.

Add the onion, carrot and sweet pepper and stir-fry for another 2-3 minutes. Add the sugar peas or mange-tout peas and the straw mushrooms and stir-fry the vegetables for 2 more minutes.

Mix the cornflour with the soy sauce and then stir this into 125 ml/4 fl oz of water. Pour this liquid over the hot vegetables and allow it to bubble up and thicken while continuing to stir-fry for a few seconds.

Immediately transfer to a warmed serving dish and garnish with spring onions or herbs, if using.

STIR-FRIED BEANS WITH GARLIC

2 tbsp vegetable oil
½ tsp salt
4 garlic cloves, coarsely chopped
2.5 cm/1 in cube of peeled fresh root ginger, finely chopped
450 g/1 lb green beans, cut into 7.5 cm/3 in lengths
125 ml/4 fl oz chicken stock

Heat a wok over a moderate heat until hot, add the oil with the salt, garlic and ginger and stir-fry for 30 seconds.

Add the green beans and stock and continue to cook for 4 minutes, or until the beans are just tender and most of the liquid has evaporated.

Serve at once.

FRIED NOODLES WITH VEGETABLES

8 dried Chinese mushrooms
350 g/12 oz Oriental noodles
3 tbsp vegetable oil
1 garlic clove, thinly sliced
2.5 cm/1 in cube of peeled fresh root ginger, finely chopped
1 onion, chopped
1 small carrot, cut across at an angle into slices
½ green sweet pepper, deseeded and cut into
bite-sized pieces
55 g/2 oz cabbage, sliced
1 tbsp soy sauce
1 tbsp sesame oil
2 tbsp raw shelled peanuts, chopped

Cover the dried mushrooms with hot water and leave them to soak for 30 minutes. Strain and remove the hard stalk (this may be either discarded or used to add flavour to stock). Slice the mushroom caps and reserve.

Cook the noodles according to the instructions on the packet and then drain well.

Heat the oil in a wok or large frying pan over a moderate heat and stir-fry the garlic and ginger for 1 minute. Add the onion and stir-fry for 2-3 minutes more. Then add the carrot, pepper, cabbage and sliced mushroom caps and stir-fry for 2-3 minutes.

Add the cooked and drained noodles and continue to cook, tossing all the ingredients together for 2-3 minutes, or until all the noodles are thoroughly heated through.

Stir in the soy sauce and sesame oil and sprinkle the chopped nuts over to serve.

TEMPURA VEGETABLES

1 egg plus 1 extra yolk, beaten
115 g/4 oz flour
about 225 g/8 oz mixed vegetables, such as courgettes,
asparagus tips, broccoli and cauliflower florets, baby spinach
leaves, carrots and deseeded sweet peppers, cut into
bite-sized pieces
vegetable oil, for deep-frying

In a bowl, make a smooth batter with the egg, flour and 175 ml/6 fl oz of water.

Dip the pieces of vegetable into the batter and deep-fry them in hot oil in a wok a few at a time. Drain on paper towels and serve immediately as they are cooked, just as they are or with a dipping sauce.

NOTE: an excellent dipping sauce for this dish may be made from equal quantities of soy sauce, fish sauce and sherry, together with a little added grated fresh root ginger.

The recipes on the following pages are salads with a sufficient protein content – be it from eggs, cheese, nuts, meat or fish – to make them nourishing and substantial meals in their own right.

CHICORY, BLUE CHEESE AND POMEGRANATE SALAD

4 large heads of chicory
1 pomegranate
225 g/8 oz beansprouts
85 g/3 oz blue cheese, such as Dolcelatte or Danish Blue
150 ml/¼ pt Basic Vinaigrette (see page 14)
4 small garlic cloves, crushed

Pull the chicory leaves apart and arrange them in a salad bowl. (Break them into pieces if they are very large, but do not cut them with a knife as this causes bruising and the base of the leaf goes pink.)

Cut the pomegranate in half and pull out the fleshy pips with a pin.

Mix the beansprouts in with the chicory and then crumble the blue cheese all over them. Sprinkle over the pomegranate seeds.

Mix the garlic into the vinaigrette and pour over the salad to serve.

Left: Leafy Green and Red Greek Salad (page 174);
right: Chicory, Blue Cheese and Pomegranate Salad

Any combination of leaves may be used in the LEAFY GREEN AND RED GREEK SALAD, such as Webb's or Loosehead with Lollo Rosso.

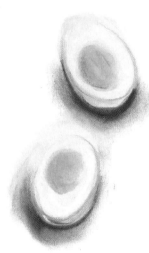

LEAFY GREEN AND RED GREEK SALAD

SERVES 6

1 head of radicchio
1 oak leaf lettuce
1 head of curly endive
115 g/4 oz Feta cheese, crumbled into large pieces
115 g/4 oz Greek olives, stoned and chopped
150 ml/¼ pt Low-calorie Yogurt Dressing (see page 14)
chopped chives, to garnish

Break all the leaves into a salad bowl and mix them together. Add the cheese followed by the olives.

Pour over the dressing and garnish with chives.

MOZZARELLA AND TOMATO SALAD WITH AVOCADO

2 buffalo mozzarella cheeses, thinly sliced
2 beef tomatoes, thinly sliced
small basil leaves, to garnish
FOR THE AVOCADO DRESSING
1 large ripe avocado
1 tbsp balsamic vinegar
1 large red onion, finely chopped
4 tbsp olive oil
salt and freshly ground black pepper

First make the dressing: halve and stone the avocado and scoop the flesh out into a bowl. Add the vinegar and mash the onion into the avocado flesh.

Gradually add the oil, mixing all the time, until it has all been incorporated. Season to taste.

On a flat serving plate, arrange the mozzarella and tomato slices in alternate rows. Either dribble the dressing over the centres of the rows or have it in a pool in the centre of the serving plate. Garnish with the basil leaves.

SPINACH SALAD WITH EGGS AND CROUTONS

SERVES 4

450 g/1 lb young spinach leaves
3 eggs, hard-boiled
3 stalks of celery, cut into slices about 6 mm/¼ in thick
225 g/8 oz croutons
85 g/3 oz freshly grated Parmesan cheese
150 ml/¼ pt Hollandaise Sauce (see page 13)
2 tbsp milk
salt and freshly ground black pepper

Remove any stalks and coarse ribs from the spinach.

Separate the egg yolks from the whites. Slice the whites finely and push the yolks through a sieve (the result should resemble mimosa blossom).

Tear the spinach leaves into a bowl. Add the celery followed by the croutons and toss gently. Add the egg whites followed by the Parmesan.

Stir the milk into the hollandaise sauce, adjust the seasoning and pour it over the salad. Sprinkle with the egg yolks and toss just before serving.

BROWN RICE SALAD WITH ORANGE, SAGE AND DATES

1 unwaxed orange
1 tbsp young sage leaves, finely chopped
115 g/4 oz stoned dates, coarsely chopped
350 g/12 oz cooked brown rice
FOR THE CASHEW NUT DRESSING
55 g/2 oz cream cheese
55 g/2 oz fromage frais
1½ tbsp cashew nut oil
1½ tbsp lemon juice
½ tbsp rock salt
2-3 tbsp Mayonnaise (see page 13)
55 g/2 oz cashew nuts, chopped
freshly ground black pepper

Pare off the peel from the orange, leaving any of the bitter white pith behind, and cut it into thin julienne strips. Stir these together with the sage and dates into the rice.

Make the dressing: blend the cream cheese and the fromage frais with the oil, lemon juice, rock salt and pepper. Fold in the mayonnaise, followed by the nuts. If the dressing is too thick, thin it down with 1-2 tablespoons of semi-skimmed milk.

Toss the salad in the dressing to serve.

PRAWN AND SHIITAKE MUSHROOM SALAD

115 g/4 oz Shiitake mushrooms
115 g/4 oz Chinese egg noodles, cooked
bunch of large spring onions, sliced
(including the green tops)
225 g/8 oz lamb's lettuce
115 g/4 oz peeled cooked prawns
1½ tbsp soy sauce
1½ tbsp Japanese rice vinegar
30 g/1 oz black sesame seeds, roasted
freshly ground black pepper

Soak the mushrooms in water for 15 minutes, then drain and squeeze out any excess liquid. Discarding any hard pieces of stem, snip the mushrooms into small pieces with kitchen scissors.

Place the noodles in a salad bowl, then add the snipped mushrooms, spring onion and lamb's lettuce. Toss together lightly, season with pepper and add the prawns.

Dress with a little of the soy sauce and Japanese rice vinegar, then sprinkle with the roasted sesame seeds.

Chill for 15 minutes before serving, dressed with the remaining soy sauce and vinegar.

SHIITAKE MUSHROOMS *have been cultivated by the Japanese on oak bark for centuries. Dried shiitakes are now widely available in healthfood stores and some supermarkets. They must be soaked in water for 30 minutes before use and the stems trimmed off and discarded. The mellow, sweet and delicate flavour of Japanese rice vinegar is an essential part of many traditional dishes, such as the raw fish sushi. Light cider vinegar may be substituted.*

In the QUAIL'S EGG AND SMOKED SALMON SALAD, smoked trout or thinly sliced raw tuna will work well as substitutes for the smoked salmon.

QUAIL'S EGG AND SMOKED SALMON SALAD

SERVES 6

bunch of watercress, stalks removed
2 cooked beetroots, thinly sliced
1 Iceberg lettuce
115 g / 4 oz smoked salmon, cut into thin strips
45 g / 1½ oz butter
6 quails' eggs
150 ml / ¼ pt Basic Vinaigrette (see page 14)
freshly ground black pepper
sprigs of dill, to garnish (optional)
1 large lemon, cut into 6 wedges, to serve

Place the watercress in little piles in the middle of 6 salad plates. Arrange the beetroot slices around the watercress.

Shred the Iceberg leaves and arrange them in a circle around the outside of the beetroot slices.

Arrange 2 strips of smoked salmon in a criss-cross on top of each pile of watercress and arrange the rest around the outside of the rings of lettuce.

Melt the butter in a frying pan over a moderate heat and fry the quails' eggs briefly until the white is just set. Sprinkle them with black pepper and then arrange one egg on top of each pile of watercress.

Dress the leaves and beetroot with the vinaigrette and serve immediately, garnished with dill sprigs, if using. Serve the lemon wedges separately for the salmon.

SUMMERHOUSE SALAD WITH ORANGE VINAIGRETTE

SERVES 6

1 large Iceberg lettuce
bunch of watercress, stalks removed
2 large avocado pears
2 large pears, peeled and sliced
170g / 6oz cooked chicken breast, coarsely chopped
FOR THE ORANGE VINAIGRETTE
1 tbsp freshly squeezed orange juice, including some flesh
150ml / ¼ pt Basic Vinaigrette (see page 14)
salt and freshly ground black pepper

Separate the lettuce leaves into a salad bowl, add the watercress and toss gently.

Halve and stone the avocados. Using a small coffee spoon, scoop out the avocado flesh and add this to the salad.

Chop the pear slices into the salad and arrange the pieces of chicken on top of the salad.

Stir the orange juice and flesh into the basic vinaigrette and adjust the seasoning, if necessary. Pour this over the salad to serve.

Left: Summerhouse Salad with Orange Vinaigrette; right: Lamb's Lettuce with Mango and Hazelnuts (page 184)

THAI CHICKEN, PRAWN AND FRUIT SALAD

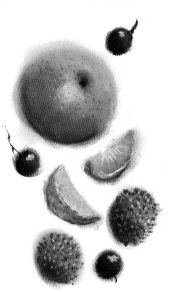

*½ mango or papaya, peeled, stoned or deseeded and cut
into bite-sized pieces*
1 orange, peeled and segmented
1 small grapefruit, preferably pink, peeled and segmented
1 pear, peeled, cored and cut into bite-sized pieces
16 seedless grapes, halved
8 lychees, peeled and stoned
2 tomatoes, cut into small pieces
*115 g/4 oz canned Chinese water chestnuts, drained
and halved*
170 g/6 oz cooked chicken, cut into bite-sized pieces
115 g/4 oz peeled cooked prawns
55 g/2 oz mixed salad leaves
4-6 shallots, thinly sliced
2 garlic cloves, thinly sliced
115 g/4 oz salted peanuts, roughly chopped, to garnish
coriander sprigs, to garnish (optional)
FOR THE DRESSING
3 tbsp sugar
juice of ½ lime
1 tbsp fish sauce
1 red chilli pepper, deseeded and chopped
1 garlic clove, crushed

The classic THAI
CHICKEN, PRAWN
AND FRUIT SALAD
*makes a spectacular
first course or light
meal. Any fruit in
season may be used
and those given here
are merely
suggestions.*

In a bowl, mix together lightly the fruit, tomatoes, water chestnuts, chicken and prawns.

Make the dressing: dissolve the sugar in 5 tablespoons of hot water and allow it to cool. Then mix in the lime juice, fish sauce, chilli and garlic.

Deep-fry the shallot and garlic slices in hot oil in a wok until crisp. Drain on paper towels.

Just before serving, pour the dressing over the salad and mix gently.

Cover a serving plate with the leaves and arrange the salad over this. Scatter over the fried shallots and garlic and the peanuts and coriander sprigs, if using, to garnish. Serve immediately.

JAPANESE-STYLE CHICKEN AND ASPARAGUS SALAD

1 tbsp sake, sherry or white wine
½ tsp salt
*about 225 g/8 oz skinless chicken breast fillets, cut across
into thin slices*
*450 g/1 lb asparagus, cut across at an angle into
4 cm/1½ in lengths*
salad leaves, to serve (optional)
*1 tsp very thin julienne strips of thinly pared zest from an
unwaxed lemon to garnish*
FOR THE DRESSING
1 tsp dry English mustard powder
2 tbsp sake, sherry or white wine
2 tbsp soy sauce

In a small bowl, mix the sake, sherry or wine with the salt. Toss the chicken pieces in this and leave to marinate for 30 minutes.

Bring 5 tablespoons of water to the boil in the bottom of a wok or very small heavy-based saucepan and cook the chicken pieces, stirring constantly, for 1-2 minutes or until just cooked. Using a slotted spoon, transfer the chicken to a bowl and allow to cool. Reserve the stock left in the pan for making the dressing and for adding to soups and sauces.

Cook the asparagus in boiling salted water for 3-4 minutes, or until just cooked but still firm. Immediately drain and refresh under cold running water, then drain again. Add to the chicken.

Make the dressing: mix together the ingredients with 1 tablespoon of the reserved stock.

Just before serving, pour the dressing over the salad and toss well to combine thoroughly. Transfer to a serving plate or dish and serve as part of an Oriental-style meal. Alternatively, make 4 individual servings piled on beds of salad leaves, if using, and serve as a Western-style first course. Either way, garnish with the lemon zest.

SALAD NIÇOISE

225 g/8 oz tiny French beans
225 g/8 oz ripe tomatoes, cut in wedges
1 green sweet pepper, deseeded and cut into strips
1 cucumber, cut into thick strips
55 g/2 oz canned anchovies, drained
55 g/2 oz stoned black olives
200 g/7 oz canned tuna fish in oil, drained and flaked
4 hard-boiled eggs, shelled and quartered
5 tbsp olive oil
1 tbsp white wine vinegar
1 garlic clove, crushed
2 tbsp chopped flat-leaf parsley
salt and freshly ground black pepper

Blanch the beans briefly until just tender and refresh in cold running water. Pat dry.

Mix the vegetables in a large salad bowl (or arrange in separate piles around the bowl). Arrange the anchovies, olives, flaked tuna and eggs over the top.

Make a dressing by vigorously mixing the oil, vinegar and garlic with seasoning. Pour this over the salad and sprinkle with parsley.

PROVENÇAL VEGETABLES WITH GOATS' CHEESE

1 small round goats' cheese, weighing about 75 g/2½ oz
(see below)
115 g/4 oz broccoli florets
115 g/4 oz fine French beans
115 g/4 oz mange-tout peas
2 small courgettes, cut into thick slices
2 large garlic cloves
4 tbsp olive oil
1 tbsp lemon juice
pinch of dried thyme
4 or 5 ripe juicy tomatoes, coarsely chopped

2 spring onions, finely chopped
salt and freshly ground black pepper
pine kernels or strips of marinated red sweet pepper, to garnish (optional)

Select a cheese which is firm but not too dry.

In a large pan of boiling salted water, blanch the vegetables in batches until just tender but still very firm to the bite: about 6 or 7 minutes for the broccoli, 5 minutes for the beans, and 2 or 3 minutes for the peas and courgettes.

Drain each batch of vegetables promptly as they are ready and refresh them under cold running water. Drain well, pat dry and leave to cool.

Make the dressing: put the cheese, garlic, oil, lemon juice and thyme in a blender. Mix until smooth.

Add the tomatoes in small batches, processing each until smooth. Add just enough to give the dressing a rich consistency which is thick but sufficiently runny to coat the vegetables. Season well.

Put the cooled vegetables in a large bowl and pour over the dressing. Toss well to coat all the ingredients thoroughly. Scatter over the spring onions and garnish with pine kernels or strips of marinated pepper, if using.

In its native South of France, SALADE NIÇOISE commonly also contains broad beans and artichokes. In Britain, lettuce and cooked potatoes are popular additions.

PARMA HAM AND FRESH FIG SALAD WITH MINT AND LIME CREAM DRESSING

SERVES 6

6 slices of Parma ham
10 mint leaves
juice of 2 limes
18 fresh figs
150 ml/¼ pt crème fraîche
170 g/6 oz radicchio or lollo rosso
salt and freshly ground black pepper
sprigs of mint, to garnish

Cut the ham into strips and cover with film to stop it drying out.

Using a pestle and mortar, bruise and crush the mint leaves in the lime juice and leave the mixture to infuse at room temperature for about 45 minutes.

Make 2 cuts halfway down each fig from the stem end to make cross-shaped incisions in their tops. Press the figs gently in their middles to open up the tops. Place on a plate, cover with film and chill for 45 minutes.

Remove the mint from the lime juice and discard, and add a pinch of salt to the juice. Gradually whisk in the crème fraîche, stirring constantly. Adjust the seasoning, if necessary.

Flood the base of 6 plates with the crème fraîche dressing. Arrange 3 figs decoratively on that. Arrange the ham strips and the salad leaves around them, garnish with the mint sprigs and serve immediately.

ASPARAGUS SALAD WITH SPICED HONEY DRESSING

450 g/1 lb asparagus
1 large carrot, peeled
1 small ripe papaya or melon, peeled, halved, deseeded and cut into bite-sized pieces
4 small hard-boiled eggs, shelled and quartered, to serve
chopped chives or other herbs, to garnish
FOR THE DRESSING
2 tbsp vegetable oil
2 tbsp lemon or lime juice
1 tbsp runny honey
¼ tsp salt
¼ tsp chilli powder or more to taste

Trim off the hard part of the asparagus, cutting away about one-third of each stem from the cut end. Cut each trimmed spear in half lengthwise, then cut each of these pieces across in two.

Cook the asparagus pieces in boiling salted water for about 5 minutes, or until just tender. Immediately drain, refresh in cold water, drain well again and allow to cool.

Using a swivel-bladed vegetable peeler, cut the carrots into long slivers. Put these in a serving bowl together with the asparagus and the fruit.

Make the dressing by combining the ingredients. Pour this over the salad, toss gently but thoroughly and divide it between 4 plates.

Arrange 4 egg quarters on each salad and sprinkle with chopped herbs to serve.

CHICKEN SALAD WITH SESAME CUCUMBER SAUCE

6 chicken fillets, skinned
1 tbsp freshly grated peeled root ginger
4 spring onions, including the green tops
2 small cucumbers
1 Iceberg lettuce, to serve
FOR THE SESAME CUCUMBER SAUCE
1 tsp peanut oil
1 tsp chilli oil
¼ tsp dry mustard
1 tbsp light soy sauce
2 tbsp tahini paste
1 tbsp rice vinegar
2 tbsp water
½ tsp salt
1 tbsp finely chopped green spring onion tops
1 tbsp roasted sesame seeds
salt and freshly ground black pepper

Place the chicken fillets in a pan with the ginger, spring onions and 700 ml/1¼ pt of water and bring to the boil. Cover and simmer gently for 4 minutes. Remove from the heat, but leave the chicken to cool in the stock.

Peel the cucumbers, reserving some of the skin. Halve them, scoop out the seeds and place the halves on beds of the lettuce arranged on 4 plates.

Using scissors, cut the drained chicken fillets into thin slivers and arrange these in the cucumber. If preparing in advance, cover with film and chill.

Make the sauce: combine all the ingredients except the spring onions and sesame seeds in a blender or food processor. Season, then add the onions and sesame seeds and toss together. Spoon this over the chicken.

Serve garnished with the reserved cucumber peel cut into thin slivers.

CHICKEN AND WATERCRESS SALAD

½ ripe melon, peeled, halved, deseeded and cut into
bite sized chunks
225 g/8 oz cooked chicken, cut into bite-sized pieces
½ bunch (about 55 g/2 oz) of watercress
FOR THE DRESSING
1 tbsp lemon juice
3 tbsp corn or sunflower oil
¼ tsp ground ginger or more to taste
salt and pepper

Mix the melon and chicken in a bowl.

Make the dressing by combining all the ingredients, seasoning it and adding a little more dry ginger, if necessary, to taste. Pour it over the chicken and melon.

Arrange the watercress on top of the salad. Just before serving, mix the watercress into the rest of the salad.

CRISPY BACON, BEAN AND PARSLEY SALAD

675 g/1½ lb canned broad beans, drained
6 slices of streaky bacon, rinds removed
10 dried apricots, sliced into thin slivers
3 tbsp coarsely chopped hazelnuts
1½ tbsp coarsely chopped parsley
6 tbsp olive oil
2 tbsp wine vinegar
1 scant tbsp coarse-grain mustard
salt and freshly ground black pepper

Rinse the beans under cold running water, drain and dry on paper towels.

Dry-fry the bacon over a moderate to high heat until crispy. Cut the cooked bacon coarsely into pieces with scissors. Drain the pieces on paper towels to remove excess fat.

Place the beans in a salad bowl. Add the bacon, apricots, hazelnuts and parsley and toss well.

Pour the oil and vinegar into a screw-top jar. Add the mustard, seal and shake vigorously. Season with salt and pepper and shake again. Pour over the salad and toss well to serve.

COURGETTE AND PURPLE BASIL SALAD

SERVES 4-6

675 g / 1½ lb courgettes, coarsely grated
3 tomatoes, coarsely chopped
2 onions, thinly sliced
1 tbsp blue poppy seeds
2 tbsp extra virgin olive oil
1 level tbsp finely snipped purple basil leaves
1 tbsp tamari sauce
1 tbsp Japanese rice vinegar
freshly ground black pepper

Put the courgettes, tomatoes, onions and poppy seeds in a salad bowl and gently mix.

Put the oil, basil, tamari, rice vinegar and pepper in a screw-top jar and shake vigorously. Dress the salad with the mixture, toss well and serve.

BABY VEGETABLE SALAD IN SOY SESAME DRESSING

115 g / 4 oz baby carrots
115 g / 4 oz baby courgettes
85 g / 3 oz baby sweetcorn
85 g / 3 oz sugar snap peas
FOR THE DRESSING
2 tbsp sesame seeds
1 tbsp lime juice (about ½ lime)
1 tbsp soy sauce
2 tbsp vegetable oil
1 tsp Oriental sesame oil

In separate pans, steam or boil the vegetables in lightly salted water until just tender but still firm. Immediately refresh in cold water, drain and leave to cool completely in a serving bowl or dish.

Toast the sesame seeds by shaking them in a dry frying pan over a moderate heat for 1 minute, or until they begin to turn brown and 'jump'.

Combine these with the remaining dressing ingredients and pour this over the vegetables. Toss until they are all well coated and serve.

WILTED ONION AND CUCUMBER SALAD

¼ cucumber, thinly sliced or cut into 'ribbons' with a swivel-bladed vegetable peeler
1 small mild onion, preferably pink, very thinly sliced and separated into rings
juice of ½ large grapefruit, preferably pink

Put the cucumber and onion slices into a salad bowl, pour over the fruit juice and mix well. Cover the bowl with film and leave for at least 12 hours to allow the onions to 'wilt'.

The remaining recipes in this chapter are salads to serve beside cheese, egg, meat or fish dishes, or to which you can add some protein to make them main course salads.

Tamari sauce is a fine Japanese soy sauce made by fermentation. If unobtainable, use a good light soy sauce. If Japanese rice vinegar is difficult to obtain, use light cider vinegar.

The salad of
LAMB'S LETTUCE
WITH MANGO
AND HAZELNUTS
*may be made using
other exotic fruits,
such as papaya or
pineapple, instead of
mango.*

The recipe for
CHANTERELLE
SALAD *may be
adapted and made
with ordinary
mushrooms, but it
will not have the
same flavour.*

LAMB'S LETTUCE WITH MANGO AND HAZELNUTS

1 large ripe mango
350 g/12 oz lamb's lettuce
115 g/4 oz roasted hazelnuts
3 tbsp crème fraîche
1 tbsp pickled green peppercorns
1 tsp lime juice
salt and freshly ground black pepper

Peel and stone the mango and coarsely chop the flesh.

Place the lamb's lettuce in a salad bowl. Sprinkle the hazelnuts over this and arrange the chunks of mango on the salad.

Mix the crème fraîche with the peppercorns and lime juice. Season and pour over the salad. Toss at the table and serve immediately.

BABY SWEETCORN AND SNOW PEA SALAD

225 g/8 oz snow peas
225 g/8 oz baby sweetcorn
55 g/2 oz flaked almonds
55 g/2 oz chopped hazelnuts
2 tbsp hazelnut oil, warmed
salt and freshly ground black pepper

Plunge the snow peas and baby sweetcorn into a pan of boiling salted water for 2 minutes to blanch them. Drain and refresh under cold running water. Pat dry and leave to cool.

Place the vegetables in a salad bowl and mix in the nuts. Season the warmed hazelnut oil and pour it over the salad.

CHANTERELLE SALAD WITH BASIL VINAIGRETTE

2 sprigs of thyme
450 g/1 lb chanterelle mushrooms
225 g/8 oz croutons
2 large purple garlic cloves, crushed
6 large basil leaves, chopped
4 tbsp Basic Vinaigrette (see page 14)
salt
4 tbsp finely chopped parsley, to garnish

Place the thyme in a pan and add 450 ml/¾ pt of water with some salt. Bring to the boil and allow to boil for 5 minutes.

Add the mushrooms, cover and reduce the heat. Simmer gently for 5 minutes. Discard the thyme, drain the mushrooms and leave them to cool.

Place the cooled mushrooms and the croutons in a salad bowl and toss lightly.

Combine the garlic and basil with the vinaigrette, then dribble this over the salad. Garnish with parsley and serve immediately.

SWEET PEPPER SALAD

1 large red sweet pepper
1 large green sweet pepper
1 large yellow sweet pepper
18 stoned black olives
3 tbsp olive oil
juice of 1 large lemon
3 garlic cloves, crushed
3 tbsp finely chopped flat-leaf parsley
salt and freshly ground black pepper

Preheat a hot grill. Halve the peppers and remove their seeds and pith.

Grill the pepper halves, skin-side upwards, until the skins are black and blistering.

Allow to cool a little and then skin them. Cut the flesh into strips and mix in a salad bowl or on a serving plate.

Finely chop half the olives and halve the others.

Make the dressing by mixing the oil, lemon juice, chopped olives, garlic and half the parsley. Season well with salt and pepper.

Dribble the dressing over the peppers and toss well. Sprinkle the salad with the remaining parsley and dot with the olive halves to serve, either still quite warm or cold.

For a light main-course salad, add about 140 g/5 oz lean bacon which has been cut into strips and dry-fried until crisp.

PUDDINGS AND DESSERTS

*T*he last course of a meal is the one in which even the most
conservative of cooks will occasionally indulge themselves in
a flight of fancy. Whether it be a simple Rhubarb and Gooseberry
Cobbler for the family or an elegant gateau like the Double Truffle
Torte for special guests, there are recipes in this chapter for all occasions.

In the spirit of *The Creative Cook*, old stand-bys are given new
life with refreshing and unusual new flavourings, like Apple Brown
Betty with Scented Geranium or Orange
and Almond Rice Pudding. There are
also lots of new ways with fruit, like
Spiced Fruit Compote with
Mascarpone, and frozen desserts
like Zabaglione Ice-cream. The
chapter also includes an amazing
array of gâteaux, pies and tarts,
such as Key Lime Pie, Chocolate
Mousse Tart and Clementine and
Strega Gâteau, which are both
impressive and tasty as well as being very
approachable for the less-than-experienced cook.

*Clockwise from the left: Pear Frangipane Tart (page 189), Crème Brûlée (page 188)
and Creamed Rice Pudding (page 188)*

The Spiced Fruit Compote with Mascarpone *makes a simple but elegant dessert. Replace the wine with apple, orange or pear juice, however, and it becomes a refreshing breakfast treat. Italian Mascarpone cheese is now widely available.*

Crème Brûlée or 'burnt cream' is more traditionally caramelized with a salamander heated in an open fire.

CREAMED RICE PUDDING

30 g/1 oz butter
55 g/2 oz pudding rice
30 g/1 oz caster sugar
strip of rind from an unwaxed lemon
300 ml/½ pt milk
300 ml/½ pt single cream
large pinch of freshly grated nutmeg
fresh fruit, fruit compote or pouring cream, to serve

Preheat the oven to 160C/325F/gas 3. Use a little of the butter to grease an 850 ml/1½ pt baking dish.

In a sieve or colander, rinse the rice under running water, then put it into the prepared dish with the sugar, lemon rind, milk and cream. Stir until the sugar is dissolved.

Bake for 1 hour, stirring twice. Dot the remaining butter over the surface and sprinkle with nutmeg.

Return to the oven and continue baking for about 45 minutes, until the rice is soft and the top is browned. Serve hot or cold, with fruit or cream.

SPICED FRUIT COMPOTE WITH MASCARPONE

450 g/1 lb mixed dried fruit, such as apricots, prunes, apple rings, pears and figs
30 g/1 oz soft light brown sugar
300 ml/½ pt sweet dessert wine
3 whole cloves
1 cinnamon stick
170 g/6 oz Mascarpone cheese
grated zest of 2 unwaxed lemons

Put all the ingredients except the cheese and half the lemon zest in a pan with 300 ml/½ pt of water.

Bring to the boil then lower the heat, cover and simmer for 45-50 minutes, until the fruit is plump

and the liquid is syrupy. Discard the cinnamon.

Serve the compote either warm or chilled, with the Mascarpone spooned over it and a little of the reserved lemon zest sprinkled over the top.

CRÈME BRÛLÉE

SERVES 6

575 ml/1 pt double cream
1 vanilla pod
4 egg yolks
2 tbsp caster sugar
4 tbsp demerara sugar
fresh fruits in season, such as summer berries or exotic fruits, to serve

Put the cream and vanilla pod in a small saucepan. Heat gently until almost boiling. Remove from the heat, cover and leave to infuse for 30 minutes.

Preheat the oven to 140C/275F/gas 1.

Place the egg yolks in a mixing bowl, add the caster sugar and beat well to mix. Reheat the cream until almost boiling. Pour this over the egg yolks, beating with a wire whisk at the same time.

Place the bowl over a pan of simmering water and whisk lightly until the mixture thickens to coat the back of a spoon. Divide the mixture between six 125 ml/4 fl oz ramekins.

Arrange the ramekins in a deep roasting pan and pour in warm water to a depth of 2.5 cm/1 in. Bake in the oven for 30-35 minutes.

Remove the ramekins from the water bath and allow to cool. Chill for at least 1 hour, or up to 24.

Preheat a hot grill. Sprinkle the demerara sugar over the tops of the ramekins. Grill for 3-4 minutes to caramelize the tops.

Allow to cool and then chill for at least 2 hours before serving, accompanied by fresh fruits.

PEAR FRANGIPANE TART

SERVES 6

85 g/3 oz butter, plus more for greasing
85 g/3 oz vanilla sugar
1 egg plus 1 extra yolk, beaten
30 g/1 oz flour
few drops almond essence
85 g/3 oz ground almonds
3 small ripe dessert pears
2 tsp lemon juice
crème frâiche or cream, to serve
FOR THE RICH SUGAR PASTRY
(makes about 450 g/1 lb)
225 g/8 oz flour
pinch of salt
115 g/4 oz butter, cubed
55 g/2 oz caster sugar
2 egg yolks
2 tbsp iced water
1 tsp lemon juice

Preheat the oven to 200C/400F/gas 6 and grease a deep 23 cm/9 in flan ring or loose-bottomed flan tin with butter.

Make the pastry: sieve the flour and salt into a bowl. Lightly rub in the butter until the mixture resembles breadcrumbs, then stir in the sugar.

Mix together the egg yolks, iced water and lemon juice. Using a palette knife, mix this into the flour to form a firm dough.

Turn the dough out on a floured surface and knead lightly. Wrap in film and chill for 20 minutes.

Use the pastry to line the prepared flan ring or tin. Prick the base and fill with baking beans. Bake blind in the oven for 10 minutes.

Remove the baking beans and return to the oven for a further 5 minutes to cook the base. Reduce the oven temperature to 180C/350F/gas 4.

Make the frangipane cream filling: beat together the butter and vanilla sugar until light and fluffy. Beat in the egg and egg yolk and then stir in the flour, almond essence and ground almonds. Spread two-thirds of this filling over the base of the prepared flan case.

Peel, core and halve the pears then slice them thinly across the width. Arrange the slices in the flan case and brush with lemon juice.

Spoon the remaining frangipane cream around the pears and bake the tart in the oven for 30-35 minutes, until the filling is firm and golden brown.

Serve warm with crème fraîche or cream.

BAKED SULTANA AND LEMON CHEESECAKE

SERVES 8

55 g/2 oz butter, plus more for greasing
225 g/8 oz digestive biscuits, crushed
icing sugar, for dusting
FOR THE FILLING
550 g/1¼ lb cream cheese
85 g/3 oz caster sugar
55 g/2 oz ground almonds
juice and grated zest of 2 unwaxed lemons
85 g/3 oz sultanas
3 eggs, beaten

Preheat the oven to 180C/350F/gas 4. Grease the base of a deep 20 cm/8 in loose-bottomed cake tin with some butter and line it with greaseproof paper.

Melt the butter in a pan and stir in the biscuits. Mix well and use to line the base of the prepared tin, pressing down well with the back of a spoon.

Make the filling: mix all the ingredients and pour into the tin. Bake for 40-45 minutes, until just set.

Allow to cool in the tin, then chill for at least 1 hour. Transfer to a serving plate and dredge with icing sugar to serve.

The term FRANGIPANE *was first used of almond-flavoured pastry cream in eighteenth-century Paris.*

KEY LIME PIE

SERVES 6-8

55 g/2 oz butter, plus more for greasing
450 g/1 lb Rich Sugar Pastry (see page 189)
4 tbsp cornflour
juice and grated zest of 4 unwaxed limes
115 g/4 oz caster sugar
3 egg yolks
FOR THE MERINGUE TOPPING
3 egg whites
pinch of salt
170 g/6 oz caster sugar

KEY LIME PIE *is so named after America's Florida Keys, the part of the world from which it originated.*

Preheat the oven to 200C/400F/gas 6 and grease a deep 23 cm/9 in loose-bottomed flan tin with butter.

Roll out the pastry and use to line the prepared flan tin. Prick the base with a fork and fill with baking beans. Bake blind in the oven for 10 minutes, then remove the baking beans and return to the oven for a further 5 minutes to cook the base. Reduce the oven temperature to 180C/350F/gas 4.

In a small bowl, mix the cornflour to a paste with a little of a measured 300 ml/½ pt of water. Put the rest of the water in a saucepan with the lime juice and sugar. Bring to the boil. Pour in the cornflour mixture, stirring constantly, and cook for 2-3 minutes until smooth and thickened.

Remove from the heat and stir in the butter and lime zest. Allow to cool slightly, then add the egg yolks and beat well. Pour the mixture into the prepared flan case and bake for 15 minutes.

Meanwhile, make the topping: put the egg whites in a large bowl with the salt. Whisk until stiff, then add half the sugar. Continue whisking until standing in stiff peaks. Add the remaining sugar and whisk again.

Pile the meringue over the partly cooked flan, swirling the surface into peaks. Return to the oven for a further 15 minutes, until the peaks of the meringue are golden brown. Serve warm or cold.

PECAN PIE

SERVES 6

FOR THE PASTRY
115 g/4 oz butter, diced, plus more for greasing
225 g/8 oz flour
pinch of salt
3-4 tbsp iced water
lightly whipped cream or vanilla ice-cream, to serve
FOR THE FILLING
170 g/6 oz pecan halves
115 g/4 oz unsalted butter
115 g/4 oz soft light brown sugar
3½ tbsp double cream
30 g/1 oz flour, sifted

Preheat the oven to 190C/375F/gas 5 and grease a 20 cm/8 in flan ring or loose-bottomed tart tin with butter.

Make the pastry: sieve the flour and salt into a mixing bowl. Lightly rub in the butter. Using a palette knife, mix in just enough iced water, a tablespoon at a time, to form a firm dough.

Knead lightly on a floured surface and roll out to line the prepared ring or tin. Prick the base and chill for at least 15 minutes.

Line the flan case with greaseproof paper then fill it with baking beans and bake blind for 10 minutes. Remove the beans and paper and return to the oven for a further 5 minutes to cook the base.

Meanwhile, prepare the filling: set aside 55 g/2 oz of the pecans and roughly chop the rest. Melt the butter with the sugar in a pan over a moderate heat, stirring, and bring to the boil. Beat in the cream and flour. Stir in the chopped nuts and bring to the boil.

Spoon into the case and arrange the reserved pecan halves on top. Bake for 20 minutes until firm.

Serve warm or cold, accompanied by lightly whipped cream or vanilla ice-cream.

Top: Pecan Pie; bottom: Key Lime Pie

AUTUMN PUDDING

SERVES 6

2 dessert apples
1 firm pear
2 tbsp lemon juice
350 g/12 oz Victoria plums, stoned and quartered
350 g/12 oz greengages, halved and stoned
115 g/4 oz caster or golden granulated sugar
200 ml/7 fl oz sweet Muscatel wine
1 cinnamon stick, halved
3 pieces of stem ginger in syrup, drained
and diced (optional)
10 large slices of white bread, crusts removed
double cream, to serve

Peel, core and chop the apples and the pear. Put the chopped fruit in a bowl and add the lemon juice. Mix well to prevent the fruit from discolouring.

Put all the fruit in a saucepan with the sugar, wine, cinnamon stick and ginger, if using. Bring to the boil, stirring frequently, then lower the heat and simmer for 15 minutes.

Use 8 slices of the bread to line the base and sides of a 1.75 litre/3 pt pudding basin. Spoon a few tablespoons of the fruit juices over the bread to moisten it and hold it in place then spoon in the fruit and the rest of the juices.

Use the remaining bread to cover the fruit. Cover the basin with greaseproof paper and a weighted plate. Chill for at least 4 hours or overnight.

Unmould the pudding on a serving plate. Serve with double cream, plain or softly whipped.

Autumn Pudding

APPLE AND BERRY CRUMBLE

450 g/1 lb tart green apples, such as Bramleys
225 g/8 oz blackberries or loganberries
85 g/3 oz caster sugar
½ tsp ground cinnamon
butter, for greasing
cream or custard, to serve
FOR THE CRUMBLE TOPPING
170 g/6 oz flour
85 g/3 oz butter, diced
55 g/2 oz demerara sugar
1 tsp grated zest from an unwaxed lemon

Preheat the oven to 180C/350F/gas 4 and grease a baking dish with butter.

First prepare the topping: sieve the flour into a mixing bowl and rub in the butter until the mixture resembles fine breadcrumbs. Stir in the sugar and lemon zest and set aside.

Peel, halve, core and thinly slice the apples. Place the slices in a bowl with the berries, sugar and cinnamon and toss lightly to mix.

Transfer the mixture to the prepared dish and sprinkle over the crumble mixture to cover completely.

Bake in the oven for about 35 minutes, until the top is golden brown. Serve hot with cream or custard.

The APPLE AND BERRY CRUMBLE lends itself to a wide range of variations. Try replacing the berries with sliced nectarines, peaches, plums, rhubarb or even raisins.

The COBBLER originated among the early American settlers and consists of a fruit filling topped with simple scone dough and baked.

RHUBARB AND GOOSEBERRY COBBLER

450 g/1 lb rhubarb, cut into 2.5 cm/1 in chunks
225 g/8 oz fresh or frozen gooseberries
55 g/2 oz soft light brown sugar
1 bay leaf
butter, for greasing
pouring or clotted cream, to serve
FOR THE SCONE TOPPING
170 g/6 oz self-raising flour
pinch of salt
45 g/1½ oz butter
30 g/1 oz caster sugar
about 100 ml/3½ fl oz milk, plus extra for glazing
1 tbsp demerara sugar, for sprinkling

Preheat the oven to 220C/425F/gas 7 and lightly grease a shallow 1.5 litre/2 ½ pt baking dish with butter.

Put the fruits in a saucepan with the sugar and bay leaf. Cook over a moderate heat, stirring frequently, for 12-15 minutes, until the fruit is almost tender.

Remove the bay leaf and spoon the fruit in an even layer into the base of the prepared baking dish.

Prepare the scone topping: sieve the flour and salt into a mixing bowl. Rub in the butter and stir in the sugar. Add the milk, mixing to form a firm dough.

Turn the dough out on a floured surface, knead lightly and roll out to a thickness of 1 cm/½ in. Using a 6 cm/2½ in pastry cutter, stamp out circles or shapes of pastry.

Arrange these on top of the fruit and brush with milk to glaze. Sprinkle the scones with the demerara sugar and bake in the oven for 15 minutes, until the cobbler topping is well risen and golden brown.

Serve hot, with pouring or clotted cream.

CHOCOLATE SPONGE PUDDINGS

SERVES 6

85 g/3 oz butter, plus more for greasing
85 g/3 oz dark chocolate, cut into pieces
100 g/3½ oz caster sugar
2 eggs
5 tbsp sour cream
115 g/4 oz self-raising flour, sifted
icing sugar, for dusting
FOR THE BITTER CHOCOLATE SAUCE
100 g/3½ oz bitter dessert chocolate
30 g/1 oz butter
3 tbsp rum or brandy

Preheat the oven to 180C/350F/gas 4. Grease 6 dariole or individual pudding moulds with butter and then line their bases with greaseproof paper.

Put the chocolate in a small saucepan with 125 ml/4 fl oz of water. Stir over a low heat until melted and smooth. Remove from the heat.

In a mixing bowl, beat the butter and sugar until light and fluffy. Beat in the eggs, one at a time. Stir in the prepared chocolate mixture then fold in alternating spoonfuls of the sour cream and flour.

Spoon the mixture between the prepared moulds. Place them on a baking sheet and bake in the oven for about 15 minutes, until just firm to the touch.

Meanwhile, prepare the sauce: put the chocolate and butter in a small saucepan with 3 tablespoons of water. Stir constantly over a gentle heat until smooth and melted. Stir in the rum or brandy.

Turn the puddings out on individual serving plates. Dredge with a little icing sugar and spoon the sauce over them to serve.

LEMON AND TREACLE PUDDING

115 g/4 oz butter, plus extra for greasing
115 g/4 oz caster sugar
finely grated zest of 2 unwaxed lemons
2 eggs, beaten
170 g/6 oz self-raising flour
4 tbsp golden syrup
cream or vanilla custard, to serve

Grease a 1.1 litre/2 pt pudding basin with butter and line the base with a disc of greaseproof paper.

Beat together the butter, sugar and lemon zest until light and fluffy. Beat in the eggs, a little at a time, and then fold in the flour.

Spoon the syrup into the bottom of the prepared basin. Spoon in the lemon sponge mixture.

Cover the basin with a layer of pleated greaseproof paper and with foil. Secure tightly with string. Place in a large pan and add enough water to come three-quarters up the basin. Cover tightly, bring to a simmer and steam the pudding for 1½–2 hours until firm, topping up the water occasionally.

Turn out on a serving plate and serve accompanied by cream or custard.

French lemon tart,
Tarte au
Citron, *is one of
the glories of
Provençal cooking.
The riper and more
fragrant the lemons,
the better the filling
will taste. Make an
orange or tangerine
tart in the same
way, using 3 large
juicy oranges or 8
tangerines in place of
the lemons and
adding 1 tablespoon
of grated zest to the
pastry.*

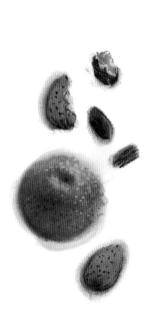

TARTE AU CITRON

SERVES 6-8

225 g/8 oz flour, plus more for dusting
85 g/3 oz icing sugar, plus more for dusting
115 g/4 oz butter, softened, plus more for greasing
4 eggs
pinch of salt
few drops of vanilla essence
5 unwaxed lemons
100 g/3½ oz caster sugar, sieved
55 g/2 oz blanched almonds, finely ground
150 ml/¼ pt double cream

Sift the flour and icing sugar into a bowl and work the butter in lightly with the fingertips. Make a well in the centre and add 1 of the eggs, the salt, vanilla and the grated zest of 1 lemon. Gradually bring the flour in from the edges and mix to a smooth dough. Leave to rest for about 30 minutes.

Preheat the oven to 180C/350F/gas 4 and grease a 27 cm/10¾ in tart pan with some butter.

Roll the rested pastry out on a lightly floured surface, and use it to line the pan. Do not remove any overhang. Chill briefly until firm.

Line with foil or baking paper, weight and place on a baking sheet. Bake blind for about 10 minutes. Remove from the oven, take off weights and paper and trim the edges. Return to the oven for 10 minutes.

Meanwhile, finely grate the zest of 2 of the remaining lemons and extract the juice from all the lemons. In a large bowl, beat the remaining eggs with the caster sugar until thick enough to form a ribbon trail. Stir in the lemon zest and juice, together with the cream, and sprinkle in the almonds.

Pour this filling into the baked pastry case as soon as it comes from the oven. Return to the hot baking sheet in the oven and bake for 30 minutes.

Preheat a hot grill. When the tart comes out of the oven, dust liberally with sieved icing sugar and flash under the grill to caramelize it. Serve hot or warm.

ORANGE AND ALMOND RICE PUDDING

SERVES 6

15 g/½ oz butter
140 g/5 oz short-grain rice
85 g/3 oz flaked almonds
85 g/3 oz sugar
1 litre/1¾ pt milk
finely grated zest and juice of 2 large unwaxed oranges
juice of 1 small lemon
150 ml/¼ pt crème fraîche or double cream
large pinch of cinnamon
1 tbsp orange blossom water, rum or orange liqueur
(optional)

Preheat the oven to 180C/350F/gas 4 and grease a large baking dish with the butter. Rinse the rice thoroughly and finely crush half the almonds.

Put the rice, sugar, milk and orange zest in a large pan and bring to the boil, stirring continuously.

Immediately transfer to the prepared baking dish and stir in the crushed almonds, orange juice, lemon juice, cream, cinnamon and orange blossom water, rum or liqueur, if using.

Bake for about 1 hour, or until the rice is tender, stirring from time to time during the first 30 minutes.

About three-quarters of the way through, spread the remaining almonds on a baking tray and put them in the oven to toast lightly.

Serve the rice pudding with the toasted almonds sprinkled on top, along with a little more cinnamon.

YOGURT, DATE AND HONEY CHEESECAKE

SERVES 8-12

45 g/1½ oz butter, melted
6 sheets of filo pastry
300 ml/½ pt Greek yogurt
6 tbsp skimmed milk
3 tbsp rice or potato flour
30 g/1 oz ground almonds
5 tbsp good mild-flavoured honey
200 g/7 oz ricotta cheese
3 eggs, lightly beaten
55 g/2 oz seedless raisins
55 g/2 oz chopped dates
zest and juice of 1 small unwaxed lemon
zest and juice of 1 small unwaxed orange
2 tbsp orange blossom water or almond liqueur
icing sugar, to dust

Preheat the oven to 190C/375F/gas 5 and grease a 27 cm/10 3/4 in tart pan with some of the butter.

Trim the sheets of filo so that they are about 30 cm/12 in square. Line the pan with them, brushing each with butter and putting it at an angle of about 60 degrees to that beneath it to fan out the edges.

Mix the yogurt and milk in a large pan and sieve the flour into it. Then add the almonds and honey. Stir until just below the boil. The mixture should become quite thick. Leave to cool slightly.

Transfer to a large mixing bowl and add the cheese and all but 1 tablespoon of the eggs. Beat in well. Stir in most of the fruit, reserving some for decoration, together with the citrus zest and juice and the orange blossom water or liqueur.

Pour into the lined pan, brush the top lightly with the reserved beaten egg and bake for about 45 minutes, or until a good light golden brown.

Dust with icing sugar and stud with the reserved fruit to serve.

TIRAMISU

SERVES 6-8

12 sponge fingers
1 tsp instant coffee
2 tbsp brandy
2 tbsp Marsala
3 eggs, separated
3 tbsp caster sugar
350 g/12 oz Mascarpone cheese
85 g/3 oz bitter chocolate

Cut the sponge fingers in half along their lengths and line the bottom of a glass trifle bowl with half the sponge pieces, cut side uppermost.

Dissolve the coffee in 2 tablespoons of boiling water and mix the brandy and Marsala into it. Use a pastry brush to paint the sponge with some of this.

Beat the egg yolks with the sugar until the mixture is thick and pale. Then beat the cheese into this mixture a spoonful at a time.

Whisk the egg whites until standing in stiff peaks and then fold these into the cheese mixture.

Break half the chocolate into tiny pieces. Spread half the cheese mixture over the sponge and stud with half of the chocolate pieces. Repeat the layers.

Finish by smoothing the top of the cheese mixture and chill overnight or for at least 4 hours.

Just before serving, grate the remaining chocolate finely over the top. Use within 24 hours.

The Italian coffee-flavoured dessert TIRAMISU *has become a great restaurant favourite in recent years. It often disappoints, however, having been made with custard rather than thick rich Mascarpone cheese. For more flavour and crunch, spread the layers of sponge with some apricot preserve and stud the top with tiny amarettini biscuits.*

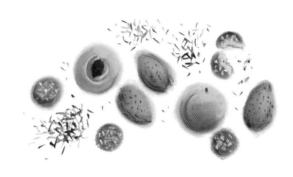

PISTACHIO BAKLAVA

MAKES ABOUT 40 PIECES

115 g/4 oz butter, melted
55 g/2 oz blanched almonds
55 g/2 oz walnuts
15 sheets of filo pastry
225 g/8 oz pistachios, shelled and chopped
1 tbsp caster sugar
½ tsp ground cinnamon
FOR THE SYRUP
450 g/1 lb caster sugar
1 cinnamon stick, broken into pieces
1 tbsp good mild-flavoured honey
2 cloves
½ tsp finely grated zest and juice from ½ small unwaxed lemon
2 tbsp orange blossom water

The Middle-eastern nut pastry cake BAKLAVA *is made with a mixture of almonds, walnuts and pistachios. Here the pistachios predominate, but the nuts may be mixed in any proportion. It is important that the nuts are not ground too finely.*

GRANITAS are Italian water ices in which the formation of crystals is encouraged to give a refreshing grainy texture.

First, make the syrup: mix all the ingredients except the orange blossom water with 250 ml/8 fl oz water in a saucepan. Place over a moderate heat and stir until the sugar has dissolved. Then bring to the boil and boil uncovered and without stirring for about 4 minutes, or until the syrup is slightly thickened. Discard the spices and stir in the orange blossom water. Allow to cool and then chill.

Preheat the oven to 160C/325F/gas 3 and grease the bottom and sides of a deep 2 cm/8 in square cake pan generously with some of the melted butter.

Toast the almonds either on a baking sheet in the oven as it warms or under the grill. Put them in a food processor or mortar with the walnuts and grind to the consistency of small breadcrumbs.

Cut the sheets of pastry roughly to fit the pan. Layer 3 sheets in the bottom of the pan, brushing each with butter and trimming as necessary. Keep the other sheets covered with a damp cloth.

Mix together the pistachios and ground nuts, caster sugar and cinnamon. Sprinkle one-quarter of this mixture over the filo base in the pan.

Continue with layers of buttered filo and nuts until all are used up, finishing with a layer of 3 sheets of pastry. Brush this well with butter and sprinkle the top with 1 tablespoon of water.

Bake for 45 minutes, then increase the heat to 220C/425F/gas 7 and cook for a further 10-15 minutes, or until the baklava is puffed and lightly golden.

As soon as it comes out of the oven pour the chilled syrup all over it. Leave to cool in the pan.

Slice in diagonal cuts about 5 cm/2 in apart and then do the same at right angles to cut the baklava into lozenge-shaped pieces to serve.

COFFEE GRANITA

170 g/6 oz good strong coffee beans, ground
85 g/3 oz sugar
2 tbsp coffee liqueur, such as Kahlúa or Tia Maria (optional)
fresh pouring cream, to serve
sugar coffee beans, to decorate (optional)

Put the coffee and sugar in a pot or large jug and pour in 1.1 litre/2 pt of boiling water. Stir, cover and leave in a warm place to infuse for about 30 minutes.

Stir again and strain through a fine sieve or muslin.

Stir in the liqueur, if using, and freeze the mixture in a mould or ice trays in the freezer for 3 or 4 hours, without stirring.

Serve topped with a little pouring cream and perhaps decorated with a few sugar coffee beans.

NOTE: this is very refreshing and not too sweet; those with a sweet tooth may like to add some more sugar to taste to the freezing mixture.

Left: Pistachio Baklava; right: Zabaglione Ice-cream (page 201) with fresh raspberries

ZABAGLIONE ICE-CREAM

SERVES 6

12 egg yolks
115 g/4 oz caster sugar
300 ml/½ pt Marsala
300 ml/½ pt whipping cream
fresh strawberries, raspberries or chopped toasted
hazelnuts, to decorate

In a bowl, beat the egg yolks together with the sugar until pale and thick. Stir in the Marsala and mix well.

Set the bowl over a water bath or on top of a double-boiler and place over a gentle heat. Stir continuously until the custard begins to thicken. Immediately remove from the heat and stand the bottom of the bowl in cold water to stop the cooking, still stirring continuously. Leave aside to cool completely.

Whip the cream until standing in soft peaks and then fold in the egg mixture.

Freeze for about 6 hours in ice trays in the freezer, taking out and stirring vigorously with a fork half-way through to break up the crystals which have formed. Use within 48 hours.

Serve in tall elegant sundae glasses, decorated with fruit or nuts.

NOTE: this makes a very rich ice-cream, but you can lighten it by adding the stiffly beaten whites of 2 or 3 of the eggs to the mixture. The remaining egg whites can be used to make meringues to serve with the ice-cream.

BAKED FIGS STUFFED WITH WALNUTS

12 ripe fresh figs
55 g/2 oz walnut halves
3 tbsp good mild-flavoured honey or soft brown sugar
3 tbsp Madeira or sweet sherry
115 g/4 oz fromage frais

Preheat the oven to 200C/400F/gas 6.

Cut a tiny slice off the bottom of each fig so that it will sit stably. Make 2 cuts down through their tops, about 2.5 cm/1 in deep, at right angles to one another. Ease the figs open with a spoon, squeezing their middles at the same time, if necessary.

In a food processor or mortar, grind most of the walnut halves coarsely, reserving the better-looking pieces for decoration. Take care not to over-process.

In a bowl mix the honey or sugar, Madeira or sherry and ground nuts into the fromage frais. Spoon this into the opened-out figs and arrange them in a baking dish.

Bake for about 15-20 minutes, until the cheese is bubbling. Arrange the reserved walnuts halves over the tops of the figs to serve.

NOTE: toasted almonds or hazelnuts work equally well in this dish, as does Mascarpone cheese.

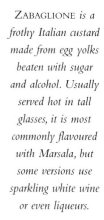

ZABAGLIONE *is a frothy Italian custard made from egg yolks beaten with sugar and alcohol. Usually served hot in tall glasses, it is most commonly flavoured with Marsala, but some versions use sparkling white wine or even liqueurs.*

Baked Figs Stuffed with Walnuts

MASCARPONE AND RASPBERRY DESSERT CAKE

32 sponge fingers
8 tbsp Marsala
170 g/6 oz raspberries, defrosted if frozen
85 g/3 oz amaretti biscuits, crushed
cocoa powder, for dusting
FOR THE MASCARPONE CREAM
30 g/1 oz custard powder
2 egg yolks
300 ml/½ pt milk
140 g/5 oz icing sugar, sifted
500 g/1 lb 2 oz Mascarpone cheese

MASCARPONE *is an Italian fresh cheese that is now readily available in our shops and supermarkets. Its sweet flavour and soft texture are ideal in the making of desserts and cakes.*

MARSALA *is a Sicilian fortified wine, like sherry, which the Italians use a great deal in cooking, but most notably in the famous frothy dessert zabaglione.*

Almond-flavoured AMARETTI BISCUITS *or Italian macaroons are widely available from good food stores.*

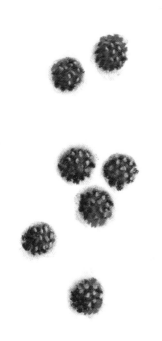

First start making the Mascarpone cream: in a large bowl, mix the custard powder and egg yolks with a little of the milk. Heat the remaining milk with a little of the sugar to just below boiling point and pour this over the custard. Return this mixture to the pan and cook, stirring continuously, until thickened. Transfer to a bowl, cover and leave to cool.

Meanwhile, line the base and sides of a 22 cm/8 ¾ in springform tin with baking parchment.

Finish the Mascarpone cream by beating the Mascarpone with the rest of the sugar. Then beat this into the cold custard until smooth and light in texture.

Set 16 sponge fingers in the bottom of the prepared tin and sprinkle over half the Marsala. Spread with half the Mascarpone cream, then sprinkle the raspberries on top. Repeat the layers of sponge fingers and Mascarpone cream.

Cover the cake with a round of baking parchment and chill for at least 8 hours, but preferably overnight.

Set the cake on a plate. Remove the sides of the tin. Turn the cake upside down on a plate and remove the base and base paper. Turn the cake back the right way up on the serving plate. Remove the top and side papers. Smooth the top and sides.

Press the sides with some of the crushed amaretti biscuits to cover them and sprinkle the rest on top of the cake. Chill until required.

Dust heavily with cocoa powder just before serving.

CHESTNUT MOUSSE CAKE WITH VANILLA CREAM

140 g/5 oz unsalted butter, softened, plus more
for greasing
225 g/8 oz caster sugar
450 g/1 lb canned unsweetened chestnut purée
grated zest of ½ unwaxed lemon
3 large (size 1) eggs, separated
150 ml/¼ pt double cream
2-3 drops vanilla essence, or to taste

Preheat the oven to 180C/350F/gas 4 and grease a 25.5 cm/10 in pie dish or flan tin with butter.

Cream the butter and sugar until pale. Beat in the chestnut purée together with the lemon zest, followed by 2 of the egg yolks. (Use the remaining egg yolk to enrich a sauce.)

Whisk the egg whites until stiff but not dry and fold them into the mixture. Pour the resulting mixture into the prepared dish or tin.

Bake for 55-60 minutes, or until a skewer inserted into the middle of the cake comes out clean.

Towards the end of this time, whip the cream and the vanilla essence until stiff.

CŒUR À LA CRÈME WITH SUMMER BERRIES

170 g/6 oz fresh cream cheese, softened
200 ml/7 fl oz double cream
1 tbsp caster sugar
white of 1 large egg, whisked until stiff but not dry
450 g/1 lb prepared seasonal soft fruits
extra sugar, to serve (optional)

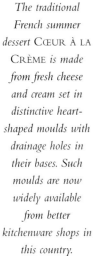

The traditional French summer dessert CŒUR À LA CRÈME *is made from fresh cheese and cream set in distinctive heart-shaped moulds with drainage holes in their bases. Such moulds are now widely available from better kitchenware shops in this country.*

Mix the cheese with the cream and the sugar. Mix in 1 tablespoon of the egg white to slacken the mixture, then carefully fold in the rest.

Dampen 4 squares of washed butter muslin and use these to line 4 heart-shaped cœur à la crème moulds. Spoon the mixture evenly into the moulds and smooth the tops.

Place these on a large plate to catch the liquid which will drain out of the holes in the bottoms of the moulds. Leave to drain and chill in the refrigerator for several hours, or overnight.

To serve: unmould each by inverting it on a plate and surround with fruit. Sprinkle the fruit with extra sugar, if wished.

Left and foreground: Cœur à la Crème with Summer Berries; top right: Raspberry Fool (page 207)

The basic RASPBERRY FOOL *recipe (see page 207) may be varied according to what summer fruit is available. Try making it with strawberries, blackberries or any ripe soft fruit. The amount of sugar added may have to be adjusted to taste, depending on the tartness of the fruit.*

TREACLE TART WITH ORANGE THYME

SERVES 6

140 g/5 oz unsalted butter, cut into small pieces, plus
more for greasing
200 g/7 oz flour
½ tsp salt
4 egg yolks
7 tbsp fresh breadcrumbs, preferably a mixture of white
and brown
4 tbsp golden syrup
2 tbsp flaked almonds
2 tbsp grated zest and the juice from ½ unwaxed lemon
1 tbsp finely chopped orange-scented thyme leaves

Preheat the oven to 200C/400F/gas 6 and grease a
24 cm/9½ in flan dish with butter.

Sift the flour with the salt into a bowl. Add the
butter and rub it in with the fingertips until the
mixture resembles breadcrumbs. Using a fork, mix the
egg yolks in lightly, together with enough cold water
to make a firm dough.

On a cold lightly floured surface, knead the dough
for 2 minutes and then roll it out to a thickness of
about 3 mm/⅛ in. Use it to line the prepared dish and
prick the base gently with a fork.

Mix the remaining ingredients together and
spread them evenly over the base. Use the pastry
trimmings to decorate the top of the tart.

Bake for 25-30 minutes on the middle shelf of the
oven, until golden. Serve hot, warm or cold.

Left: Apple Brown Betty with Scented Geranium; right: Treacle
Tart with Orange Thyme

APPLE BROWN BETTY WITH SCENTED GERANIUM

SERVES 4-6

9 slices of stale brown bread, crusts removed
55 g/2 oz softened butter
900 g/2 lb cooking apples, peeled, cored and sliced
3 tbsp golden syrup
1 tbsp finely chopped scented geranium leaves
Greek yogurt, custard or cream, to serve

Preheat the oven to 160C/325F/gas 3.

Spread the slices of bread generously with butter and cut each slice into quarters.

Place a layer of one-third of the bread quarters over the base of a pie dish. Cover this with half the apple, dribble one tablespoon of golden syrup over and then sprinkle over half of the geranium leaves.

Repeat with a second similar layer and finish with a layer of overlapping bread quarters to cover. Spread this with the remaining syrup.

Bake for 50 minutes, then increase the temperature to 190C/375F/gas 5 and bake for 10 minutes more, until crisp and golden brown. Serve hot, warm or cold with yogurt, custard or cream.

MARIGOLD AND APRICOT SORBET

SERVES 4-6

3 tbsp sugar
325 g/11 oz canned apricot halves in syrup, drained
1 egg white, whisked until stiff
juice of 1 lemon
petals from 2 marigold (calendula) heads

In a saucepan dissolve the sugar in 150 ml/¼ pt water. Bring to the boil and cook until it is syrupy, stirring constantly. Allow to cool.

Purée the apricots in a blender or food processor, then strain this through a fine sieve. Stir in the egg white and lemon juice. Then mix this into the syrup.

Put the mixture into an ice-cream maker or in ice trays with half the marigold petals sprinkled into it. If using an ice-cream maker, follow the manufacturer's instructions; otherwise place the trays in a freezer until just set, whisking several times with a fork to disperse large crystals as it freezes.

Serve in chilled glass dishes, decorated with the remaining marigold petals.

RASPBERRY FOOL

225 g/8 oz raspberries
1 tbsp sugar, or more to taste
300 ml/½ pt double cream
mint or lemon balm leaves, to decorate (optional)

Reserving a few perfect berries for decoration, mash the fruit with the sugar. (Do not use a food processor; the texture is nicer if the purée isn't too smooth.)

Whip the cream until stiff, then fold this into the purée. Chill in the refrigerator.

Serve decorated with the reserved whole berries and the leaves, if using.

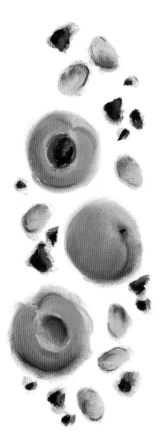

APRICOT CHOCOLATE TART

SERVES 6

FOR THE PASTRY
170 g/6 oz flour
115 g/4 oz butter, cut into small pieces
30 g/1 oz caster sugar
1 tsp almond essence
1 egg
FOR THE FILLING
2 egg yolks
85 g/3 oz caster sugar
45 g/1½ oz flour
300 ml/½ pt milk
30 g/1 oz plain chocolate
4 tbsp double cream
450 g/1 lb apricots, halved
15 g/½ oz flaked almonds, toasted
4 tbsp apricot jam

To make the pastry: sift the flour into a bowl, add the butter and rub it in finely with the fingertips. Stir in the sugar, almond essence and egg and mix together with a fork to form a firm dough.

Knead the dough on a lightly floured surface until it is smooth. Roll it out thinly and use to line a 23 cm/9 in diameter loose-based fluted tart tin. Chill for 30 minutes.

Preheat the oven to 200C/400F/gas 6.

Bake the pastry case blind for 15-20 minutes, until lightly browned at the edge.

While the case is baking make the filling: in a bowl, whisk together the egg yolks, one-third of the sugar, the flour and 1 tablespoon of the measured milk until smooth. In a saucepan, bring the remaining milk and the chocolate to the boil, whisking, and pour over the egg mixture, whisking continuously. Return the mixture to the saucepan and cook gently, whisking well, until the custard has thickened.

Remove the saucepan from the heat and whisk in the cream. Pour the custard into the pastry case and leave until cold.

Place the remaining sugar in a saucepan with 5 tablespoons of water and bring to the boil, stirring. Add the apricot halves, cover and cook gently for 2-3 minutes until tender. Using a slotted spoon, remove the apricots from the syrup and arrange them over the custard filling. Scatter over the almonds.

Add the apricot jam to the syrup in the saucepan and bring to the boil. Boil for 1 minute, then sieve into a bowl. Leave to cool slightly.

Pour the apricot syrup evenly over the apricots to glaze and then leave until cold.

PRUNE AND ARMAGNAC TART

SERVES 6

FOR THE PASTRY
115 g/4 oz flour
85 g/3 oz butter, cut into small pieces
30 g/1 oz caster sugar
1 egg yolk
FOR THE FILLING
20 stoned no-soak prunes
4 tbsp Armagnac or brandy
1 tbsp clear honey
1 tbsp demerara sugar
125 ml/4 fl oz double cream
2 eggs
30 g/1 oz hazelnuts, halved
TO DECORATE
icing sugar

To make the pastry: sift the flour into a bowl, add the butter and rub it in finely with the fingertips. Stir in the sugar and egg yolk and mix together with a fork to form a firm dough.

Knead the dough on a lightly floured surface until it is smooth. Roll it out thinly and use to line a 20 cm/8 in diameter loose-based fluted tart tin. Chill for 30 minutes.

Preheat the oven to 200C/400F/gas 6.

Bake the pastry case blind for 10-15 minutes, until lightly browned at the edge and cooked at the base.

While the pastry case is baking make the filling: place the prunes and Armagnac or brandy in a small saucepan and warm through gently until hot, taking care not to over-heat. Cover and leave until cold.

Beat the honey, sugar, cream and eggs together until well blended. Strain the Armagnac or brandy into the mixture and place the prunes in the pastry case.

Stir the filling, pour it over the prunes and return the tart to the oven for 20 minutes. Scatter the hazelnuts over the tart and return it to the oven for a further 10 minutes, or until the filling has set.

Dust with icing sugar and serve warm or cold.

ROSÉ PEAR TART

SERVES 6

FOR THE PASTRY
115 g/4 oz flour
85 g/3 oz butter, cut into small pieces
55 g/2 oz walnuts, finely chopped
30 g/1 oz caster sugar
1 egg
FOR THE FILLING
300 ml/½ pt rosé wine
200 g/7 oz caster sugar
5 small pears, peeled, quartered and cored
2 egg yolks
45 g/1½ oz flour
1 tbsp rose water
300 ml/½ pt milk
4 tbsp double cream
2 tsp powdered gelatine

To make the pastry: sift the flour into a bowl, add the butter and rub it in finely with the fingertips. Stir in the walnuts, sugar and egg and mix together with a fork to form a firm dough.

Knead the dough until smooth. Roll it out thinly and use to line a 20 cm/8 in square loose-based fluted tart tin. Chill for 30 minutes.

Preheat the oven to 200C/400F/gas 6.

Bake the pastry case blind for 15-20 minutes, until lightly browned at the edges.

While the pastry case is baking make the filling: place the wine and 175 g/6 oz of the sugar in a saucepan and heat gently, stirring until the sugar has dissolved. Add the pears and bring to the boil. Cover and cook very gently for 10-15 minutes, until the pears are tender. Leave to cool.

In a bowl, whisk together the egg yolks, remaining sugar, the flour and rose water until smooth. Bring the milk to the boil in a saucepan and pour it over the egg mixture, whisking all the time. Return the mixture to the saucepan and cook gently, whisking well, until the custard has thickened. Remove from the heat and whisk in the cream. Pour into the pastry case and leave to cool.

Using a slotted spoon, transfer the pears to a large plate. Blend the gelatine with 2 tablespoons of water and stir this into the wine syrup, then heat gently, until dissolved. Leave until almost set.

Meanwhile, cut half of the pear quarters into about 4 thin slices each, keeping the quarters together with the rounded sides on the right hand side. Slice the remaining pear quarters in the same way, with the rounded sides on the left.

Arrange 5 of the pear quarters on the custard filling and press lightly to spread them evenly; place another 5 quarters cut in the other direction and spread similarly. Repeat the process with the remaining pear halves in different directions.

When the jelly has begun to set, spoon it over the pears and chill until set. Remove from the tin.

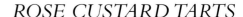

NORMANDY APPLE TART

FOR THE PASTRY
140 g/5 oz flour
85 g/3 oz butter, cut into small pieces
30 g/1 oz caster sugar
2 egg yolks
FOR THE FILLING
115 g/4 oz unsalted butter, softened
125 g/4½ oz caster sugar
3 egg yolks
2 tbsp double cream
115 g/4 oz ground almonds
2 tbsp crumbled lavender heads
4 dessert apples, peeled, halved and cored
4 tbsp apricot jam, boiled and sieved

Normandy, being the apple-growing region of France, strongly features apples in its traditional cookery. There are many variations of this traditional tart and the addition of the sweet scent of lavender is particularly rewarding.

To make the pastry: sift the flour into a bowl, add the butter and rub it in finely with the fingertips. Stir in the sugar and egg yolk and mix to a firm dough.

Knead the dough until it is smooth. Roll it out thinly and use to line a 23 cm/9 in diameter loose-based fluted tart tin. Chill for 30 minutes.

Preheat the oven to 200C/400F/gas 6.

To make the filling: in a bowl, beat together the butter and 115 g/4 oz of the sugar until light and fluffy. Add the egg yolks one at a time, beating well after each. Stir in the cream and fold in the almonds.

Scatter the lavender over the base of the pastry case. Then spread the mixture over these.

Slice the apple halves very thinly, keeping the halves together. Place one half in the centre of the filling and arrange the remaining 7 evenly around it. Press each apple half gently to spread out the slices.

Bake for 15 minutes, then sprinkle the remaining sugar over the apples. Reduce the oven temperature to 180C/350F/gas 4 and bake for a further 40-45 minutes until the filling is lightly browned.

Allow to cool before removing the tart from the tin. Brush the top evenly with the apricot jam glaze.

ROSE CUSTARD TARTS

MAKES 8

FOR THE PASTRY
115 g/4 oz flour
85 g/3 oz butter or margarine, cut into small pieces
55 g/2 oz ground almonds
55 g/2 oz caster sugar
1 egg, beaten
FOR THE FILLING
2 eggs + 2 extra yolks
2 tbsp rose water
1 tbsp flour
175 ml/6 fl oz milk
300 ml/½ pt single cream
225 g/8 oz wild strawberries or stoned cherries

To make the pastry: sift the flour into a bowl. Add the butter or margarine and rub it in finely with the fingertips. Stir in the ground almonds, sugar and egg and mix with a fork to form a firm dough.

Knead the dough on a lightly floured surface until it is smooth. Roll it out thinly, and use to line eight 11 cm/4½ in loose-based fluted tart tins. Chill for 30 minutes.

Preheat the oven to 200C/400F/gas 6.

Bake the pastry cases blind for 10-15 minutes, until lightly browned at the edges. Reduce the oven temperature to 180C/350F/gas 4.

Place the eggs, egg yolks, rose water and flour in a bowl and whisk until smooth. Whisk in the milk and cream and pour the mixture into the pastry cases. Dot with the fruit.

Return the tarts to the cooler oven for 45-50 minutes, until the custard has just set. Allow to cool.

A Rose Custard Tart

CARROT AND PASSION CAKE

170 g/6 oz raisins
300 ml/½ pt sunflower oil, plus more for greasing
225 g/8 oz plain flour
2 tsp baking powder
1 tsp bicarbonate of soda
1 tsp salt
2 tsp ground cinnamon
4 eggs
2 tsp natural vanilla essence
225 g/8 oz caster sugar
170 g/6 oz light Muscovado sugar
225 g/8 oz walnut pieces, chopped
450 g/1 lb carrots, finely grated and excess moisture squeezed out
FOR THE PASSION FRUIT ICING
4 passion fruit, halved
225 g/8 oz icing sugar, sifted
1 tsp lemon juice
225 g/8 oz butter, softened
115 g/4 oz curd or cream cheese

Put the raisins in a small saucepan with just enough water to cover and simmer for about 10 minutes until they are well plumped up. Leave to go cold and then drain thoroughly.

Preheat the oven to 180C/350F/gas 4. Grease three 23 cm/9 in cake tins with oil and line the bases with greaseproof paper.

Sift the flour, baking powder, bicarbonate of soda, salt and cinnamon together.

Place the eggs, vanilla, sugars and oil in a large bowl and whisk until thick. Fold in the flour mixture, followed by the walnuts, raisins and carrot.

Transfer the mixture to the prepared tins and bake for about 25 minutes, until risen and just firm to the touch. Allow the cakes to cool in the tins, then carefully turn them out on cooling racks.

Make the passion fruit icing: place the pulp from the passion fruit in a saucepan with 2 tablespoons of the sugar, the lemon juice and 2 tablespoons water. Simmer for 2-3 minutes, until the pulp loosens from the seeds. Pass the contents of the pan through a fine sieve and leave to go cold.

Beat the butter until smooth, then beat in the remaining icing sugar, a little at a time. Beat in the cream cheese and stir in the passion fruit purée.

Use a little of this mixture to sandwich the cakes together, then use the rest to cover the top and sides of the cake.

PAVLOVA PALETTE

whites of 4 eggs (about 175 ml/6 fl oz)
pinch of salt
225 g/8 oz caster sugar
2 tsp cornflour
1 tsp vinegar
1 tsp natural vanilla essence
575 ml/1 pt double cream, whipped to soft peaks
selection of prepared fruits in season
icing sugar, for dusting

Preheat the oven to 150C/300F/gas 2.

Draw a 25 cm/10 in circle on a piece of baking parchment and set it on a baking tray.

Whisk the egg whites with a pinch of salt until stiff, then whisk in the sugar, 1 tablespoonful at a time, adding the cornflour to the last spoonful. Quickly whisk in the vinegar and vanilla.

Transfer the mixture to the parchment and shape it evenly, making a slight dip in the centre. Bake for 1 hour, then switch off the oven and leave it to go cold while still in the oven.

Spread the whipped cream over the top of the cold pavlova, then cover with an abstract arrangement of fruits. Dust with icing sugar.

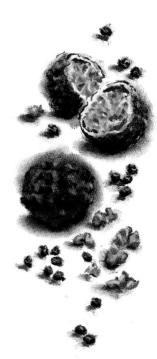

A classic of Antipodean cooking which has become an international favourite, the PAVLOVA *meringue cake was devised in honour of the great Russian prima ballerina when she toured Australia early this century.*

DOUBLE TRUFFLE TORTE

FOR THE SPONGE LAYERS
55 g/2 oz plain flour, plus more for dusting
115 g/4 oz caster sugar, plus more for dusting
2 tbsp cornflour
4 tbsp cocoa powder, plus more for dusting
4 eggs
butter for greasing
FOR THE DARK TRUFFLE LAYER
85 g/3 oz plain chocolate
2 tbsp milk
115 g/4 oz unsalted butter
115 g/4 oz caster sugar
75 g/2½ oz cocoa powder, sifted
3 egg yolks
200 g/7 oz crème fraîche
FOR THE WHITE TRUFFLE LAYER
85 g/3 oz best-quality white chocolate
115 g/4 oz unsalted butter
115 g/4 oz caster sugar
75 g/2½ oz ground almonds
3 egg yolks
200 g/7 oz crème fraîche

Preheat the oven to 190C/375F/gas 5. Butter three 20 cm/8 in sandwich tins and line the bases with greaseproof paper. Dust the sides with a mixture of equal parts flour and caster sugar, then shake out any excess. Sift the flours and cocoa together.

Place the eggs and sugar in a large bowl set over a saucepan of simmering water and whisk with a hand-held electric whisk until thick and foamy (the whisk should leave a thick trail in the mixture).

Fold in the flour mixture and divide between the tins. Bake for 10-15 minutes, until just firm to the touch. Turn out and allow to cool on wire racks.

Line base and sides of a 20 cm/8 in springform tin with a 8.5 cm/3½ in collar of baking parchment.

Make the dark truffle layer: melt the chocolate with the milk and stir until smooth. Leave to cool.

Beat the butter and sugar together in a bowl until light and fluffy, then beat in the chocolate mixture, cocoa, egg yolks and crème fraîche.

Place one layer of sponge in the prepared tin and spread the dark truffle mixture on top. Set a second sponge on top and press lightly. Chill until required.

Make the white truffle layer: melt the chocolate and stir until smooth. Leave to cool.

Beat the butter and sugar together in a bowl until light and fluffy, then beat in the chocolate, ground almonds, egg yolks and crème fraîche.

Spread the white truffle mixture on top of the second sponge layer and cover with the last sponge. Press down lightly and chill for 24 hours.

Unmould and dust with cocoa powder to serve, cut in very thin wedges.

The little sweets known as chocolate TRUFFLES, *due to their physical similarity to the equally flavourful little black truffle fungus, are traditionally given as Christmas gifts in France. They are classically flavoured with rum or praline but brandy, whisky, champagne and vanilla truffles are also common.*

PEAR GALETTE

FOR THE PASTRY
85 g/3 oz toasted skinned hazelnuts, finely ground
85 g/3 oz butter
3 tbsp caster sugar
125 g/4½ oz plain flour
pinch of salt
FOR THE FILLING
900 g/2 lb dessert pears, peeled, cored and chopped
1 tbsp apricot jam
finely grated zest of ½ an unwaxed lemon
1 tbsp cut mixed peel
2 tbsp currants
2 tbsp sultanas
TO DECORATE
about 8 tbsp whipped cream
8 toasted skinned hazelnuts
icing sugar, for dusting

First make the pastry: place all the ingredients in a food processor and pulse until evenly combined. Chill for at least 20 minutes.

Cut the dough in half and roll out each piece to form a 23 cm/9 in round on a circle of non-stick parchment. Chill on baking trays for 20 minutes.

Preheat the oven to 190C/375F/gas 5 and bake the pastry rounds for 20 minutes, until golden. Cut one round into 8 even wedges. Leave them to go cold.

Make the filling: place the ingredients in a pan and cook over a moderate heat, stirring occasionally, for about 15 minutes until the pears are soft and all the juice has evaporated. Leave to go cold.

Just before serving, place the uncut pastry round on a serving plate and spread with filling. Set the wedges on top and dust with icing sugar. Decorate with piped 'shells' of cream and top with hazelnuts.

Left to right: Marzipan Gâteau (page 219), Pear Galette and Coconut Cheesecake with Strawberry Coulis (page 218)

COFFEE WALNUT GÂTEAU

2 tbsp espresso coffee granules dissolved in 2 tbsp boiling water
6 eggs
225 g/8 oz caster sugar
115 g/4 oz walnut pieces, finely ground
170 g/6 oz plain flour
1 tsp baking powder
2 tbsp walnut oil
4 tbsp apricot jam
12 sugared coffee beans
butter, for greasing
FOR THE COFFEE BUTTERCREAM
1 tbsp espresso coffee granules
8 tbsp milk
4 egg yolks
115 g/4 oz caster sugar
250 g/8½ oz unsalted butter, diced

Preheat the oven to 180C/350F/gas 4. Butter two 20 cm/8 in cake tins and line with greaseproof paper.

Make a sponge mixture as on page 215, adding the coffee to the eggs and sugar, and the walnuts to the sifted flour. Fold in the walnut oil.

Divide between the tins and bake for 25 minutes. Allow to cool in the tins, then turn out on racks.

Make the buttercream: in a small pan over a gentle heat, dissolve the coffee in the milk. Whisk the egg yolks and sugar in a bowl then pour on the milk and stir well. Return to the pan and cook gently, until thick enough to coat the back of a spoon. Sieve, cover and leave to cool. Whisk in the butter, a little at a time, to make a thick buttercream.

Split each cake in half and sandwich in pairs with a little buttercream. Sandwich the two cakes together with jam. Reserving about 6 tablespoons, use the rest of the buttercream to cover the top and sides. Pipe 12 rosettes around the top using the reserved buttercream. Top each with a coffee bean.

The egg custard for the coffee buttercream used in the COFFEE WALNUT GÂTEAU may also be thickened by cooking it in the microwave oven for 3 minutes, whisking after each minute.

In French cooking a COULIS is a runny purée or sauce of raw or cooked vegetables or fruit. Fruit coulis are popular accompaniments to all sorts of desserts, especially frozen ones.

COCONUT CHEESECAKE WITH STRAWBERRY COULIS

FOR THE BASE
100 g/3½ oz butter, softened
55 g/2 oz caster sugar
75 g/2½ oz plain flour, sifted
1 tsp baking powder
1 large egg, beaten
55 g/2 oz desiccated coconut
FOR THE FILLING
225 g/8 oz cream or curd cheese
3 eggs, separated
115 g/4 oz caster sugar
30 g/1 oz plain flour
150 ml/¼ pt coconut milk
1 tbsp lemon juice
FOR THE STRAWBERRY COULIS
350 g/12 oz ripe strawberries, hulled
about 55 g/2 oz icing sugar
squeeze of lemon juice
TO DECORATE
150 ml/¼ pt double cream, whipped to soft peaks
2 fresh strawberries, quartered
1 tbsp shredded coconut, toasted

First make the base: beat the ingredients together in a bowl until creamy. Using a palette knife, spread a thin layer of the mixture on the sides of a 23 cm/9 in non-stick springform tin. Spread the rest on the base. Chill for at least 20 minutes.

Preheat the oven to 160C/325F/gas 3.

Make the filling: beat the cream cheese, egg yolks and half the sugar in a bowl until smooth, then beat in the flour and coconut milk.

Whisk the egg whites until fairly stiff, then continue whisking while adding the lemon juice, a little at a time. Then whisk in the remaining sugar a spoonful at a time. Fold this into the cheese mixture and transfer to the prepared tin.

Bake for 35 minutes, until lightly golden. Switch off the oven and leave the cheesecake in it for 10 minutes before removing. Allow to go cold.

Make the strawberry coulis: put the strawberries in a blender or food processor and purée until smooth. Sweeten and add lemon juice to taste. Then pass through a fine sieve to remove seeds, if wished.

Unmould the cheesecake and decorate with rosettes of whipped cream, strawberry quarters and a little toasted shredded coconut. Serve accompanied by the strawberry coulis.

LEMON SYRUP GÂTEAU

225 g/9 oz caster sugar, plus more for dusting
115 g/4 oz plain flour, plus more for dusting
2 unwaxed lemons
4 eggs
2 tbsp lukewarm water
55 g/2 oz cornflour or potato flour
1 tsp baking powder
butter, for greasing
FOR THE FILLING AND TOPPING
575 ml/1 pt double cream
3 tbsp icing sugar
45 g/1½ oz shelled pistachio nuts, very finely chopped
8 fresh strawberries, to decorate

Preheat the oven to 190C/375F/gas 5. Butter a 23 cm/9 in round cake tin and line the base with greaseproof paper. Dust the sides of the tin with a little caster sugar and flour. Shake out any excess.

Finely grate the zest of one lemon and pare the zest of the other. Extract the juice from them both.

In a large bowl set over a saucepan of simmering water, whisk the eggs with the lukewarm water, 140 g/5 oz of the sugar and the grated lemon zest until thick and mousse-like (the whisk should leave a thick trail in the mixture). Remove from the heat.

Sift the flours and baking powder together and carefully fold them into the mixture. Transfer to the prepared tin and bake for about 25 minutes, until risen and just firm to the touch.

Allow to cool in the tin, then unmould on a wire rack. When cold, split horizontally into 3 layers.

Place the prepared lemon zest and all the lemon juice in a pan with the remaining sugar and 300 ml/ ½ pt water. Heat gently until the sugar dissolves, then boil until the liquid is reduced to about 175 ml/6 fl oz. Pass this syrup through a fine sieve and leave to cool. Brush the cooled syrup over one of the cut surfaces of each layer of sponge.

Make the filling: whip the cream with the icing sugar to stiff peaks. Use a generous third of this to sandwich the cake layers back together.

Cover the top and sides of the cake with most of the remaining cream. Press the pistachios into the sides of the cake. Using a piping bag fitted with a star nozzle and filled with the remaining cream, pipe a ring of shell shapes around the rim of the cake.

Chill until required, then decorate with fruit.

MARZIPAN GÂTEAU

30 g/1 oz butter, melted, plus more for greasing
115 g/4 oz caster sugar, plus more for dusting
55 g/2 oz plain flour, plus more for dusting
4 eggs
finely grated zest from ½ an unwaxed lemon
30 g/1 oz cornflour
½ tsp baking powder
30 g/1 oz ground almonds
FOR THE FILLING AND TOPPING
500 g/1 lb 2 oz white marzipan
about 5 tbsp egg whites (about 2 eggs)
about 8 tbsp best-quality raspberry jam
55 g/2 oz flaked almonds, lightly toasted

Preheat the oven to 180C/350F/gas 4. Grease a 22 cm/8¾ in springform tin with butter, then line the base with greaseproof paper. Coat the sides with a little sugar and flour and shake out any excess.

In a large bowl set over simmering water, whisk the eggs, sugar and lemon zest until thick and mousse-like. Remove from the heat and continue whisking until cool.

Sift the flour, cornflour, baking powder and ground almonds together and fold them into the mixture, followed by the melted butter.

Transfer the mixture to the prepared tin and bake for about 25 minutes, until risen and golden and just firm to the touch. Allow to cool in the tin, then unmould on a wire rack. (This cake is best made the day before.)

Make the filling: place half the marzipan and 3 tablespoons of the egg white in a food processor and pulse until sooth and soft enough to spread.

Split the cake in half horizontally and then sandwich the layers together with about 6 tablespoons of the jam. Set it on a baking tray.

Use the pulsed marzipan to cover the top and sides of the cake, then press the toasted almonds all over the sides to cover them completely.

Preheat the oven to its highest setting.

Put the rest of the marzipan in a food processor with 5 teaspoons of egg white and pulse until smooth enough to pipe. Using a piping bag fitted with a small star nozzle and starting in the centre of the cake, pipe about 10 loops of the marzipan mixture to the outside edge to create the impressions of petals of a flower. Pipe a rosette in the centre.

Bake the cake for about 10 minutes, until golden brown. Then remove from the oven and leave to cool. Fill each 'petal' with about ½ teaspoon of jam and leave it to go completely cold.

Ready-made white marzipan – now more popular than the yellow variety due to its natural colouring – is available from all good supermarkets. Made from sugar, ground almonds, glucose syrup and invert sugar syrup, it must always be kneaded thoroughly before using or rolling.

The curd cheese
RICOTTA, *so*
popular in all sorts of
Italian dishes, is now
commonly available
in our shops and
supermarkets. Its
delicious sweet
flavour makes it a
popular dessert on its
own with fruit or
honey. Use sieved
cottage cheese if you
can't find any ricotta.

The bitter-sweet
Italian liqueur
STREGA *is brewed*
using over 70 herbs.
Miniatures are
available from better
off-licences and good
food stores.

ITALIAN HAZELNUT CAKE

115 g/4 oz skinned hazelnuts
115 g/4 oz butter, softened, plus more for greasing
115 g/1 oz caster sugar
4 eggs, separated
115 g/4 oz ricotta or curd cheese
2 tsp finely grated zest from an unwaxed lemon
30 g/1 oz plain flour, sifted
pinch of salt
TO DECORATE
115 g/4 oz plain chocolate, melted
6 tbsp apricot jam, warmed
300 ml/½ pt double cream whipped to soft peaks
icing sugar, for dusting

Preheat the oven to 200C/400F/gas 6 and roast the nuts for 15-20 minutes. Leave to cool, then grind them to a fine powder.

Reduce the oven setting to 190C/375F/gas 5. Grease a 25 cm/10 in shallow cake tin or flan tin with butter and line the base with greaseproof paper.

Cream the butter with two-thirds of the sugar in a large bowl until almost white, then beat in the egg yolks, cheese and lemon zest. Fold the hazelnuts and flour into the creamed mixture.

Whisk the egg whites with a pinch of salt until standing in soft peaks. Whisk in the remaining sugar and then fold this into the creamed mixture.

Transfer the mixture to the prepared tin and bake for about 25 minutes. Leave to cool in the tin, then transfer to a cooling rack.

To decorate: spread the chocolate thinly on a marble slab or smooth plastic work surface and leave to set. Using a large knife held at a 45 degree angle to the surface of the chocolate and with the blade facing away from you, scrape curls from the chocolate and set these on a tray in the refrigerator to harden.

Spread the surface of the cake with jam, then top with whipped cream and the chocolate curls. Finally, dust with icing sugar.

CLEMENTINE STREGA GÂTEAU

FOR THE FRUIT LAYER
350 g/12 oz candied whole clementines
115 g/4 oz caster sugar
150 ml/¼ pt Strega liqueur
FOR THE SPONGE LAYERS
115 g/4 oz soft tub margarine or softened butter, plus
more for greasing
115 g/4 oz caster sugar
2 eggs
85 g/3 oz self-raising flour
30 g/1 oz cocoa powder, sifted
FOR THE CHOCOLATE MIXTURE
285 g/10 oz chocolate hazelnut spread
285 g/10 oz plain chocolate, melted

First make the fruit layer: place the candied fruit in a saucepan and just cover with water. Bring to a fast boil, then remove from the heat and leave to go cold in the liquid. Drain, reserving 125 ml/4 fl oz of the cooking liquid.

Mince or pulse the fruit in a food processor, then mix it with the reserved liquid and the sugar in a saucepan. Cook over a moderate heat for 10-15 minutes, stirring occasionally, until thick and syrupy (rather like marmalade). Remove from the heat and stir in two-thirds of the Strega. Leave to go cold.

Preheat the oven to 190C/375F/gas 5. Grease two 900 g/2 lb loaf tins with butter and line the bases with greaseproof paper.

Make the sponge layers: cream the margarine or butter and sugar together until almost white, then beat in the eggs one at a time. Divide the mixture in half and fold 50 g/2 oz flour into one portion and the remaining flour and cocoa powder into the other.

Spread one mixture in each tin, making a dip in the centre of each. Bake for about 20 minutes, until risen and just firm to the touch. Allow to cool on wire racks, then trim the crusts to give two layers each about 2 cm/¾ in thick.

Line a 900 g/2 lb loaf tin with cling film. Make some chocolate mixture by mixing 225 g/8 oz of each of the ingredients together. Pour half of this mixture into the base of the tin and freeze until solid.

Set one layer of sponge on top of the frozen chocolate layer and moisten with half the remaining Strega. Top with the fruit mixture, followed by the other sponge layer and moisten with the last of the Strega. Spread the remaining chocolate mixture on top and freeze for about 1 hour until solid.

Make up the remaining chocolate mixture by mixing the remaining ingredients. Unmould the cake and spread the sides with it.

Chill until set, then cut the gâteau into thin slices to serve.

Top: Italian Hazelnut Cake; bottom: Clementine Strega Gâteau

NORFOLK TREACLE TART

SERVES 8

FOR THE PASTRY
170 g/6 oz flour
115 g/4 oz butter, cut into small pieces
1 tbsp lemon juice
FOR THE FILLING
225 g/8 oz golden syrup
30 g/1 oz butter
6 tbsp single cream
2 eggs, beaten
grated zest and juice from 1 unwaxed lemon
55 g/2 oz white breadcrumbs

To make the pastry: sift the flour into a bowl, add the butter and rub it in finely with the fingertips. Stir in the lemon juice and 2 tablespoons of cold water and mix together with a fork to form a firm dough.

Knead the dough on a lightly floured surface until smooth. Roll it out thinly and use to line a 23 cm/ 9 in diameter ovenproof tart plate, reserving the pastry trimmings. Chill for 30 minutes.

Preheat the oven to 200C/400F/gas 6.

To make the filling: place the golden syrup in a saucepan and heat gently until just melted. Remove the pan from the heat, add the butter and stir until melted. Then beat in the cream, eggs, lemon zest and juice until well blended.

Sprinkle the breadcrumbs over the pastry case and pour the mixture over the top. Roll out the pastry trimmings, cut them into thin strips and use to make a lattice design over the top.

Bake in the oven for 40-45 minutes, until the pastry is golden brown and the filling has set. Allow to cool in the dish and serve warm or cold.

Clockwise from the top: Fruit Bakewell Tart; Rum and Butterscotch Tart (page 224); Norfolk Treacle Tart

FRUIT BAKEWELL TART

SERVES 6

FOR THE PASTRY
115 g/4 oz flour
55 g/2 oz margarine, cut into small pieces
1 tsp caster sugar
FOR THE FILLING
3 tbsp redcurrant jelly
85 g/3 oz each redcurrants, white currants
and blackcurrants
85 g/3 oz soft margarine
85 g/3 oz caster sugar
55 g/2 oz ground almonds
55 g/2 oz self-raising flour
2 eggs, beaten
1 tsp almond essence
30 g/1 oz flaked almonds
TO DECORATE
icing sugar

To make the pastry: sift the flour into a bowl, add the margarine and rub it in finely. Stir in the sugar and 2 tablespoons of cold water and mix to a firm dough.

Knead the dough until smooth. Roll out thinly and use to line a 20 cm/8 in diameter loose-based fluted tart tin. Chill for 30 minutes.

Preheat the oven to 180C/350F/gas 4.

To make the filling: spread the redcurrant jelly over the base of the case. Reserve a few strands of each type of fruit for decoration, and remove the remainder from their stalks. Scatter over the jelly.

Beat together the margarine, sugar, almonds, flour, eggs and almond essence for 1-2 minutes.

Spread this mixture over the fruit in the pastry case. Scatter the flaked almonds evenly over the top and bake for 45-50 minutes, until the sponge has risen and feels firm when pressed lightly in the centre.

Cool in the tin, then remove carefully. Dust with icing sugar and decorate with the reserved fruit.

BAKEWELL TART, *or pudding as it was sometimes called, is named after the town of Bakewell in Derbyshire. The layers were traditionally separated by crushed raspberries or raspberry conserve, to add moisture.*

TREACLE TART *is said to have originated in Essex. The Norfolk variety introduced eggs, cream and lemon.*

KENTISH
STRAWBERRY
TART *is named
after the Kentish
strawberry trifle
which is used in this
recipe, enclosed in a
light crisp almond
pastry. Trifles were
very popular in
Victorian England.
They were made
using light sponge
cakes soaked in
sherry, brandy or
Madeira, layered
with fruit – Kentish
strawberries being
the most popular –
and covered with a
rich egg custard.*

RUM AND BUTTERSCOTCH TART

SERVES 6

FOR THE PASTRY
170 g/6 oz flour
115 g/4 oz butter
30 g/1 oz caster sugar
1 egg
FOR THE FILLING
115 g/4 oz soft dark brown sugar
55 g/2 oz butter
45 g/1½ oz flour
300 ml/½ pt milk
150 ml/¼ pt single cream
2-3 tbsp dark rum
TO DECORATE
4 tbsp whipped cream
chocolate coffee beans

To make the pastry: sift the flour into a bowl, add the butter and rub it in finely with the fingertips. Stir in the sugar and egg and mix together with a fork to form a firm dough.

Knead the dough on a lightly floured surface until smooth. Roll it out thinly and use to line a 23 cm/9 in diameter ovenproof tart dish. Chill for 30 minutes.

Preheat the oven to 200C/400F/gas 6.

Bake the pastry case blind for 15-20 minutes, until lightly browned at the edge and cooked at the base.

While the case is cooling, make the filling: place the sugar, butter, flour, milk and cream in a saucepan. Whisk together continuously over a moderate heat and bring to the boil. Cook gently for 1-2 minutes, until the sauce is thick and smooth. Stir in the rum.

Pour the filling into the pastry case and leave until cold. Decorate the top with whipped cream and the chocolate coffee beans.

KENTISH STRAWBERRY TART

SERVES 8

FOR THE PASTRY
115 g/4 oz flour
55 g/2 oz ground almonds
115 g/4 oz butter, cut into small pieces
30 g/1 oz caster sugar
1 tsp almond essence
1 egg
FOR THE FILLING
1 egg + 1 extra yolk
1 tsp vanilla essence
30 g/1 oz caster sugar
30 g/1 oz flour
300 ml/½ pt milk
3 tbsp strawberry jam
10 sponge fingers, cut into halves
2 tbsp Madeira
225 g/8 oz strawberries, sliced
300 ml/½ pt double cream, whipped
TO DECORATE
strawberry slices and strawberry leaves

Make the pastry: sift the flour into a bowl, stir in the almonds, add the butter and rub in finely. Stir in the sugar, almond essence and egg and mix to a firm dough.

Knead the dough until smooth. Roll it out thinly and use to line a 28 x 18 cm/11 x 7 in oblong ovenproof fluted tart dish. Chill for 30 minutes.

Preheat the oven to 200C/400F/gas 6.

Bake the pastry case blind for 15-20 minutes, until lightly browned at the edges.

While the case is baking, make the filling: in a bowl whisk together the egg, egg yolk, vanilla essence, sugar and flour until well blended. Place the milk in a saucepan and bring it to the boil. Whisking continuously, pour the milk over the egg mixture. Return to the pan and continue whisking over a low heat until the custard thickens. Allow to cool.

Spread the pastry case with jam. Dip the sponge fingers into the Madeira, turning to coat well. Arrange them over the jam. Cover with strawberry slices.

Fold two-thirds of the whipped cream into the custard and spread evenly over the strawberries.

Place the remaining cream in a piping bag fitted with a small star nozzle. Pipe ropes of cream across the tart and decorate with strawberry slices and leaves.

IRISH APPLE TART

SERVES 6

FOR THE PASTRY
85 g/3 oz flour
30 g/1 oz butter, cut into small pieces
1 tsp caster sugar
225 g/8 oz floury potatoes, cooked and sieved
FOR THE FILLING
675 g/1½ lb apples, thinly sliced
30 g/1 oz caster sugar
1 tsp ground cloves
150 ml/¼ pt sour cream
2 tsp clear honey

To make the pastry: place the flour in a bowl, add the butter and rub it in finely with the fingertips. Stir in the sugar and potato and mix to a soft dough.

Roll the dough out thinly and use to line a 23 cm/ 9 in diameter ovenproof tart plate.

Preheat the oven to 190C/375F/gas 5.

Mix together the apples, sugar and cloves and pile the mixture into the pastry case. Bake for 20-25 minutes, or until the apples are almost tender.

Stir the apples, spread the sour cream over the top and drizzle with honey. Bake for a further 5-10 minutes, until the cream has set. Serve warm or cold.

Kentish Strawberry Tart

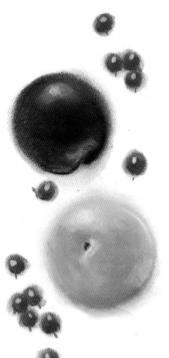

PLUM AND SOUR CREAM TART

SERVES 6

FOR THE PASTRY
170 g/6 oz flour
115 g/4 oz butter, cut into small pieces
30 g/1 oz caster sugar
3 tbsp sour cream
FOR THE FILLING
55 g/2 oz amaretti biscuits, crushed
4 tbsp sour cream
55 g/2 oz light soft brown sugar
225 g/8 oz red plums, halved
225 g/8 oz yellow plums, halved
4 tbsp redcurrant jelly

To make the pastry: sift the flour into a bowl, add the butter and rub it in finely with the fingertips. Stir in the sugar and sour cream and mix together with a fork to form a firm dough.

Knead the dough on lightly floured surface until it is smooth. Roll it out thinly and use to line a 20 cm/8 in diameter loose-based fluted tart tin, reserving the trimmings. Chill for 30 minutes.

Preheat the oven to 190C/375F/gas 5.

To make the filling: in a bowl, mix together the crushed biscuits, sour cream and brown sugar. Spread the mixture over the pastry case and arrange the plums on top, alternating the colours.

Roll out the pastry trimmings thinly and cut out 12 thin strips. Arrange these over the plums in a lattice design. Trim off the ends and press the strips on to the edge of the pastry case.

Bake in the oven for 35-40 minutes, or until the pastry is lightly browned and the plums are tender. Leave to cool.

Heat the redcurrant jelly until melted, then pour it in between the pastry lattice to glaze the tart. Leave to set.

PEACH AND PASSION TART

SERVES 8

FOR THE PASTRY
170 g/6 oz flour
115 g/4 oz butter, cut into small pieces
30 g/1 oz caster sugar
1 egg
FOR THE FILLING
2 eggs
100 ml/3½ fl oz double cream
55 g/2 oz caster sugar
strained juice from 3 passion fruit
6 peaches, skinned and halved
30 g/1 oz pistachio nuts, shelled
4 tbsp apricot jam, boiled and sieved

To make the pastry: sift the flour into a bowl, add the butter and rub it in finely with the fingertips. Stir in the caster sugar and egg and mix together with a fork to form a firm dough.

Knead the dough on a lightly floured surface until it is smooth. Roll it out thinly and use to line a 23 cm/9 in diameter ovenproof tart dish. Chill for 30 minutes.

Preheat the oven to 200C/400F/gas 6.

Bake the chilled pastry case blind for 10-15 minutes, until lightly browned at the edge and cooked at the base. Reduce the oven temperature to 160C/325F/gas 3.

While the case is baking make the filling: place the eggs, cream, sugar and passion fruit juice into a bowl. Beat together until well blended.

Pour the mixture into the pastry case and return it to the oven for 30-40 minutes, until the custard has set. Leave to cool.

Arrange the peaches over the custard filling and decorate with pistachio nuts. Brush the top with the apricot jam glaze and leave to set.

MINTED CURRANT TART

SERVES 6

FOR THE PASTRY
115 g/4 oz flour
85 g/3 oz butter, cut into small pieces
30 g/1 oz caster sugar
1 egg yolk
FOR THE FILLING
350 g/12 oz redcurrants
350 g/12 oz white currants
2 sprigs of mint
4 tbsp cornflour
115 g/4 oz caster sugar
TO DECORATE
sprigs of mint

To make the pastry: sift the flour into a bowl, add the butter and rub in finely with the fingertips. Stir in the sugar and egg yolk and mix to a firm dough.

Knead the dough until it is smooth. Roll it out thinly and use to line a 20 cm/8 in diameter loose-based fluted tart tin. Chill for 30 minutes.

Preheat the oven to 200C/400F/gas 6.

Bake the pastry case blind for 15–20 minutes, until lightly browned at the edge.

While the case is baking, make the filling: place half each of the redcurrants and white currants together with the mint in a saucepan with 250 ml/8 fl oz of water. Bring to the boil and cook for 2 minutes. Pour the contents of the saucepan into a sieve over a bowl and rub through the fruit, discarding the stems and pips.

Blend in the cornflour with 4 tablespoons of water in a saucepan. Add the strained fruit purée, stir well and bring to the boil. Allow to cool for 5 minutes, stir in the sugar and pour the mixture into the pastry case. Leave until cold.

Decorate the top of the tart with the remaining redcurrants and white currants and fresh mint sprigs.

TARTE FRANÇAISE

SERVES 8

375 g/13 oz frozen puff pastry, defrosted
FOR THE FILLING
6 tbsp apricot jam, boiled and sieved
170 g/6 oz full-fat cream cheese
3 tbsp plain natural yogurt
3 tsp clear honey
1 tsp vanilla essence
450 g/1 lb mixed soft fruits, such as cherries, raspberries,
strawberries, apricots, peaches, plums, stoned and sliced
as necessary

Roll the pastry out on a lightly floured surface to make an oblong about 30 x 20 cm/12 x 8 in. Lightly flour the pastry surface and then fold the pastry in half lengthwise to make a long narrow oblong.

Measure 2.5 cm/1 in down from the top of one narrow edge and cut across the fold to within 2.5 cm/1 in of the open edge. Repeat at the bottom.

Cut a line 2.5 cm/1 in in from the open edge to join up with the side cuts. Remove the centre piece from the 'frame', open out the pastry and roll out and trim to match the size of the pastry 'frame'.

Place the oblong on a wetted baking sheet, brush the edges with water and place the frame on top. Press the edges together to seal well. Cut up the edges with a knife to form flakes. Mark a design on the top of the edges. Prick the base and chill for 30 minutes.

Meanwhile, preheat the oven to 220C/425F/gas 7.

Bake the pastry case for 15–20 minutes, until risen and golden brown. Allow to cool on a wire rack and brush the base with some of the apricot jam glaze.

Beat the cream cheese, yogurt, honey and vanilla essence together in a bowl until well blended. Spread the mixture evenly over the base of the pastry tart and cover with an arrangement of soft fruits. Brush well with the remaining glaze and leave to set.

MARINATED MELON FILLED WITH FRUIT

SERVES 6-8

1 large cantaloupe melon
1 small ripe mango
85 g/3 oz muscat grapes
350 g/12 oz mixed summer fruit, including sweet
cherries, raspberries, strawberries and redcurrants
2 tbsp lemon juice
1 tbsp rose or orange blossom water
2 tbsp Kirsch, Maraschino or Grand Marnier
2-3 tbsp caster sugar
small pinch of salt

Cut a thin slice off the bottom of the melon so that it will sit stably. Cut a 'lid' off the top. Scoop out and discard the seeds. Then scoop out the flesh with a melon baller or spoon, taking care not to pierce the skin.

Peel the mango and chop the flesh into pieces the same size as the pieces of melon. Reserving a few on their stalks for decoration, remove the seeds from the grapes if necessary and halve if large.

Mix the melon flesh with the prepared mango and grapes and half the summer fruit. Mix the lemon juice, rose or orange blossom water and 1 tablespoon of liqueur and stir in all but 1 tablespoon of the sugar and the salt until it has dissolved. Use to dress the fruit, tossing gently to coat well and leave to macerate in the refrigerator for at least 2 hours.

Dissolve the remaining sugar in the remaining liqueur and swirl this mixture around the inside of the melon shell. Put the 'lid' back on the melon shell and leave it to chill with the other fruit.

Just before serving, pile the fruit mixture into the chilled melon shell along with the macerating juices. Arrange the remaining summer fruit so that it spills decoratively from the top.

Melon shells make a delightful way of serving a whole range of dishes in summer. Make ice-cream using the mashed melon flesh mixed with 5 beaten egg yolks and 85 g/3 oz sugar. Beat the mixture over a gentle heat until thick and then fold in 450 ml/¾pt whipped double cream. Flavour with lemon or lime juice and port, if wished. Freeze, stirring from time to time. Pile into the well-chilled shell, and serve with fruit or raspberry purée.
Alternatively, mix the melon flesh with citrus segments and chopped mint or chunks of avocado, apples and grapes. Dress with a light vinaigrette made with lemon or lime juice and serve in the melon shells as refreshing starters

CRUMBED APPLES WITH ORANGE AND CRANBERRY SAUCE

170 g/6 oz fine fresh white breadcrumbs
1 tbsp sugar
¼ tsp ground cinnamon
2 good-quality eating apples, such as Cox's, peeled,
cored and sliced very thinly
1 large egg, beaten
85 g/3 oz unsalted butter
flour, for coating
FOR THE SAUCE
150 ml/¼ pt fresh orange juice
1 tsp arrowroot, dissolved in a little water
2 tbsp ready-made cranberry sauce

Mix together the breadcrumbs, sugar and cinnamon. Dip the apple rings first in flour, then in beaten egg and then in the breadcrumb mixture, shaking off any excess each time.

Gently heat the butter in a large frying pan (or two smaller ones - or work in batches) over a moderate heat and fry the apple rings, turning them once, until they are crisp and golden. Keep them warm, if necessary.

Meanwhile, make the sauce: combine the ingredients in a small saucepan and heat, stirring continuously, until the sauce thickens.

Pour a little sauce on each of 4 warmed plates, top these pools of sauce with a circle of overlapping cooked apple rings and drizzle over the remaining sauce. Serve at once.

Crumbed Apples with Orange and Cranberry Sauce; right:
Honey and Lemon Dream Pudding (page 231)

HONEY AND LEMON DREAM PUDDING

140 g/5 oz unsalted butter, plus more for greasing
115 g/4 oz sugar
115 g/4 oz runny honey
5 eggs, separated
75 g/2½ oz flour
grated zest and juice of 2½ unwaxed lemons
300 ml/½ pt milk

Preheat the oven to 180C/350F/gas 4 and generously grease a shallow 1.75 litre/3 pt ovenproof dish with butter.

In a large bowl, cream the butter and sugar together until pale. Beat in the honey followed by the egg yolks. Stir in the flour, followed by the lemon zest and juice and then the milk. The mixture may look a little curdled at this stage.

Whisk the egg whites until stiff but not dry, and then fold these into the mixture.

Pour this into the prepared dish and stand it in a large roasting pan. Pour boiling water into the pan to come halfway up the sides of the dish.

Bake for 35-40 minutes, or until the sponge topping is golden and feels firm to the touch in the middle.

This pudding is best served straight from the oven but is also good cold, when the sauce sets to a thick lemon curd.

CHOCOLATE MOUSSE TART

SERVES 6

FOR THE PASTRY
170 g/6 oz flour
115 g/4 oz butter or margarine, cut into small pieces
30 g/1 oz caster sugar
1 egg yolk
FOR THE FILLING
170 g/6 oz plain chocolate
15 g/½ oz white chocolate
3 eggs, separated
2 tbsp dark rum

To make the pastry: sift the flour into a bowl, add the margarine or butter and rub it in finely with the fingertips. Stir in the sugar, egg yolk and 1 tablespoon of water and mix to a firm dough.

Knead the dough until it is smooth. Roll it out thinly and use to line a 36 x 10 cm/14 x 4 in loose-based fluted tranche tin. Chill for 30 minutes.

Preheat the oven to 200C/400F/gas 6.

Bake the pastry case blind for 15-20 minutes, until lightly browned at the edges.

While the case is cooling make the filling: place the plain and white chocolate in separate clean, dry bowls over hot water. Stir occasionally until the chocolate has melted. Stir the egg yolks and rum into the plain chocolate until well blended and thick.

Whisk the egg whites in a clean bowl until stiff. Gradually add the egg white to the plain chocolate mixture, folding it in well after each addition.

Pour the plain chocolate mixture into the flan case, shaking gently to level. Place the melted white chocolate in a greaseproof paper piping bag, fold down the top and snip off the point.

Pipe parallel lines of white chocolate across the chocolate filling. Draw a cocktail stick across the white chocolate lines to feather them. Leave to set.

CHESTNUT TART

SERVES 6

FOR THE PASTRY
170 g/6 oz flour
85 g/3 oz butter or margarine, cut into small pieces
1 tbsp chocolate spread
FOR THE FILLING
425 g/15 oz canned unsweetened chestnut purée
200 g/7 oz fresh soft cheese
2 tbsp Marsala
115 g/4 oz white chocolate, melted
150 ml/¼ pt single cream
55 g/2 oz plain chocolate, melted
TO DECORATE
white and dark chocolate curls

To make the pastry: sift the flour into a bowl, add the butter or margarine and rub it in finely with the fingertips. Stir in the chocolate spread and 2-3 tablespoons of cold water and mix to a firm dough.

Knead the dough until it is smooth. Roll it out thinly and use to line a 23 cm/9 in diameter loose-based fluted tart tin. Chill for 30 minutes.

Preheat the oven to 200C/400F/gas 6.

Bake the pastry case blind for 15-20 minutes, until lightly browned at the edges. Allow to cool on a wire rack.

While the case is cooling make the filling: place half the chestnut purée, the cheese and Marsala in a food processor and process until smooth. Stir into the white chocolate until well blended.

Place the remaining chestnut purée and the cream in the food processor and process until smooth. Add the plain chocolate and blend well.

Spread half the plain chocolate mix over the case and spread the white chocolate mix over it evenly.

Put the remaining plain chocolate mixture in a piping bag fitted with a plain nozzle. Pipe a lattice on top and decorate with chocolate curls.

MOCHA WALNUT FLAN

SERVES 6

FOR THE PASTRY
115 g/4 oz flour
85 g/3 oz butter, cut into small pieces
55 g/2 oz walnuts, finely chopped
30 g/1 oz soft light brown sugar
1 egg
FOR THE FILLING
300 ml/½ pt milk
55 g/2 oz plain chocolate
55 g/2 oz unsalted butter
1 tsp instant coffee granules
1 tbsp cornflour
2 egg yolks
2 tbsp Tia Maria
150 ml/¼ pt single cream
150 ml/¼ pt whipping cream, whipped to soft peaks
TO DECORATE
chocolate coffee beans and chocolate curls

To make the pastry: sift the flour into a bowl, add the butter and rub it in finely. Stir in the walnuts, sugar and egg and mix to a firm dough.

Knead the dough until it is smooth. Roll it out thinly and use to line a 23 cm/9 in diameter loose-based tart tin. Chill for 30 minutes.

Preheat the oven to 200C/400F/gas 6.

Bake the pastry case blind for 15-20 minutes, until lightly browned at the edges.

While the case is baking make the filling: place the milk, chocolate, butter and coffee in a pan and heat gently until the chocolate has melted. Blend the cornflour, egg yolks and liqueur together, add this to the pan and bring to the boil, stirring. Cook for 1 minute.

Off the heat, stir in the cream and pour into the pastry case. Leave until cold.

Pipe the whipped cream over the tart and decorate with chocolate coffee beans and curls.

PECAN CHOCOLATE TART

SERVES 8

FOR THE PASTRY
200 g/7 oz flour
½ tsp baking powder
140 g/5 oz butter or margarine, cut into small pieces
55 g/2 oz caster sugar
grated zest of 1 unwaxed lime
1 egg
FOR THE FILLING
140 g/5 oz caster sugar
85 g/3 oz butter or margarine
2 eggs, beaten
1 tbsp cornflour
170 g/6 oz pecan nuts, ground
85 g/3 oz plain chocolate, chopped into small pieces
2 tbsp chocolate liqueur
TO DECORATE
pecan nuts

To make the pastry: sift the flour and baking powder into a bowl, add the butter or margarine and rub it in finely with the fingertips. Stir in the sugar, lime zest and egg and mix to a firm dough.

Knead the dough until it is smooth. Roll it out thinly and use to line a 25 cm/10 in tart dish, reserving the trimmings. Chill for 30 minutes.

Preheat the oven to 190C/375F/gas 5.

To make the filling: place the sugar and butter or margarine in a bowl and beat until light and fluffy. Add the eggs a little at a time, beating well after each addition. Fold in the cornflour, pecan nuts, chocolate and chocolate liqueur until evenly blended.

Pour the mixture into the pastry case and use the pastry trimmings to make a lattice across the top. Bake for 45-50 minutes, or until the filling has set.

Allow to cool in the dish and decorate with pecan nuts. Serve warm or cold, cut in wedges.

ITALIAN CHEESE TART

SERVES 6

FOR THE PASTRY
115 g/4 oz flour
85 g/3 oz butter or margarine, cut into small pieces
30 g/1 oz caster sugar
grated zest of 1 unwaxed lemon
white of 1 egg
FOR THE FILLING
55 g/2 oz glacé fruits, chopped
30 g/1 oz plain chocolate, chopped into small pieces
30 g/1 oz raisins
1 tbsp Marsala
225 g/8 oz ricotta or cream cheese
30 g/1 oz caster sugar
1 egg, separated + 1 extra egg yolk

To make the pastry: sift the flour into a bowl, add the butter or margarine and rub it in finely with the fingertips. Stir in the sugar, lemon zest and egg white and mix with a fork to form a soft dough.

Knead the dough until it is smooth. Roll it out thinly and use to line an 18 cm/7 in diameter loose-based fluted tart tin. Chill for 30 minutes.

Preheat the oven to 200C/400F/gas 6.

Bake the pastry case blind for 10-15 minutes until lightly browned at the edges. Reduce the oven temperature to 180C/350F/gas 4.

While the case is baking make the filling: place the glacé fruits, chocolate, raisins and Marsala in a bowl and stir well to mix.

Place the cheese in another bowl. Add the sugar and egg yolks and beat well. Whisk the egg white in a third bowl until stiff. Fold this into the cheese mixture, together with the mixed fruits, and spread the filling over the pastry.

Bake in the cooler oven for 45-50 minutes, until the filling has set and the pastry is golden brown. Leave in the tin to cool.

BELGIAN TART

SERVES 6

FOR THE PASTRY
115 g/4 oz cream cheese
55 g/2 oz butter, softened
200 g/7 oz flour
30 g/1 oz cornflour
30 g/1 oz caster sugar
FOR THE FILLING
2 tbsp coconut strands
2 tbsp soft light brown sugar
3 tbsp apricot jam
2 nectarines, sliced
TO DECORATE
strips of fresh coconut
more nectarine slices

To make the pastry: place the cream cheese and butter in a bowl, beat until smooth. Stir in 2 tablespoons of water, the flour, cornflour and sugar and mix with a fork to form a firm dough.

Knead the dough on a lightly floured surface until it is smooth. Roll it out thinly and use two-thirds of the pastry to line a 20 cm/8 in loose-based fluted tart tin. Chill for 30 minutes.

Preheat the oven to 200C/400F/gas 6.

Make the filling: shred the remaining pastry and trimmings on a coarse grater. Mix together the coconut and sugar in a bowl.

Spread the apricot jam over the base of the pastry case and cover with the sliced nectarines. Top with the grated pastry and sprinkle with the coconut mixture.

Bake in the oven for 35-40 minutes, until lightly browned. Serve warm or cold. Decorate with strips of coconut and slices of nectarine.

Left: Mascarpone and Raspberry Dessert Cake (page 202);
right: Chocolate Refrigerator Cake (page 241)

BAKING

The varied recipes in this section are for all those occasions when you wish you had a piece of cake or a little something to offer friends when they drop in for tea or coffee. The recipes are characterized by an amalgamation of unusual textures and exciting flavours to memorable effect, like Poppy Seed and Strawberry Cake or Date, Pear and Walnut Cake. All are reasonably easy to make and the instructions are so clear and uncomplicated that it is almost impossible not to produce wonderful results every time – be it something as simple-sounding as Fudge Brownies or as exotic as Red Berry Griestorte. So if you want to make an impressive cake for an elegant afternoon tea at home or simply have something nice in the pantry for coffee in the morning, like a mature gingerbread, dip into this chapter and enjoy every last crumb.

MOIST CHOCOLATE SQUARES

MAKES 9

75 g/2½ oz butter, softened, plus more for greasing
115 g/4 oz plain chocolate, broken into pieces
3 eggs, separated
75 g/2½ oz ground almonds
75 g/2½ oz icing sugar, sifted
1 tbsp plain flour, sifted
pinch of salt
cocoa powder, for dusting
icing sugar, for dusting

Preheat the oven to 180C/350F/gas 4. Grease a 19 cm/7½ in square cake tin with butter and line the base with greaseproof paper.

In a small bowl, melt the chocolate with 2 tablespoons of water either in a microwave oven or set over a saucepan of simmering water.

Remove from the heat and beat in the butter until evenly incorporated.

Beat in the egg yolks one at a time. Then stir in the ground almonds, icing sugar and flour.

Whisk the egg whites with a pinch of salt until stiff. Then carefully fold in the chocolate mixture.

Transfer to the prepared tin and bake for 20 minutes, until risen and just firm to the touch.

Allow to cool in the tin. Trim the edges, if necessary, and then cut into 9 squares. Dust with cocoa powder and icing sugar.

RUM BABAS

MAKES 8

2 tbsp dark rum
55 g/2 oz seedless raisins
55 g/2 oz currants
115 g/4 oz butter, melted, plus more for greasing
1 sachet (6 g/1½ tsp) 'easy-blend' dried yeast
225 g/8 oz strong plain or plain flour
55 g/2 oz caster sugar
4 eggs, beaten
FOR THE SYRUP
140 g/5 oz caster sugar
5 tbsp dark rum

Mix the 2 tablespoons of rum and the dried fruit in a bowl, cover and leave for at least 1 hour or up to 24 hours.

Grease 8 large (about 150 ml/¼ pt) individual brioche moulds with butter.

Mix the yeast, flour and sugar in a large bowl. Then beat in the butter and eggs until the mixture is light in texture. Beat in the fruit and rum.

Half-fill the moulds with the mixture, then cover and leave to rise in a warm place until the mixture reaches the top of the tins.

Preheat the oven to 200C/400F/gas 6.

Bake the babas for 15-20 minutes, until golden brown and just firm to the touch. Leave to cool a little, then unmould into a shallow dish.

Make the syrup: in a small saucepan set over a moderate heat, dissolve the sugar in 200 ml/7 fl oz of water. Once the sugar is completely dissolved, bring to a simmer and continue to simmer for 5 minutes. Stir in the rum and remove from the heat.

Immediately pour the hot syrup over the babas and leave until they have absorbed all the syrup.

COCONUT AND CHERRY MACAROONS

MAKES 10

whites of 2 eggs
85 g/3 oz icing sugar, sifted
115 g/4 oz desiccated coconut
115 g/4 oz ground almonds
55 g/2 oz glacé cherries, chopped
1 tbsp dark rum or dry sherry

Preheat the oven to 150C/300F/gas 2 and line a baking tray with baking parchment.

Combine all the ingredients in a bowl and then shape the mixture into 10 round cakes.

Place these on the baking tray and bake for 20 minutes until lightly golden.

Leave to cool on a wire rack.

FUDGE BROWNIES

MAKES 9

85 g/3 oz butter, diced, plus more for greasing
85 g/3 oz best-quality white chocolate, broken into pieces
2 eggs
½ tsp natural vanilla essence
¼ tsp salt
170 g/6 oz light Muscovado sugar
85 g/3 oz self-raising flour
75 g/2½ oz walnut pieces, chopped

Preheat the oven to 180C/350F/gas 4. Grease a 20 cm/8 in square tin with butter and line the base with greaseproof paper

Place the chocolate and butter in a bowl set over simmering water and heat gently until they have just melted.

Beat the eggs, vanilla, salt and sugar together in another bowl until thickened. Then stir in the flour and melted chocolate mixture, followed by the walnuts.

Transfer this mixture to the prepared tin and bake for 30 minutes, until risen and just firm to the touch.

Allow to cool in the tin and then cut across into 9 square pieces.

BROWNIES *are classics of American baking. Chopped nuts, such as pecans, or shredded coconut are often added to the mixture.*

If preferred, the traditional Austrian gâteau GRIESTORTE may be made as two smaller cakes rather than one big one as described here

SYRUPY GRAPEFRUIT CAKE

115 g/4 oz soft tub margarine
115 g/4 oz caster sugar
2 eggs
170 g/6 oz self-raising flour
½ tsp baking powder
pinch of salt
finely grated zest of 1 and juice of 2 firm unwaxed grapefruit
8 tbsp icing sugar
butter or vegetable oil for greasing

Preheat the oven to 180C/350F/gas 4. Grease a 20 cm/8 in square tin with butter or oil and line the base with greaseproof paper.

Place the margarine, sugar, eggs, flour, baking powder, salt and grapefruit zest in a large bowl and beat well with a wooden spoon for 1-2 minutes, until the mixture has a soft dropping consistency. Transfer to the prepared tin and level the surface of the mixture.

Bake for about 30 minutes, until risen and just firm to the touch. Allow to cool in the tin.

Place the grapefruit juice and icing sugar in a saucepan and bring to the boil. Continue to boil for about 3-4 minutes, until slightly syrupy.

Prick the top of the cake all over with a skewer and pour the syrup over it. Leave to go cold in the tin.

Unmould the cake and cut it into fingers. Dust with extra icing sugar if wished.

PEAR GRIESTORTE WITH ALMONDS AND GINGER

SERVES 12-16

6 eggs, separated
225 g/8 oz caster sugar, plus more for dusting
juice and grated zest of 1 unwaxed lemon
115 g/4 oz fine semolina
30 g/1 oz ground almonds
30 g/1 oz ground ginger
3 drops of vanilla essence
6 ripe dessert pears, peeled and sliced
450 ml/¾ pt double cream, whipped to soft peaks
sprigs of mint, to decorate
butter, for greasing
flour, for dusting
icing sugar, for dusting (optional)

Preheat the oven to 180C/350F/gas 4.

Grease two 20 cm/8 in diameter cake tins with butter and line their bases with discs of greaseproof paper (this is unnecessary if using non-stick pans). Butter the greaseproof discs and then dust them and the sides of the pans with flour followed by caster sugar.

In a large bowl, beat the egg yolks and sugar together until pale, creamy and light. Add the lemon juice and continue beating until the mixture thickens. Stir in the semolina, almonds, ginger and lemon zest and mix thoroughly. Whisk the egg whites to stiff peaks and gently fold them into the mixture.

Spoon into the prepared tins and cook for 30-40 minutes. The mixture will rise dramatically owing to the proportion of egg to starch. Do not open the oven or the mixture will subside!

Allow the cakes to cool, then split them across horizontally. Stir the vanilla essence and some of the pear slices into the whipped cream. Sandwich all the sponge layers together with this mixture and then top with the remaining pear slices. Dust with extra icing sugar, if wished, and decorate with mint.

CHOCOLATE REFRIGERATOR CAKE

55 g/2 oz walnut pieces
55 g/2 oz blanched almonds
55 g/2 oz sultanas
55 g/2 oz glacé cherries, chopped
225 g/8 oz digestive biscuits, crushed
140 g/5 oz plain chocolate, melted
1 large egg, beaten
3-4 tbsp dark rum, or more to taste
TO DECORATE (OPTIONAL)
4 tbsp whipped cream
2 Maraschino or glacé cherries, cut into thin wedges

Preheat the oven to 180C/350F/gas 4 and line a 20 cm/8 in flan tin with foil.

Place the nuts on a baking tray and roast them for 20 minutes until golden.

Roughly chop the roasted nuts and combine them with the fruit and biscuit crumbs in a large bowl. Stir in the chocolate. Add the egg and 3-4 tablespoons rum. Check the taste and add a little more rum if wished.

Press the mixture into the prepared tin and chill for at least 4 hours or preferably overnight.

Unmould the chilled cake and cut into 12 wedges.

If wished, top each wedge with a swirl of whipped cream and a piece of cherry.

MINCEMEAT CAKE

115 g/4 oz soft tub margarine
85 g/3 oz light Muscovado sugar
2 eggs
75 g/2½ oz self-raising flour
75g/2½ oz wholemeal self-raising flour
½ tsp baking powder
1 tbsp warm water
225 g/8 oz best-quality mincemeat
butter or vegetable oil, for greasing
FOR THE ICING
170 g/6 oz icing sugar, sifted
2 tbsp mandarin or tangerine juice

Preheat the oven to 160C/325F/gas 3. Grease a 20 cm/8 in round cake tin with butter or oil and line the base with greaseproof paper.

In a large bowl, combine all the ingredients for the cake and beat well with a wooden spoon for about 2 minutes, until the mixture has a soft dropping consistency. Transfer to the prepared tin and level the surface.

Bake for about 40 minutes, until risen and just firm to the touch.

Allow to cool in the tin and then transfer to a wire rack to cool completely.

Make the icing by mixing the icing sugar with the juice until smooth and spread this over the top of the cake. Leave to set.

Roasting the nuts before adding them to the CHOCOLATE REFRIGERATOR CAKE *adds an extra depth of flavour. If wished, replace the almonds and walnuts with an equal quantity of other nuts such as pecans, hazelnuts, brazils or macadamia nuts.*

MINCEMEAT CAKE *is a clever way of using up mincemeat left over after Christmas.*

One of the secrets of good GINGERBREAD is to leave it to mature as this allows the flavour to develop – especially this one, which contains chopped stem ginger. Once the cake is cool, wrap it and leave it for a few days before icing it.

Warm CINNAMON CAKE is ideal served straight from the oven on its own or with some vanilla ice-cream. Leftover individual wedges may successfully be freshened in the microwave oven.

VERY GINGERBREAD WITH LEMON ICING

115 g/4 oz butter, plus more for greasing
125 g/4½ oz plain flour
pinch of salt
1 tsp ground mixed spice
1 tbsp ground ginger
125 g/4½ oz wholemeal flour
45 g/1½ oz demerara sugar
85 g/3 oz stem ginger, chopped
115 g/4 oz black treacle
115 g/4 oz golden syrup
1 tsp bicarbonate of soda
125 ml/4 fl oz warm milk
1 large egg, beaten
FOR THE LEMON ICING
55 g/2 oz icing sugar, sifted
2½ tsp lemon juice

Preheat the oven to 180C/350F/gas 4. Grease a 20 cm/8 in square tin with butter and line the base with greaseproof paper.

Sift the plain flour, salt and spices into a large bowl then stir in the wholemeal flour, demerara sugar and chopped ginger.

In a saucepan, warm the butter, treacle and syrup together until the butter just melts.

Dissolve the bicarbonate of soda in the milk and add this to the dry ingredients together with the treacle mixture and egg. Beat the mixture well until smooth.

Transfer to the prepared tin and bake for 40-45 minutes, until risen and firm to the touch.

Allow to cool slightly in the tin, then unmould and leave to cool completely on a wire rack.

Make the icing: mix the icing sugar and lemon juice in a bowl until thick and smooth. Drizzle this over the cake in a random pattern and leave to set. Cut into squares to serve.

WARM CINNAMON CAKE

225 g/8 oz plain flour
1 tbsp baking powder
½ tsp salt
115 g/4 oz caster sugar
115 g/4 oz white vegetable fat or soft tub margarine
1 egg
6 tbsp milk
butter, for greasing
vanilla ice-cream, to serve (optional)
FOR THE TOPPING
3 tbsp plain flour
3 tbsp caster sugar
1 tbsp ground cinnamon
45 g/1½ oz white vegetable fat or soft tub margarine

Preheat the oven to 200C/400F/gas 6. Grease a 25 cm/10 in cake tin with butter and line the base with greaseproof paper.

First make the topping by sifting the dry ingredients together and rubbing in the fat.

Then make the cake: sift the dry ingredients into a bowl and add the vegetable fat, egg and milk. Beat for 1 minute with a wooden spoon until smooth and then transfer to the prepared tin.

Sprinkle evenly with the topping and bake for about 25 minutes, until well risen (don't be tempted to press it with your finger to check if it's cooked – the sugar in the topping will be very hot!).

Serve straight from the oven, as it is or with vanilla ice-cream.

Left: Very Gingerbread with Lemon Icing; right: Warm Cinnamon Cake

ESPRESSO COFFEE
GRANULES *are
instant coffee
granules that contain
a small percentage of
real ground coffee to
give a more
authentic taste.
Available from most
supermarkets, they
are very useful for
adding a good
flavour to cakes and
icings. Always
dissolve them in a
little boiling water
before use.*

ONE-STAGE COFFEE CAKE

170 g/6 oz soft tub margarine
170 g/6 oz caster sugar
3 eggs
170 g/6 oz self-raising flour
1 tsp baking powder
pinch of salt
*1 tbsp espresso coffee granules, dissolved in 1 tbsp
boiling water*
butter or vegetable oil, for greasing
8 sugared coffee beans, to decorate
FOR THE FILLING
85 g/3 oz butter, softened
*1 tbsp espresso coffee granules, dissolved in 1 tbsp
boiling water*
170 g/6 oz icing sugar, sifted
FOR THE ICING
85 g/3 oz icing sugar, sifted
*1½ tsp espresso coffee granules, dissolved in 2½ tsp
boiling water*

Preheat the oven to 180C/350F/gas 4. Grease two
20 cm/8 in sandwich tins with butter or oil and line
the bases with greaseproof paper.

Place all the ingredients for the cake in a large
bowl and beat well with a wooden spoon for 1-2
minutes until mixed to a soft dropping consistency.

Divide the mixture between the tins and bake for
about 25 minutes, until risen and just firm to the
touch. Allow to cool slightly in the tin, then transfer
to cooling racks and leave to go cold.

Make the filling: beat the butter in a bowl until
soft and almost white, then stir in the coffee solution
and beat in the icing sugar. Use two-thirds of this
mixture to sandwich the cakes together.

Make the icing: mix the icing sugar and coffee
solution together until smooth and then spread this
over the top of the cake. Leave to set.

Using a piping bag fitted with a medium star
nozzle, pipe 8 rosettes of the remaining filling around
the rim of the cake and decorate each one with a
sugared coffee bean.

ANNIE'S FAT-FREE FRUIT LOAVES

MAKES 2

450 g/1 lb sultanas
300 ml/½ pt cold tea
1 egg, beaten
200 g/7 oz light Muscovado sugar
285 g/10 oz self-raising flour
butter, for greasing

Soak the sultanas in the tea overnight.

Preheat the oven to 160C/325F/gas 3. Grease two
450 g/1 lb loaf tins with butter and line the bases
with greaseproof paper.

Place all the ingredients in a bowl and beat
together until evenly combined.

Divide the mixture between the prepared tins and
bake for about 1¼ hours, until risen and firm to the
touch (a fine metal skewer inserted into the centre of
the cake will come out clean and hot to the touch).

Leave to cool in the tins, then unmould on a wire
rack. Serve cut into slices, with or without butter.

TUTTI-FRUTTI CAKE

170 g/6 oz soft tub margarine
170 g/6 oz caster sugar
3 eggs
170 g/6 oz self-raising flour
pinch of salt
1 tsp baking powder
55 g/2 oz assorted glacé fruits, such as coloured cherries
and angelica, finely chopped
butter or vegetable oil, for greasing
FOR THE FILLING
150 ml/¼ pt double cream, whipped to soft peaks
4 tbsp apricot preserve

Preheat the oven to 180C/350F/gas 4. Grease two 20 cm/8 in sandwich tins with butter or oil and line the bases with greaseproof paper.

Place all the ingredients for the cake except the glacé fruits in a large bowl and beat well with a wooden spoon for 1-2 minutes, until the mixture has a soft dropping consistency.

Divide the mixture between the two tins and level the surface. Sprinkle the chopped fruit evenly over the surface of one of the cakes.

Bake the cakes for about 25 minutes, until risen and just firm to the touch. Allow to cool slightly and then unmould and transfer to cooling racks.

Make the filling by combining the cream and apricot preserve and use this to sandwich the cakes together with the fruit topped cake uppermost.

NOTE: for a more professional finish, bake the cake for 10 minutes before sprinkling over the glacé fruits.

Centre: Tutti-frutti Cake; top and bottom: Annie's Fat-free Fruit Loaves

COCONUT CAKE

170 g/6 oz butter, softened, plus more for greasing
170 g/6 oz caster sugar
3 tbsp warm water
3 eggs
125 g/4½ oz self-raising flour
140 g/5 oz desiccated coconut

Preheat the oven to 180C/350F/gas 4. Grease a 20 cm/8 in round cake tin with butter and line the base and sides with a double thickness of greaseproof paper.

Cream the butter and sugar until almost white. Beat in the water, 1 tablespoon at a time. Then beat in the eggs one at a time.

Sift in the flour, then add all but 2 tablespoons of the coconut. Fold this into the creamed mixture until evenly combined.

Transfer to the prepared tin and level the surface. Sprinkle with the remaining coconut and bake for about 45 minutes, until risen and golden and just springy to the touch.

Allow to cool slightly in the tin and then unmould on a cooling rack.

BANANA LOAF

115 g/4 oz butter, diced, plus more for greasing
225 g/8 oz self-raising flour
½ tsp salt
170 g/6 oz golden caster sugar
115 g/4 oz sultanas
55 g/2 oz pecan nuts, chopped
115 g/4 oz glacé cherries, halved
2 eggs, beaten
450 g/1 lb (peeled weight) ripe bananas, mashed

Preheat the oven to 180C/350F/gas 4. Grease a 900 g/2 lb loaf tin with butter and line the base with greaseproof paper.

Sift the flour and salt into a large bowl and rub in the butter until the mixture resembles fine crumbs.

Stir in the sugar, sultanas, nuts and cherries until evenly coated with the mixture.

Add the eggs and bananas to the mixture and beat well until evenly incorporated.

Transfer to the prepared tin and bake for about 1 hour 10 minutes, until risen and just firm to the touch. Allow the cake to cool in the tin, then unmould on a cooling rack.

Desiccated coconut gives the COCONUT CAKE *a moist crumbly texture that is further enhanced by leaving the cake to mature for a couple of days. Wrap it carefully and store in a cool dry place.*

BANANA LOAF *tastes better if made using well-ripened bananas with blackening skins. The cake also develops in flavour if wrapped and stored for a few days before eating.*

SUNSHINE MARBLE CAKE

170 g/6 oz butter, softened, plus more for greasing
170 g/6 oz caster sugar, plus more for dusting
170 g/6 oz plain flour, plus more for dusting
3 tbsp juice and finely grated zest from
1 large unwaxed orange
3 eggs, separated
2¼ tsp baking powder
30 g/1 oz ground almonds
1½ tbsp hot water
pinch of salt

Preheat the oven to 180C/350F/gas 4. Grease a 22 cm/8¾ in (1.5 litre/2½ pt capacity) kugelhopf mould with butter. Sprinkle liberally with caster sugar and flour and shake well to coat the inside of the tin evenly. Shake out any excess.

Cream the butter and sugar until almost white, then divide the mixture into two equal portions.

To one portion, add the orange juice a little at a time. Then add the orange zest and egg yolks and beat thoroughly.

Sift half the flour with 1½ teaspoons of baking powder and fold this into the orange mixture together with half the ground almonds.

To the other portion of butter mixture, add the hot water and beat well.

Sift the remaining flour, baking powder and ground almonds together.

Whisk the egg whites with a pinch of salt until stiff. Then fold alternate spoonfuls of them and the sifted flour mixture into the hot water and butter mixture.

Place alternate spoonfuls of the orange mixture and this white mixture in the prepared tin.

Bake for about 40 minutes, until risen and just firm to the touch. Allow the cake to cool in the tin until just cool enough to handle, then immediately unmould on a cooling rack.

BLACKBERRY AND APPLE RIPPLE CAKE

170 g/6 oz butter, softened, plus more for greasing
200 g/7 oz caster sugar
3 eggs
170 g/6 oz self-raising flour
225 g/8 oz blackberries
2 dessert apples, peeled, cored and grated

Preheat the oven to 180C/350F/gas 4. Line the base of a 23 cm/9 in round cake tin with greaseproof paper and grease it with butter.

Cream the butter with 170 g/6 oz of the sugar in a large bowl until almost white, then beat in the eggs one at a time until thoroughly incorporated. Fold in the flour.

Spoon about two-thirds of the mixture into the prepared tin.

Mix the blackberries, apples and remaining sugar. Spoon this over the cake mixture and then drop spoonfuls of the remaining cake mixture over the top in a random pattern until it is all used up.

Bake for about 1 hour, until risen and golden and just firm to the touch. Leave to cool in the tin.

The two-tone marbling effect in the SUNSHINE MARBLE CAKE *is produced by separating the eggs and using the yolks in one mixture and the whites in the other.*

Any soft berry fruits, such as raspberries, loganberries, blueberries or small strawberries may be used in place of the blackberries in the BLACKBERRY AND APPLE RIPPLE CAKE.

JEWELLED FRUIT CAKE

225 g/8 oz butter, softened, plus more for greasing
85 g/3 oz ground almonds
225 g/8 oz light Muscovado sugar
300 ml/½ pt beaten egg (5 large eggs)
255 g/9 oz plain flour
1 tbsp mixed spice
450 g/1 lb seedless raisins
450 g/1 lb sultanas
140 g/5 oz cut mixed peel
3 tbsp orange juice
4 tbsp sherry or dark rum
225 g/8 oz glacé cherries
TO DECORATE
4-6 tbsp apricot jam, warmed and sieved
6 glacé cherries
2 glacé pears, quartered
3 glacé orange slices, halved
3 glacé pineapple slices, halved
2 wedges of glacé apple
2 slices of glacé kiwi, halved
30 g/1 oz whole blanched almonds, toasted

Preheat the oven to 150C/300F/gas 2. Line the base and sides of a 23 cm/9 in round cake tin with a double thickness of greased greaseproof paper, then wrap the outside with a thick layer of brown paper or newspaper.

Place the ground almonds in a frying pan and cook over a moderate heat, stirring all the time, until evenly toasted. Leave to cool.

Cream the butter and sugar together in a large bowl until pale and fluffy. Beat in the egg a little at a time until evenly combined.

Fold in the flour, spice and ground almonds. Then stir in the fruit, orange juice and sherry or rum and mix thoroughly. Lastly, stir in the cherries.

Transfer the mixture to the prepared tin and level the surface.

Bake for about 3 hours, until just firm to the touch (and a fine metal skewer inserted into the centre of the cake comes out piping hot and clean). Leave to cool in the tin.

To decorate: unmould the cooked cake and brush the surface with some of the warmed apricot jam. Arrange the glacé fruit and toasted nuts attractively over the surface of the cake and brush with the remaining jam.

CHERRY STREUSEL CAKE

115 g/4 oz butter, softened, plus more for greasing
200 g/7 oz caster sugar
3 eggs
140 g/5 oz self-raising flour
115 g/4 oz ground almonds
225 g/8 oz glacé cherries, quartered
30 g/1 oz flaked almonds

Preheat the oven to 180C/350F/gas 4. Grease an 18 cm/7 in cake tin with butter and line the base and sides with a double thickness of greaseproof paper.

In a bowl, cream the butter and 115 g/4 oz of the sugar until almost white. Beat in 2 whole eggs, one at a time. Then separate the third egg and add the yolk. Reserve the white for the topping.

Combine the flour, half the ground almonds and the cherries and fold this into the creamed mixture. Transfer to the prepared tin and level the surface of the mixture.

Make the topping by combining the remaining ingredients and scatter this on top of the cake.

Bake for about 1-1¼ hours, until risen and golden (a fine metal skewer inserted into the centre of the cake should come out clean and feel piping hot to the touch).

Allow the cake to cool in the tin, then unmould on a cooling rack.

SRI LANKAN FRUIT CAKE

170 g/6 oz butter, softened, plus more for greasing
115 g/4 oz seedless raisins
170 g/6 oz sultanas
115 g/4 oz assorted glacé fruits
115 g/4 oz crystallized ginger
55 g/2 oz cut mixed peel
115 g/4 oz glacé cherries, halved
115 g/4 oz cashew nuts or blanched almonds
225 g/8 oz ginger preserve
2 tbsp dark rum
170 g/6 oz caster sugar
3 eggs, separated, plus 3 extra yolks
1 tsp finely grated zest from ½ an unwaxed lemon
¾ tsp ground cardamom
½ tsp ground cinnamon
½ tsp ground nutmeg
½ tsp ground cloves
1 tbsp natural vanilla extract
115 g/4 oz semolina

Preheat the oven to 150C/300F/gas 2. Grease a 20 cm/8 in round tin with butter and line with a double thickness of greaseproof paper. Wrap the outside of the tin with newspaper or brown paper.

Finely chop all the dried and crystallized fruit except the cherries. Coarsely grind or finely chop the nuts. Combine the chopped fruits, nuts, cherries, ginger preserve and the rum. Cover and leave while preparing the cake, or for up to 24 hours.

Cream the butter and sugar until almost white then beat in all the egg yolks, one at a time. Then beat in the lemon zest, spices and vanilla. Stir in the semolina followed by the fruit until evenly mixed.

Whisk the egg whites until stiff, then fold them into the fruit mixture.

Transfer to the prepared tin and level the surface. Bake for about 2½ hours, until just firm to the touch. Allow to cool in the tin.

When using GLACÉ CHERRIES, *as in the* CHERRY STREUSEL CAKE, *it is always a good idea to wash and dry them thoroughly to remove excess sugar syrup. Then mix them with some of the flour, as this helps prevent them from drifting to the bottom of the cake during cooking.*

YVONNE'S YOGURT CAKE

125 ml/4 fl oz vegetable oil or 115 g/4 oz melted butter,
plus more for greasing
125 ml/4 fl oz natural yogurt
170 g/6 oz caster sugar
2 eggs
170 g/6 oz plain flour
1½ tsp baking powder
finely grated zest of 1 unwaxed lemon or 1 tbsp orange
blossom water
strawberry or raspberry jam or fresh berries to serve
(optional)

Preheat the oven to 180C/350F/gas 4. Grease the base of a 22 cm/8¾ in round cake tin with oil or butter and line the base with greaseproof paper.

Mix the yogurt and sugar in a large bowl until smooth, then beat in the oil or melted butter and eggs until well combined.

Sift the flour and baking powder together and beat them into the mixture. Then stir in the lemon zest or orange blossom water.

Transfer the mixture to the prepared tin and bake for about 45 minutes, until risen and just firm to the touch. Allow to cool in the tin then transfer to a cooling rack.

Serve with jam or fresh berries, if using, to accompany morning coffee.

Clockwise from the top: Poppy Seed and Strawberry Cake, Cherry Streusel Cake (page 249) and Yvonne's Yogurt Cake

POPPY SEED AND STRAWBERRY CAKE

115 g/4 oz poppy seeds
250 ml/8 fl oz milk
225 g/8 oz butter, softened, plus more for greasing
225 g/8 oz light Muscovado sugar
3 eggs, separated
225 g/8 oz wholemeal flour
1½ tsp baking powder
pinch of salt
6 tbsp best-quality strawberry jam, warmed

Place the poppy seeds and milk in a saucepan and bring to the boil. Then remove from the heat and leave to infuse for at least 20 minutes (leaving it for longer won't matter).

Preheat the oven to 180C/350F/gas 4. Grease a 22 cm/8¾ in round cake tin with butter and line the base and sides with a double thickness of greaseproof paper.

Cream the butter and sugar together in a large bowl until light and fluffy, then beat in the egg yolks one at a time.

Mix the flour and baking powder together and fold alternate large spoonfuls of this and the poppy seed mixture into the creamed mixture.

Whisk the egg whites with a pinch of salt until stiff and then fold these into the mixture.

Transfer to the prepared tin and level the surface. Bake for about 1-1¼ hour(s), until risen and just springy to the touch. Allow to cool in the tin, then unmould on a cooling rack.

Brush the top of the cake with the warmed jam and leave to go cold.

YVONNE'S YOGURT CAKE *is a French plain sweet cake to be eaten for breakfast or with morning coffee, on its own or with jam.*

Before making the POPPY SEED AND STRAWBERRY CAKE *it is essential to soak the poppy seeds in the milk to soften them which makes the cake more moist. Any fruit jam can be used to top the cake once it is baked, then it may be served with the appropriate fresh fruit.*

CHOCOLATE SPONGE

115 g/4 oz butter, softened, plus more for greasing
115 g/4 oz self-raising flour
1 tsp baking powder
30 g/1 oz cocoa powder
3 tbsp boiling water
3 tbsp golden syrup
115 g/4 oz caster sugar
3 eggs, beaten
150 ml/¼ pt double cream, whipped to soft peaks
icing sugar, for dusting

When adding the eggs to the CHOCOLATE SPONGE *mixture stir in a spoonful of the flour, if necessary, to prevent curdling.*

Traditional to Viennese pâtisserie, GRIESTORTE *is commonly made using semolina and probably owes its origins to Turkish influence.*

Preheat the oven to 180C/350F/gas 4. Grease a 22 cm/8¾ in cake tin with butter, then line the base with greaseproof paper.

Sift the flour and baking powder together into a bowl. In another bowl mix the cocoa, water and golden syrup together until smooth.

In a large bowl, cream the butter and sugar until almost white. Then beat in the eggs a little at a time. Fold in the flour, then the cocoa mixture.

Transfer the mixture to the tin and bake for about 35 minutes, until risen and just firm to the touch.

Allow to cool slightly, then unmould on a rack. Leave the tin over the cake until cold.

To serve, split the cake horizontally and fill with whipped cream. Dust the top with icing sugar.

RED BERRY GRIESTORTE

225 g/8 oz caster sugar, plus more for dusting
6 eggs, separated
juice and finely grated zest of 1 unwaxed lemon
115 g/4 oz ground rice or semolina
30 g/1 oz ground almonds
pinch of salt
170 g/6 oz red berries
150 ml/¼ pt double cream, whipped to soft peaks
butter, for greasing
icing sugar, for dusting

Preheat the oven to 180C/350F/gas 4. Grease two 20 cm/8 in sandwich tins with butter and line the bases with greaseproof paper. Sprinkle the sides of the tin with caster sugar to coat them evenly. Shake out any excess.

Whisk the egg yolks, about three-quarters of the sugar and the lemon juice in a large bowl until thick and pale. Then stir in the lemon zest, ground rice or semolina and the ground almonds until smooth.

Whisk the egg whites with a pinch of salt until stiff, then whisk in the remaining sugar a little at a time.

Fold the egg yolk mixture into the egg whites and divide the resulting mixture between the prepared tins.

Bake for about 30 minutes, until risen and just firm to the touch. Allow to cool slightly in the tins then unmould on cooling racks.

Fold the red berries into the whipped cream and use this to sandwich the cakes together. Dust the top with icing sugar.

APPLE SAUCE CAKE

450 g/1 lb cooking apples, peeled, cored and chopped
225 g/8 oz caster sugar, plus more for dusting
30 g/1 oz glacé cherries, chopped
30 g/1 oz toasted flaked almonds
30 g/1 oz currants
1 tbsp chopped angelica
115 g/4 oz butter, softened, plus more for greasing
225 g/8 oz plain flour, plus more for dusting
1 egg
1 tsp bicarbonate of soda
pinch of salt
115 g/4 oz icing sugar, sifted
1 tbsp apple juice
glacé fruits, to decorate (optional)

Place the apples in a saucepan with 55 g/2 oz of the caster sugar and cook gently to a purée (about 10 minutes). Continue cooking over a medium heat, stirring all the time, for about another 5 minutes until the purée is really thick. Leave to go cold then stir in the cherries, almonds, currants and angelica.

Preheat the oven to 180C/350F/gas 4. Grease a 24 cm/9½ in ring tin with butter, then dust the inside with a little sugar and flour. Shake off any excess.

Cream the butter and half the remaining caster sugar until almost white, then beat in the remaining caster sugar and egg.

Sift the flour, bicarbonate of soda and salt together and fold this into the creamed mixture. Stir in the apple purée and transfer the mixture to the prepared tin.

Bake for about 35 minutes, until risen and firm to the touch. Allow to cool slightly in the tin, then unmould on a wire rack and leave to go cold.

Mix the icing sugar with the apple juice to give a thick smooth icing and drizzle it over the cooked cake. Decorate with extra glacé fruits, if using, and leave to set.

DATE, PEAR AND WALNUT CAKE

115 g/4 oz stoned dates
115 g/4 oz date syrup or malt extract
125 ml/4 fl oz vegetable oil
125 ml/4 fl oz natural yogurt or buttermilk
2 eggs
140 g/5 oz wholemeal flour
½ tsp bicarbonate of soda
1 tsp ground cinnamon
½ tsp ground mixed spice
85 g/3 oz walnut pieces
2 ripe pears
4 tbsp apricot jam, warmed and sieved
butter or vegetable oil, for greasing

Place the dates in a small saucepan with 150 ml/¼ pt water and cook until all the water has evaporated to produce a soft date purée. Leave to cool.

Preheat the oven to 180C/350F/gas 4 and grease a 23 cm/9 in springform tin with butter or oil.

Place the date syrup or malt extract in a large bowl with the oil, yogurt or buttermilk and the eggs and beat until smooth. Then beat in the date purée.

Mix the flour, bicarbonate of soda and spices together and fold them into the date mixture with the walnuts. Transfer to the prepared tin.

Peel, quarter and core the pears. Then cut each quarter into thin slices without cutting right through the top of each piece. Fan out the slices of each pear quarter and place them attractively on top of the cake mixture.

Bake for about 45-50 minutes, until the cake is risen and just firm to the touch.

Allow to cool in the tin, then transfer to a cooling rack. Brush with the warmed and sieved apricot jam and leave to go cold.

INDEX

Page numbers in *italic* refer to the illustrations

ACKNOWLEDGEMENTS
The Authors have provided the recipes on the pages indicated below.

Richard Cawley: *11, 30-1, 40, 48-53, 64 (right), 66, 73, 75, 84, 92 (right), 93 (right), 106, 108, 111, 120-36, 161, 164-5, 170-1, 178, 181 (left), 182 (left), 183 (right), 203-4, 207 (right), 230-1*
Lewis Esson: *34-9, 42, 56-63, 74, 76-7, 89-90, 100-2, 152 (right), 174 (bottom), 179, 185, 196-201, 228*
Janice Murfitt: *46-7, 85 (left), 148-51, 208-10, 223-7, 232-4*
Lyn Rutherford: *18-19, 25-7, 64 (left), 70-1, 78, 81-2, 86, 94-5, 103-5, 107, 110, 114-17, 141-2, 162-3 (left), 188-95*
Sally-Ann Scott: *10, 12-17, 20-4, 28, 45, 65, 80, 85 (right), 92 (left), 96-7, 109, 112, 140, 144-9 (left), 152 (left), 157-9, 163 (right), 166-8, 172, 174 (top), 175-6, 180, 181 (right), 182 (right), 183 (left), 184, 202, 206, 207 (left)*
Jane Suthering: *213-21, 238-53*

The publishers thank the photographers for their kind permission to reproduce the photographs on the following pages:

Julie Fisher: *2, 32-3, 37, 43, 54-5, 58, 61, 63, 77, 88, 91, 98-9, 199, 200, 228-9*
Michelle Garrett: *52, 67, 118-19, 122-3, 125, 126-7, 130-1, 134-5, 137, 151, 153, 211, 212, 214, 216, 221, 222, 225, 235, 236-7, 243, 245, 248, 250, 252*
Deborah Patterson: *6, 8-9, 15, 23, 26, 68-9, 79, 87, 95, 104, 117, 138-9, 143, 147, 154-5, 156-7, 158, 160, 161, 169, 172-3, 177, 180, 188, 191, 192, 195*
Pia Tryde: *29, 41, 44, 72-3, 83, 85, 113, 204-5, 206, 230-1*

The publishers also thank Jackie Boase, Roísín Neiold, Jane Newdick, Debbie Patterson and Sue Skeen for food styling, and Richard Cawley, Meg Jansz, Janice Murfitt, Lyn Rutherford and Jane Suthering for food for photography.